gHost

ALSO BY
KATHERINE RAMSLAND

gHost

INVESTIGATING THE OTHER SIDE

KATHERINE RAMSLAND

THOMAS DUNNE BOOKS

ST. MARTIN'S PRESS ⚌ NEW YORK

THOMAS DUNNE BOOKS.
An imprint of St. Martin's Press.

GHOST: INVESTIGATING THE OTHER SIDE. Copyright © 2001
by Katherine Ramsland. All rights reserved. Printed in
the United States of America. No part of this book may
be used or reproduced in any manner whatsoever without written permission except in the case of brief quo-
tations embodied in critical articles or reviews. For
information, address St. Martin's Press, 175 Fifth
Avenue, New York, N.Y. 10010.

www.stmartins.com

All photos courtesy of the author

Designed by Lorelle Graffeo

Library of Congress Cataloging-in-Publication Data

Ramsland, Katherine M.
    Ghost : investigating the other side / Katherine
Ramsland.—1st ed.
        p.   cm.
    Includes bibliographical references and index.
    ISBN 0-312-26164-0
    1. Ghosts—United States.   2. Ramsland,
Katherine M.   I. Title

    BF1472.U6 R35 2001
    133.1'0973—dc21

                                        2001041725

First Edition: October 2001

10   9   8   7   6   5   4   3   2   1

This book is for Christian, wherever he is.

CONTENTS

ACKNOWLEDGMENTS

Many people made a contribution to this book, some of whom were enormously instrumental in my learning and understanding. For help and inspiration, I wish to thank Charles Adams III, "Frodo Baggins," Stanley Bard and the Chelsea staff, Elizabeth Baron, Stuart Lee Brown, Susan Burger, Chanda, Tom Chiolo, Corrine, Amanda Corzelo, David Craig, Mark DiIonno, Nora Doan, David Douthat, Sarah Estep, the Farnsworth House staff, Mary Farrelly, Dorothy Fiedel, Rick Fisher, Bas van Fraassen, Fuzzy, Marie Gallagher, Adele Gamble, Judy Garwood, Sharon Gill, the Gold Club personnel, Christina Guentner, the wait staff at Harry's Seafood Bar & Grill, Richard Hatem, Ming & Jimmi Hower, the Inn at Jerome, Jennifer, Donna Johnston, Michael Johnston, Henry Johnston, Barbara Johnston, Keith, Miss Kitty, Dean Koontz, Mimi Lansou, Lawanda, Lizzie Borden B & B, the Logan staff, Mark Macy, Jana Marcus, Mariah, John McDougall, Martha McGinn, Sally McGinn, Merlin, Larry Montz, Nora Natale, Mark Nesbitt, Patti O'Day, Dave Oester, Ed Okonowitz, Ruth Osborne, Ken Paris, Liza Price, Harvey Ray, Rosemary, Seth, Sidney and Kathy Smith, John Timpane, Southern Nights B&B, Mark Spivey, the wait staff at Jimmy's, Dennis Schuyler, Karl Silvius, Maggie Smith, "Steve," Terry Stouch, Troy Taylor, Todd, Priscilla Tollefson and Ron

Wheeler at Garden Gate Farm, Barbara Trimmer, Sue Trombino, Arthur V., Pelli Wheaton, Wraith, Jeanne Youngson, Victor Zammit, the authors of all the ghost books, all the people who had a ghost story to tell me, and the discoverers of EVP.

Of those, I want to say special thanks to my teachers, companions, and assistants on my adventurers. I certainly couldn't have done it alone. Mike Epperson has been especially enthusiastic and helpful with promoting my work, so many thanks to him.

I was skeptical of doing a book like this, since I didn't really believe I'd discover much, so I thank my agent, Lori Perkins, who kept saying, "It would be perfect for you." Little did either of us know what was in store.

I'm also grateful that my editor, Barry Neville, was so excited about it and so easily scared. His ideas about how to shape it improved the material and made it educational as well as entertaining. Emily Hopkins, too, who came on board with great enthusiasm.

I also want to thank the support staff at St. Martin's Press for their dedication to making this story into a book.

PREFACE

Not long ago, I investigated a subculture created by people who view themselves as vampires. I moved among them, listened to their stories, and gained a fair sense of how they see the world. Then I wrote up my experiences in a book called *Piercing the Darkness*. End of story. Or so I thought. Then something happened that propelled me into yet another adventure. This time it involved ghosts.

While moving among the vampires, I acquired a haunted ring. This wasn't just any old haunted ring, but a ring that had belonged to a murderer. Not only that, he had thought he was a vampire. In fact, he had allegedly killed himself to "bleed into the spirit world" and return as a ghost to possess his former partner-in-murder and thereby become a more powerful vampire. That's why he now haunted this ring. Before dying, he had given it to his partner, who claimed to have experienced its effects. It was quite a story. Yet when I decided to see if a spirit really could possess a ring, I happened upon an even better story.

I've always had an interest in ghosts and have listened to ghost tales my whole life. Some appear credible, some don't. For myself, I want proof—or at least enough detail to make me think. A medium who says there's a ghost standing in the corner talking to me is dubious.

One who offers the ghost's name, Social Security number, unlisted phone number, and other specifics that all check out but could be known only through the deceased person—that would get my attention. Even so, I still consider all natural explanations before accepting a ghost.

I've developed my mind through reasoning and psychological observation. I have a Ph.D. in philosophy and master's degrees in both forensic and clinical psychology. I've done research for a former FBI agent, assisted with court reports, done painstaking research for my other books, and practiced as a psychotherapist. I also taught philosophy for fifteen years at a major university, with a specialty in logic and in psychological ideologies. I know how the braiding of ambiguity, suggestion, and poor logic can become dogma that substitutes for proof. I saw that many times in student papers.

In the real world as well, I've noticed that stories about angels, aliens, and ghosts are equally rife with such earnest mistakes. It might be fairly assumed that many alleged sightings of supernatural entities are the result of wishful thinking, the need to believe, suggestibility, or even commercial exploitation. In fact, investigators estimate that from 70 to 98 percent of all "hauntings" have natural explanations or are the result of tricks. That's not to say that all tales are fabricated, but only that many tend to be constructed more from hope and skewed perceptions than with reason and genuine evidence.

Even so, I won't go as far as some psychologists, who dismiss all of this as "experienced anomalous trauma." Some insist that anyone who has psychic visions or ghostly encounters has a disorder, from sleep paralysis to full-blown psychosis. As a therapist, I frequently encounter people who confess to alien abduction experiences, past lives, transformation into animals, and other such anomalies. I have never quite taken either side: I listen, but I don't fully accept or dismiss such a description. I try to work within it. With ghosts, too, I'm aware that there's a lot of psychological meat mixed in the sauce of paranormal experience, but I don't believe it's *entirely* psychological.

To investigate the ghost world, my plan was to explore in the manner of an *X-Files* or *Nightstalker* type of detective, using the same openness that I adopted in the vampire subculture, but ready to expose a hoax. I practiced what I call "phenomenological bracketing." In other words, I tried to suspend my beliefs as much as possible so that I could listen openly to what I was told by those whose chosen lifestyles were different from mine. I became part of their world, followed their instructions, and attempted to see things from their perspective so that I could fully understand. If I had to take a bath in wormwood to participate in a séance, I did. If I needed to buy equipment or go through a home-study course to be a certified ghost hunter, I did. If I had to spend the night alone in a haunted building, I did. And as I did these things, I learned about ghost photography, paranormal meter readings, the recording of ghost voices, the various ways that what we call a ghost can make itself understood, and the kind of person who is most likely to have such experiences.

Often, what I heard from one person on the best approach to the paranormal contradicted what I heard from someone else, so I'll say right up front that I probably broke everyone's rules in one way or another. I simply immersed myself in whatever "world" I was in and performed those rituals as instructed—even if someone else had warned me not to.

Was I scared? Absolutely. In fact, if there's anything I'm scared of, it's a ghost. Going to a vampire club at midnight is a snap compared to being in a room alone with a ghost. It doesn't have to be the ghost of a murderer. Just any ghost will do. I don't even have to believe in them to be scared. I sometimes think the only reason I didn't die of a heart attack in some situations is because I knew it would put me *closer* to the ghosts.

Nevertheless, that was no reason to refrain from going forward to investigate my haunted ring. In fact, it was incentive. Once I realized that I had a ring that came with a ghost and that the ghost was rather mean, I had every good reason to find out if there was anything to it. I went into the paranormal realm with serious doubt. I emerged from it amazed. I can honestly say that I've seen things that baffle me, experienced things that surprised me, learned things that gave me pause, and above all, acquired a new understanding of possibilities that has altered my life.

I'm not convinced that just anyone can have a ghost encounter, but I believe that most of us can develop a greater degree of receptivity to it. If that were to happen, I think we'd learn a lot more about the possibilities than we currently know. And if it's true that "ghosts" seem to be communicating about what the other world is like, I think most of us would *want* to know, because it would profoundly affect how we live.

Just to be clear, this is no ordinary ghost book. It's not a ghostly directory or collection of folklore, nor even an attempt to explain it all in scientific terms. It's also not a guide for finding your inner medium. It's my adventure in the ghost world, from my early blundering efforts at a vigil to ultimately becoming a fully established ghost hunter. Although my initial motivation was to find out about my ring, I soon wanted to know everything I could discover about ghosts—*any* ghost. There is much more to this realm than I originally had thought, and while I still don't believe all that I hear, I certainly had experiences that made me revise much of what I thought I knew.

Something is out there.

The Claiming of Christian

"BE CAREFUL WHAT YOU HUNT FOR . . ."

—1—

It's always the same. I pick a place specifically for its reputation for ghosts, make a reservation to spend the night, and then find myself alone in a haunted room, listening, waiting breathlessly, and wondering what I'm doing there. In particular, why was I in a room where the ghost gets into bed with the guests?

On this night I was in the 17Hundred90 Inn, a fourteen-room B&B on Lincoln Street in Savannah, Georgia's historic district. It stood on a foundation over three hundred years old, near the Colonial Park Cemetery. The ghost is "Anna," a former owner's daughter, for whom the place had been built. One day she watched the man she loved sail away and then in a fit of despair threw herself from the third-floor balcony to her death. Since 1820, people have reported her presence, which they say fills the air with deep sadness and an overwhelming sense of loss. Sometimes the phone rings in what was once Anna's room, but no one is on the line and the call never goes through the switchboard. Several women have even reported that Anna tried to climb into bed with them. By day, that had sounded terrific. I was ready for that. By night, it was another story.

My second-floor room had an antique four-poster bed, a desk, and a daybed with romantic dimmer lights. During the night, it turned out to be really dark. Drapes so heavy that Scarlett O'Hara could have used them for a winter dress covered the only window. I thought about sitting on the daybed to commence my vigil, but decided instead to get under the four-poster's covers. If I were lucky, I'd drift off to sleep. Better to do that in bed than *out there*.

As I lay there on my back, I listened. My auditory focus was so sharp I could have heard a coyote howl in Montana. Yet that was not what I was listening for.

I swallowed, trying not to breathe. I kept hoping my eyes would grow used to the dark and I'd be able to see. I turned my head to the left, toward where the bathroom door stood open across the room. I couldn't really see it, but I knew there was a lot of empty space over in that direction. Almost like an empty stage upon which something could emerge. I could almost feel it gathering.

I heard a door slam somewhere in the building. A phone rang in another room. The sounds were too distant to startle me. I was waiting for something else, something much closer.

Gripping the bedcovers in my hands, I peered around once more. It was *really* dark. And cold. I felt the dense, chilly air against my face and thought about pulling the covers all the way up. I wanted to just hide. However, since childhood I've harbored a superstition that ghosts are most attracted to the one who's scared. They look for specific signs, and pulling covers over your head is an obvious one. I tried to make it appear as if I was just lying there, unaware and unafraid, just going to sleep. Not thinking about ghosts at all. That way Anna might just pass me by and find someone else.

Then I heard something. I tensed. Slowly I turned my head to the left again. It had come from over there. Something was moving in one corner of my room, near the bathroom. My heart beat in the rhythm of "fight or flight."

I held my breath. I imagined a woman in a long dress slowly approaching with malevolent intent. Her entire focus was on me. She *knew* I was scared. Was that a swish of a cotton slip against the rug? I felt the air change. There was a slight breeze in there. I thought it was growing colder. I was sure it was. My face was freezing.

"Why am I doing this?" I silently wondered. "Why do I always do this?" I was quite literally terrified. Whatever was there, I didn't want to see it.

I swallowed and hoped that "it" could not hear my telltale heart.

This was silly; I knew better, but I could actually lie in desperate fear for hours on nights like this. I'd done it many times before, and each time I wondered why. I had come all this way and had devoted the entire day to preparing myself in great anticipation for just this moment. I wanted to see a ghost. But-not-right-there-in-the-dark-all-by-myself-wondering-where-the-ghost-was-and-what-it-was-doing.

I thought only of those stories that described Anna lifting the covers and climbing under the sheets. I waited for the tug of the blankets from the other side or the touch of cold fingers on my face. I thought for sure that the mattress had been pressed down near my feet, as if someone had sat on it. I tried to breathe evenly and remind myself that ghosts don't harm anyone. Or most of them don't, anyway. Surely this one wouldn't. I had nothing to be scared about.

No, there was something here. It was close. I could feel it leaning toward me. I closed my eyes tight. *Don't touch me, please don't.*

—2—

Since childhood, I've wanted to see a ghost. I don't know why. Maybe it's for the adrenaline rush. I had even wished fervently for a ghost companion, like something out of *The Ghost of Dibble Hollow,* in which a boy befriended a male ghost his own age who led him on an exciting adventure. I actually prayed for it. (However, when night fell I always shakily reneged—"Not tonight, please not tonight!") In any event, nothing ever happened.

The story of my life is that I'm always the one sitting *next* to the person who saw a ghost, or staying in a haunted place the night *before* someone got scared out of his wits. I was always the one who *heard* about the experience, never had one. And when I heard that there were kids who claimed to be able to see ghosts, I was envious. I wanted to do that. In fact, that ability even appeared to be in my own family. I felt like the spiritual runt of the litter.

My grandmother was a water witch. I recall how she once walked the dry ground outside her house with a wishbone-shaped dowsing stick to successfully locate water for a new well. Most recently, as she sat in her room in an elder-care home, she saw a nurse enter, sit at the desk, and begin to write. The only problem was, there was no chair.

My mother, too, has had paranormal experiences. At age six she went with her parents to visit people at a cottage on Wisconsin's Lake Butte de Mort, where an Indian battle once had raged. Growing bored of the adults, she had wandered toward the stairs. Just as she put her foot on the first step, she sensed something in the darkness above. She hesitated, unsure whether to continue. Something up there felt sinister. Suddenly the woman who lived there stopped her with, "No, dear, don't go up the stairs. We don't use that part of the house anymore." My mother never learned why.

She's also had visual experiences. Once, her neighbors had a car parked in their driveway. The car belonged to a woman who had recently committed suicide. As my mother drove home one day and emerged from her own car, she glanced over and saw the deceased woman sitting in the driver's seat, just staring straight ahead.

These incidents don't upset her like they would me, but one sighting did shake her up. Her father—my grandfather—died at the age of seventy-four from cancer, which had left us all deeply bereft. We had memories of working with him out on a piece of property where he grew Christmas trees. Shortly after his death, my mother went out there to get a tree. She walked around, located one she liked, and cut it down. As she was dragging it back toward the car, she saw the figure of her father standing near the barbecue pit. She stopped to look, and he waved as if to let her know that he was fine. Then he was gone.

"It seems that when I come across things like that," she told me, "I haven't been trying to look for them. They're just all of a sudden there."

I've heard that this ability runs in families. My sister and brother both say they have seen ghosts. Mike's experiences were in Vietnam, but Donna saw hers in the same house where a school chum reported an odd event. David Douthat, who had lived there, told me, "There was something different about that house." One night when he was about eleven, he woke up to the sounds of a party downstairs. His parents often entertained, so it was no surprise to hear talking, laughing, and clinking glasses. "I didn't recall that anyone was coming," he said, "but I got up and went out to the banister by the stairway. I saw no lights. I sat at the top of the stairs and thought it was weird that people were down there. I went down a few steps, leaned over the railing, and looked. I could still hear them. But when I got to the bottom of the steps, it was totally quiet and my hair stood up." Instead of investigating further, he went back to bed.

It's unfair. From my early youth, I have wanted to see a ghost, and it seemed so easy for others. That's why I became an amateur ghost hunter, a sort of Fox Mulder of the ghost world. Like him, part of me *wants* to believe, but I crave the indubitable experience of an entity gracing me with its presence. I want to know for sure. I've had a few eerie experiences, but I was never quite convinced that any of them was a true encounter.

Finally, I got a unique opportunity from a source I least expected. In my hunt for vampires for *Piercing the Darkness,* a man came hunting for me. He wanted to tell me about his own experience, but he gave me more than a story. He gave me a ghost. To explain, it means first going back to the vampires.

—3—

When a reporter named Susan Walsh mysteriously disappeared in 1996 while investigating Manhattan's vampire cults, I decided to pick up where she left off. I hoped to find some clues to her whereabouts, but more interesting to me was who these people were. So I acquired fangs and adopted a vampire name, Malefika, to go undercover.

For the most part, people who call themselves vampires are just having fun. They identify with the vampire for various reasons, whether to dress up in romantic clothing, find community, or achieve transcendence in the aura of a larger-than-life creature; they're not out to hurt anyone.

However, there are those few hovering at the edge of the subculture that adopt the bloodsucker's persona to empower themselves with its deadly energy. They view themselves as being beyond good and evil and may become violent. Rod Ferrell, sixteen, led a band of kids to Florida, where he murdered an elderly couple after "crossing over" their daughter into his vampire cult. Richard Trenton Chase drank the blood of his murder victims. Here and there, the vampire inspires bloodthirsty acts. I'd heard of these killers but did not expect to encounter any during my foray into vampire culture. I should have been better prepared.

Enticed by the erotic communiqués from an elusive "vampire" whom I dubbed, Wraith, I agreed to meet him on his terms: I would not know his name; our encounter would take place at night; and no one could accompany me. Ever mindful that Susan Walsh was still missing, I agreed but remained guarded.

Wraith's directions led me out to the woods, to an unfamiliar and isolated spot. No one knew where I was and I knew little about this guy, except that he had claimed his story was "dark" and spiked with hints of madness. By this time, I'd spoken to hundreds of people in this maligned subculture and had found them mostly engaged in a fantasy. I expected something similar from Wraith. To me, this dark place was all about atmosphere, like telling a ghost story around a campfire.

I found Wraith as compelling as Mina must have found the exotic Count Dracula. Surprisingly, Wraith adopted none of the typical vampire trappings—fangs, makeup, black attire, exotic jewelry. Instead, he wore a white T-shirt, jeans, and "stomper" boots. His dark hair was short and his face almost angelic. Tall and lean, he talked with a polished Southern accent in a charmingly measured manner that proved to be a blend of sophisticated ideas and poetic phrasing. Regardless of the potential danger, I was enraptured with the way he verbally shaped his experiences as if with the skilled fingers of a potter.

Throughout the night, Wraith slowly led me through a tale that grew increasingly violent and sadistic. He'd had a lover and partner, he said, who was a vampire. His name was Christian and he liked to torture his "prey"—young men he picked up in various places. According to Wraith, Christian was as alluring as a model, and he showed me a picture he'd torn from a magazine of a tall blond man who he claimed looked similar.

"I burned all of the photos I had of him," Wraith told me, "because he wanted me to. But this is what he looked like."

Although I wasn't sure that I wholly believed his story, I could see why Wraith might have fallen for someone who looked like this. Christian apparently had been tall and lean, with blue eyes beneath a shock of light blond hair.

But he had a mean streak. When torturing young men failed to satisfy him, he began to kill them. Although Wraith hinted that these were hired hits, he also told me about how Christian had killed two girls. His methods were cruel. Wraith, who had exchanged blood with him, had been forced (by his account) to accompany Christian as his unwilling accomplice. Yet he admitted to me that he'd also been energized by Christian's evil acts.

"He was so free," Wraith said. "He was fully present to what he wanted. That's what a vampire is. Fully present to his hunger and his own survival, no matter how vulnerable the victim. There was an excitement about being with him, a thrill, a constant mystery and unpredictability. There was poetry in his madness."

I hadn't quite believed this story at first, because it was introduced through fantastic tales of spooky visitations and underground cults, not to mention a photo cut from a magazine. However, even fantasy addicts spin their tales off truths, and Wraith's descriptions of the murders sounded authentic. I wasn't sure why he was confessing to me. I also wasn't sure where this Christian was. I wondered if I was being set up.

As the night wore on and the woods around us seemed to grow increasingly dense, Wraith continued the story. His apparent acceptance of Christian's violence and his lack of genuine reaction chilled me. Though he claimed reticence, I saw no evidence of it in the telling of his story. Then he got to a part that seemed to actually disturb him. Despite what the two of them secretly had shared, it appeared that they had drifted apart. Christian wanted to leave him, and Wraith found himself feeling utterly lost. I asked him where Christian was now. Had he actually left?

Without answering, Wraith led me through the thickening woods to another place, equally dark and surrounded by a thicket, where Christian had ended his life: He had committed suicide by slashing open both of his carotid arteries. However, he had not given up the world altogether. Wraith claimed that Christian had returned as a ghost—a *vampire ghost.*

"I felt the sensation of something running through me," Wraith said about the day he had visited the suicide site. "And there he was, standing in the woods, looking at me with a smile. I freaked out and ran to the car, but he was already there in the passenger seat. He began to speak to me, telling me not to cry, that he hadn't left me. He said I'd feel him inside me the rest of my life, and that we were now more powerful together as vampires."

Wraith actually seemed to think that Christian had killed himself so that he could join his spirit with Wraith's to hunt together as a single organism—one heart, one soul. He gave me a few chilling examples of just how Christian would possess him.

"I went one night to a club that was like a large, dark cave, with split-level dance floors and flashing lights. The place was filled with muscled young men. Christian appeared at the bar [as a ghost] in a classic predator pose, directing my attention to his favorites. He pointed out a small boy leaning against the far wall. An easy mark. Christian was at his side in a second, licking his neck, getting him ready. I didn't know what this boy could feel, but I thought he could hear Christian whispering in his ear. I walked down, not sure this was what I wanted, but I had no choice. Whatever Christian wanted, he got.

"The boy was happy to see me come up to him and I took him

on the dance floor. At alternate times, I saw Christian possessing him to dance with me and felt him possessing me to entice the boy. Christian wanted to do something mean, but I resisted. I saw Christian standing outside us both, watching me. Within moments, he was inside the boy, kissing me. The boy's mind was Christian, and I was lost to him. And if you think Christian was mean in life, you should have seen him as a ghost. Most of the time, he scared me."

This account, which went into much more detail, disturbed me. I had heard of ghostly possessions, some of them blamed for murders, illnesses, and even psychoses, but I'd never heard such a vivid description.

"Did you kill anyone under his direction?" I asked. I knew that Wraith could very well have been carrying out his own violent inspiration and blaming some imagined entity.

He did not admit to that, but told me about the ways that Christian had tormented him with dreams, poltergeist activity, and even by blocking other relationships. Christian, it seemed, was a possessive spirit. Wraith was clearly disturbed about being haunted but was unwilling to exorcise him. "I don't know what he'd do if I ever tried that," he said quietly.

I continued to query him about things that made little sense: Why would Christian commit suicide? Why, when he was breaking up with Wraith, would he return after death to merge with him? How could he, as a ghost, force Wraith to do things against his will?

Wraith fielded these questions with responses so enigmatic that I began to think something was up. It occurred to me that Christian might not have killed himself after all. In fact, I suspected something more sinister. Finally, to my peril, I confronted him. "Did you murder him?" I asked.

Wraith stared at me, aghast. "No!" he protested. "I loved him!"

"But he was leaving you."

"I *needed* him. I wouldn't have killed him."

I wasn't satisfied. In fact, as I ruminated over this story, it just didn't sit right. I did believe that Christian had killed people and that Wraith had been involved, but it was the nature of Wraith's participation that failed to add up. Finally, I realized what was bothering me.

"Despite what you want me to believe about Christian," I said, "he was just a sadistic sociopath. *You* are the vampire. You're the manipulator. You've wanted me to believe you were helpless, but that's a lie. You've been deceiving me all along."

Slowly he smiled. There was something malicious in the way he looked at me, but I continued. "You clearly made no attempt to dissuade Christian from doing these things. You wanted him to kill. You stayed with him because he was doing what you wanted him to do. And he knew it. He knew *you,* that you'd do anything to keep him going."

Wraith's smile broadened, but he said nothing.

"You encouraged him, supported him. You were attracted to him because he took you into this bloody arena. He acted out what you couldn't do yourself. You set him in motion and fed off him. You were *worse* than him because you exploited his sickness—you amplified it." I went on to theorize that Wraith had planted some kind of trigger that made Christian decide to die. "You got him all obsessed with the spirit world and when he wanted to break up, you used your trigger. If he was finished, he had to die. It's the perfect murder."

Wraith was amused. "If you think I'm so clever," he said, "wouldn't I have done the same with you? I've been talking to you for some time now. Maybe I planted a trigger in you, too."

I hadn't thought of that. The sudden realization made me tremble. Here I was standing alone in the woods with a man who might have been the real killer all along. I couldn't really tell anymore. I'd found myself liking him, even feeling sorry for him, but he had craved that vicious life. He wasn't struggling with his conscience.

He moved closer to me. I took a step back. How easy it would be for him to reach out and grab me.

"Think about this," he said. "Christian is still here. He inspires what I do. He feeds off me. So ultimately, *he's* the vampire."

I was surprised. "You really think you have a vampire ghost?"

"The vampire never dies. He's alive. He's here." Wraith showed me a silver ring that he wore on his right forefinger. "This was Christian's. He gave it to me."

I reached over and touched it. Wraith didn't move, so after a moment I gripped it and pulled it off his finger. "Now you can be free of him," I said. It was a psychological ploy, but he didn't react. He made no move to take the ring back.

"I won't be free of him," he stated.

"If you don't have the ring to remind you . . ."

He shrugged. I smiled and put the ring in my pocket.

"Take it," he said. "But watch out. He comes with it."

I didn't believe that for a second. Yet I did feel that our talk had come to an end. There seemed nothing more to say. I fingered the ring, inclined to give it back, but something in me wanted to keep it.

Wraith just watched me. I wondered if he was reevaluating how much he had disclosed and whether it might not be wiser to add me to his list of victims. I thanked him quickly for his story and then turned and walked away. I wanted to get to my car as fast as I could.

I imagined him following me, grabbing me, hitting me with something to silence me. I had an urge to start running. I listened for his footsteps, but all I heard were his final startling words.

"You'll see him in your dreams," he promised from somewhere behind me. "He won't leave you alone. I give him to you. Now he's all yours."

—4—

I thought about just dropping the ring or tossing it into the woods, but I didn't. Instead when I got home, I put Christian's ring on a silver chain and kept it close by. It hung next to my computer as I wrote the tale, and I took it with me on my book tour. Although I did not believe that Christian was there in spirit, it was fun to warn others of the possibility. Everyone wanted to touch the ring, and some claimed to feel heat emanating from it. But nothing happened to me. I never felt compelled to hunt for "fresh kill" or drink blood. A few lightbulbs went out and some things seemed misplaced, but that's about it. However, I did have strange dreams. Since Wraith still called me every couple of months, I told one to him.

"I was in an old building," I said. "As I climbed the stairs to the top floor, a bat flew at me. I knocked it away but found it gripping my hand with its wings. I felt it bite me. When I finally shook it off, I saw tiny teeth marks on my ring finger, right hand. I knew I had been infected."

Wraith had laughed. "That's one of his favorites. The bat is Christian. It's symbolic of the infection he brings. He'll make you ill to let you know he's there. He plans to be with you a lot more now. He'll become part of you. He waits till your guard is down and then he's there."

"What do you think he wants?"

"He wants you for his next host. He likes your sense of adventure."

"Right," I countered. "This is all from suggestion. You told me he'd come in my dreams, so I had dreams."

"I'm sure he's happy you think that. Like not believing in the devil. It makes you vulnerable. Just be warned: He's hard to handle. Do you want to give him back?"

I pondered this. Maybe I finally had what I'd asked for since childhood: my own ghost. So I said no.

"I didn't think so."

Then I wondered if my response had been wise. There was another dream, more disturbing, that I had not mentioned. One night I awoke at about 4:00 A.M. and felt paralyzed, as if I were tied up. I could hardly breathe. It had seemed as if something implike was in the room, circling the bed at a terrific speed while I lay there unable to move. It felt quite real and I had been terrified. Only later did it occur to me that it might have something to do with this ring. Throughout the following day, the dream haunted me.

These dreams made me wonder about the things that Wraith had told me. I didn't believe that Christian had killed himself. If indeed he had been found in the woods with both carotid arteries slashed, then he did not do that himself. I asked two different physicians about this, and they agreed that it would be quite difficult: Once you've managed to get through one artery with all the surrounding muscle, you bleed so fast that you're pretty much gone. I was convinced that Christian had been murdered. If that were true, then other parts of the story were also suspect. Was Christian actually a ghost who was now haunting me? Or was he perhaps trying to show that the story that Wraith had told was wrong? Did he have some unfinished business? If so, he had to be a little more obvious. Even a vivid and terrifying dream was open to interpretation.

Wraith had mentioned something that now felt like an itch in a place that I would never be able to scratch. He'd said he had written the truth about what he and Christian had done in a book and kept this diary in a locked gray metal box. He teased me with the possibility of getting a look, but then had insisted that no one would ever see it. "I should just burn it," he said.

I urged him not to. I hoped that one day I might discover it and learn what had really happened. However, I told no one else about the existence of this book or the gray metal box and did not reveal it in my vampire book. Even so, I was to find that one does not easily hide such information in the spirit world. As for me, I did not expect ever to see Wraith again. He would certainly not invite me to, and I would not seek him out. Or so I thought.

—5—

Several months after our encounter, he called to say that Christian would make himself known to me by Halloween. I waited and waited, hoping (and fearing) a manifestation. I wanted to see this guy, even if he was some sort of sadistic entity.

Weeks went by and nothing happened. I didn't realize then that this would be the pattern. What I wanted or expected would rarely coincide with what occurred.

Finally, it was the night before Halloween. I felt vaguely disappointed as I prepared for a trip to New York City. I had half hoped that Wraith's prediction would come true—that this time I would be the one who saw the ghost, not the one who heard about someone else's sighting. I was in a rush, so I scooped the spare change from my purse to make room for Halloween essentials and unceremoniously dumped several dozen coins on my coffee table. I then grabbed a clay skull necklace, knocking over two Mexican Day of the Dead skeleton figurines, and rushed out. I wish now that I had knocked over a lot more things.

That night I met Rosemary, a vampiress who claimed to have psychic powers. She was tall with long black hair, a perfect figure, and exotic eyes lined heavily in black. She wore a shiny purple shawl over a tight black dress, and decorated herself with exquisite necklaces and rings. Her skin was pale, and her lips were bright red. She had known Susan Walsh, she told me, and had felt moved to meet me. Her smooth manner and entrancingly deep voice suggested practiced sensuality.

I had Christian's ring around my neck, and Rosemary took it in her hand. "The name I get from it," she said, "is Michael." I shrugged. I didn't know any Michael.

Rosemary had come to give me a candle that she had blessed specifically for me against the forces of evil. That surprised me. Why would she think I was in danger? She urged me to light it as soon as possible because she did not want the same thing to happen to me as had happened to Susan. I accepted it but was determined not to light it that night. There was one more day for Christian to make an appearance. He might be a bad ghost, but he was a ghost. I'd take whatever I could get. I figured that afterward if I needed to I could light Rosemary's candle and shoo him away. Of course, I could not have known what was to come.

On the way home, I got to thinking about Rosemary's reaction to the ring. Perhaps Wraith had used a false name to tell me about his former partner. Maybe his name had been Michael. Or maybe "Michael" referred to the first man that Wraith believed Christian had murdered—their vampire mentor. He'd talked about the leader of a vampire cult who'd been found stabbed to death in his home. His name was Michael. Had the ring been his and had Christian taken it from his corpse? Or had Wraith killed Michael and just called him Christian to disguise him? Wraith had told me a few things about Michael, but I couldn't recall the details.

Suddenly I felt a little sick. That the ring might have been passed from one person to another, at least two of whom had ended up dead, seemed a bit like a mummy's curse. I took it from around my neck and dropped it into my purse. I returned very late that night and fell into bed.

The next day, I went through my mail. There was an envelope from the director of the workshop I had recently given for the Los Angeles County library staff. They had sent a photo of me onstage, which they said had captured something rather strange. They thought I ought to see it. I looked closely. Behind me were streaks of some kind of whitish, feathery aura, almost like a contrail. It was not part of the background and appeared to be unrelated to the lighting. The woman who sent it claimed that no other photo from the workshop had shown such an image. I was curious. The phenomenon was intriguing, but I sure hoped that was not going to be the extent of Christian's "manifestation."

The phone rang. I forgot about the photo and sat on the couch to talk with the friend who had called. After a few minutes of conversation, I happened to glance at the table where I had dumped the change from my purse. My eyes widened. I stopped talking and sat up straight. I shook my head.

It couldn't be.

The coins were now stacked into four perfectly ordered piles of quarters, dimes, nickels, and pennies.

I stared at them. I had not done that. I distinctly recalled the disorganized clatter of the coins as I'd emptied my purse onto the table, and besides, I never stack coins. I'm not that kind of person. No one had been in my apartment. What in the world?

Then it came to me. It was Halloween.

Christian's deadline.

My eyes traveled to the two figurines that I'd knocked over in my haste the night before. They now stood upright.

Wraith!

I hung up the phone and rushed out to look at the doorframe. I didn't put it past him to break in and set all this up, just to make his prediction "come true." Yet that thought was even more disturbing than a ghostly visitation. I examined the door handle and frame minutely. There was no sign of tampering and no other way in.

Psychokinesis? Had he stacked those coins with his mind? Or had I, with my determination to witness a manifestation, subconsciously moved matter with mental energy? I didn't buy it. But did I believe it was a ghost?

I took a breath and thought about this. Until that point, I had not really believed that this ring was haunted. Now I wasn't so sure. It was time to get help.

—6—

I didn't know anyone who knew much about haunted possessions, but Rosemary had told me about a psychic named Steve (not his real name) who helped her try to locate Susan Walsh, the missing reporter. Since he knew her, he was obviously comfortable with the vampire scene and could be a good contact. I decided to call her to set something up.

We all met at a long, narrow coffee shop one evening on a nondescript street in the Lower East Side of Manhattan. It was decorated with abstract art, hung on green walls. Rosemary looked as if she were going to a modeling appointment rather than a reading, and I soon learned that poise was part of her persona. She was always polished, precise, and ready for a photograph.

She introduced me to Steve. To my surprise, he was blind. He had gray hair, a stocky build, and a loud, infectious laugh that immediately put me at ease. He took his work seriously, but not himself. He struck me as Hollywood's version of the head of a gypsy clan who could afford to be amused by the world because he had a few tricks up his sleeve. Steve had been approached, he told me, with every question you could imagine, and he felt sorry for those who just could not get along without answers.

Rosemary picked up the ring to examine it as Steve had me shuffle a large tarot deck that he used "to give his impressions some direction." Rosemary pointed out to me that a tiny cross had been scratched onto the ring, along the outside rim. We both thought that was strange. "Maybe it stands for Christian," I surmised.

For an opening card, I picked the Ace of Pentacles—new birth—and the number thirty-four. Steve took the card and then said with confidence, "He was heavy into pills of some kind." I wasn't sure about that, but the fact that Christian always seemed to have money, though his family was poor, might indicate drug money.

Steve laid out an arrangement that included the Tower, the Emperor, the two of Wands, and the seven and Queen of Swords. He named each of them correctly. I was impressed with his psychic ability. He was right on target with every card. Then I felt one of the cards and realized that each had Braille pinpoints on it. He was "reading" them with his hands.

"I think I know what the deal is here," he said. I felt a thrill of anticipation. He knew nothing of my story except that Christian was said to be a killer and was now dead himself. Steve picked up the ring and held it. "Ooooh," he murmured. "Okay, now I'm going to ask you a question. Were you told anything about the circumstances under which he is reputed to have killed?"

"Yes."

"Okay, my feeling is that it was not your standard, 'I'm pissed, I'm gonna get you' type of situation. This involves a mix of sex and violence."

Right so far, but then weren't most killings?

"It was a game," Steve went on, "and whoever it was, was supposed to get away. There's something about bad drugs. Then he left. He fled the scene. Did he murder? Yes. Did he intend it? No, but also yes. He's killing his mother in absentia or both parents. This is where the anger is from. He never understood the power of his rage. What were you told?"

I was thrown. It sounded like Steve was doing a reading of Wraith. Had Wraith killed Christian as part of a game? But there was a question, and I needed to answer it.

"I was told that he'd killed several people as a hit man."

"That's what I thought," said Rosemary, nodding gravely. "That was my impression."

Steve seemed doubtful but offered to explore it. "Give me a number between one and nine."

"Seven," I said. I didn't believe I was tuning into these numbers psychically, as I was told. Each time he asked, I had to scramble to think of one, but he might say I was unknowingly getting them from some subliminal place.

Steve picked a card and laughed. "Well, he may have said that he did that, but I has me doubts. I has me doubts." He did not say what he really thought.

"Now," said Steve, "another question is, can you use this ring like a telephone? Yes. But you have to intend to. You have to make an effort."

Now we were getting somewhere. A telephone! "How?" I asked.

"I don't think you want to," said Rosemary with a warning look.

"No, you don't want to," Steve echoed her.

"Yes, I do."

"No," said Rosemary. "Believe me."

Well, I just wanted to know how, not to actually do anything, but I didn't press it.

"What you'd do," Rosemary explained, "is turn your own anger energy on. You might not be like him, but you'd do things that you might not really want to do. It's better not to mess with this."

"Okay, then," I said, "has he manifested himself to me in some way and will he hurt me?"

"That's a good question." Steve said, and picked up the cards. "Pick a number between one and nineteen."

"Seven," I said.

"Oh, that's interesting!" Steve exclaimed to himself, staring upward as he went through the cards. "Oh, yeah!" He was silent for a moment and then said, "Only in a dream did he manifest himself to you. You were just about to wake up and you had a sense of being tied."

I sat up, startled. That was the dream that had so disturbed me. I had wondered if it had been Christian's way to get my attention. Now I *really* had something to ask.

"I heard a story about Christian's death and I'm not convinced about it," I went on. "I'd like to ask how you think he died."

Steve handed me the deck to shuffle, and I picked the number six. Again, the Ace of Pentacles came up, along with the King of Cups, Page of Wands, and a sleeping figure with swords running through him. Steve looked thoughtful as he said, "He was not alone when he died."

That was significant, I thought. That was my own feeling.

He asked for a number and Rosemary gave him seven. Steve pulled a card and said, "He wanted it. Unconsciously, he wanted out."

"Was he in trouble?"

Steve smiled. "He knew he would be. The stuff was escalating. He opted out."

I asked for more and the reading went on for a while longer, but without significant information. It was not clear that I was in any kind of danger, but it was also not clear that I wasn't. Steven and Rosemary both warned me that there was a lot of power in this ring and I needed to be careful with it. Whatever spirit was around it would want something from me if I tried to use it. Rosemary thought I should just put it in a box and leave it alone.

Since this was the first psychic reading I'd had, I wasn't sure what to think, but I decided that I ought to seek out others who could educate me about ghosts. Since Steve had come so close to things I knew without knowing anything himself, I was convinced that there was enough weirdness in this reading—coupled with what had happened with those coins in my apartment—to warrant further investigation.

Thus, I made a decision. I would try to find out whether Christian did indeed haunt the ring. In fact, if I could use it as a phone, all I needed . . . hey! Spare change. Maybe those coins were a sign to "call" him on this "phone."

I made some inquiries and soon began my journey into the world of mediums, channelers, psychics, exorcists, and ghost hunters. I decided to start my quest in the Garden of Good and Evil, and that's how I ended up in the room with "Anna."

2 *Ghosts in the Garden of Good and Evil*

—1—

In my room at the 17Hundred90 Inn, I was engaging in what many ghost hunters call the "vigil." It's a basic exercise, and it was all I really knew at that point about ghost hunting. I'd read about this as a teenager in some ghost hunter's handbook when I'd first begun to look for ghosts in earnest.

The idea is to spend the night awake in a haunted place, watching for signs of a presence. You write down everything unusual and later check out all the possible sources for that activity. I'd done it many times in the past in places like cemeteries and battlefields, but without real success. Although my intention in coming to Savannah was to seek out a ghost expert, I figured it couldn't hurt to throw in a night at a haunted B&B as well.

According to what I'd read, ghost hunters generally work in pairs, so they have a witness. They also use recording equipment of some sort, like cameras and meters. I had neither equipment nor a willing partner. If Anna showed up, I'd have to deal with her on my own. I might live to tell about it, but I'd have no witness to back me up. I knew that no serious ghost hunter would support such a vigil, but I wasn't there to prove anything to anyone else. This was strictly for me. I wasn't going to visit a place like Savannah—a Southern city that embraces its ghosts—without trying to spot one. In addition, Savannah offered good potential for finding an authority on the paranormal. I had the name of a man whose tour I had attended on a prior visit, and I hoped to get him alone.

Ghosts are to the South as works of art are to Italy: They're part of daily life and you find them everywhere. No matter where you go, someone has a story to tell. The first one I ever heard from a Southerner was told by my father, a native of Tennessee. One evening, when he was a boy, he saw the dark figure of a man run across the street in front of him. He was scared but curious, so he pursued the man, chasing him in the dark across a muddy area. He lost the guy, but the next day he went back. When he looked at the ground, he saw only one set of tracks—his. He swore it was the truth.

In fact, among my many previous attempts at a vigil, I had found more people in the South than anywhere else who could speak easily on the topic of ghosts. Encouraged by this, I felt sure I would find someone in Savannah, and I did.

I went by train and sat next to a young man named Ron, who sported a short, army-style haircut. It wasn't long before we were talking about the supernatural. He was from Savannah, although he had also lived in California. He told me about a house there that his mother had owned in which Mexican workers refused to sleep because they claimed that "things" pressed on their chests at night to stop them from breathing. Ron thought that was pretty strange.

"Have you ever heard of anything like that?" he asked.

In fact, I had. Such night visitations were generally referred to as the "Old Hag" phenomenon, from the medieval notion that witches would "ride" on someone's chest at night to cause paralysis and suffocation. This kind of story has been around since ancient times, and in her book, *The Encyclopedia of Ghosts and Spirits,* Rosemary Ellen Guiley claims that 15 percent of the population worldwide has experienced the Old Hag attack. Different cultures interpret it in different ways, from an enemy's magic to malevolent fairies to sleep disorders. What is common about the experience is that the victim suddenly wakes up, feels a weight on his chest, and finds he cannot move or scream. As he loses consciousness, the attack ceases. However, he's left feeling exhausted afterward.

Some experiences begin with the sound of footsteps, others with

gHost

the feeling that someone is looking at you or about to touch you. The victim may experience a terrible odor or see a pair of bright red eyes and hear rasping breath. He may choke or feel his breath drawn from his body. Inevitably, he feels threatened, and the attack can happen at any time during the day or night.

As a kid I read an article in a newspaper about a house not far away in Detroit, Michigan, in which strange things happened to a man in a back bedroom. At first he only had nightmares. Then, after others repeatedly saw and felt things in the room, he made a deliberate effort to check it out. He went in one day and lay on the bed. Someone touched him, and he rolled over to find himself face-to-face with an ugly old woman with stringy gray hair and a revolting smell. She drooled and hissed at him. He got up, grabbed his family, and fled from the place. Police came in to search, but detected only faint traces of a foul odor.

Professor David Hufford wrote a book on this phenomenon entitled *The Terror That Comes in the Night*. His research indicates that this kind of experience spans many cultures and that at least 15 percent of adults report it. I suppose he believes that makes the experience merely psychological, but I don't think I would find that reassuring if some old woman hovered over *me*.

I told Ron that I had booked a room in the 17Hundred90 Inn, and he said, "Oh, that *is* haunted." Just the way he said it made me shiver with delight. Maybe . . . just maybe . . .

He asked me to let him know if anything happened.

For the rest of the trip I looked through some of the ghost research I had done so far and thought about the theories I'd heard that purported to explain ghosts. There were numerous ideas, including dismissing all sightings as hallucination or imagination. I wasn't willing to do that, although I still was not entirely convinced by some of the tales I'd heard. Yet, when two people who don't know each other describe the same phenomenon, it's not so easy to dismiss. I have run across that from time to time. I also once heard a tape recording of a ghostly voice crying, "Help me," and that had seemed real enough, although I knew that the person could have faked the recording. Photos did not convince me, either, because it's too easy to manipulate photography. In fact, many ghost photos from the nineteenth-century spiritualist movement had been faked. I would have to take a picture of my own before I'd believe that kind of evidence.

One idea I had read about was the electrical impulse wave theory. During periods of stress, such as during a suicide or murder, the brain waves become more active, and it's possible that they might produce an image that somehow imprints itself on the atmosphere of a certain place and remains there after the person has died. It may be that during stress, the person thought about a better time in his life, such as walking through a garden or looking out a window, and that's the image that transfers. This fits with the reports of ghosts who continue to walk on the same floor or stairs they knew in life even after the floor has been raised or the stairs dismantled.

Yet how would this explain sightings of ghost animals or vehicles like trains, planes, ships, and cars? Others speak of time slips, where they find themselves in a completely different place, seeing people there as ghosts. Reports of ghostly experiences are varied and no single theory quite covers all incidents.

A common idea is that people who want to see ghosts "feed" energy into the phenomenon and thus make it occur, which amounts to a sort of telepathic psychokinesis, particularly if they can make an object move or a door open by itself. In fact, in 1972 a group of eight people in Canada, the Toronto New Horizons Research Foundation, had actually produced numerous paranormal events after designing a ghost and concentrating together on him. They named him Philip; gave him a tragic history as an English aristocrat and a reason to have returned as a ghost; and designed his likes and dislikes, habits and customs. For some time nothing happened. Yet when they left off concentrating and decided to just have fun and relax, they got results: raps or "answers" on the table in response to songs and questions, the "answers" being in perfect accord with the invented personality. Then the table began to move and once even shot across the room. There were cool breezes and metal bending, and all of this was captured on videotape. When one member told "Philip" that they had made him up, the phenomena ceased. It picked up again when the group resumed "belief" in his existence. One might assume, then, that all such phenomena are psychological in nature.

That theory doesn't fit with my own experience. If we "feed" entities with our desire to experience them, I've been sending out enough energy to satisfy a phantom army. I'd also heard many reports from people who never wanted to see a ghost, didn't even believe in them, and yet still saw them. It may be that our own psychology makes a contribution, but I can't reduce the phenomena merely to the mind.

If ghosts are not telepathic images, are they spirits or souls of those who have died? Again, the ghostly vehicles would not fit this theory, but it's still not so easy to dismiss. Mediums believe that only people who have the gift can contact these spirits and that the spirits often have messages for those they have left behind, but I had never seen a convincing demonstration of this. Also, there seemed to be ghostly manifestations that I came to understand as residual hauntings in which ghosts repeatedly go through a scenario—which includes ghostly images of people who did not die in that same context. In other words, a haunting of a victim running from a killer will include not only the victim but the killer—although only one of them actually died. The whole thing, if true, seemed too mindless to be contacted, let alone have a message to offer. In addition, I wasn't sure how I felt about mediums or exorcists who send spirits to "the light." Since we don't really know what a ghost is, how can we tell that this is a proper or effective procedure? Just because some spirit ceases to haunt an exorcised place (and they don't always), maybe it just went to some other place or figured that if it wanted to stay, it would have to be quiet.

There are also ghosts of the living. There are reports on record of people seeing the apparition of someone they knew when that person was alive and well in some other place. Some theorists call that bilocation, others astral projection. Whatever it is, if it actually can happen, then it tends to support the notion that we have some sort of spiritual counterpart that can manifest in a ghostly image.

Then there's the issue of poltergeists—those trickster spirits that move things around, throw stuff across the room, rattle doors, hit people, and otherwise make life difficult. Most ghost hunters are now of the mind that this is an energy manifestation from living people, typically adolescent or preadolescent children. In other words, a poltergeist is not a ghost.

I had read that people have a one in ten chance of seeing a ghost at some point during their lives. In fact, one book listed the typical features associated with those most likely to have a paranormal encounter:

- *A female in her mid-forties.*
- *Has an advanced degree in a mental health field.*
- *Has a parent or grandparent with psychic ability.*
- *Was an only child.*
- *Has a tendency toward bilateral dominance.*
- *Has talent in the arts.*
- *Was/is an exceptional student or dyslexic or both.*
- *Has a photographic memory.*
- *Has a need to be alone.*

- *Has experience as a mediator.*
- *Has a need for a regular dose of nature.*
- *Has or had an endocrine dysfunction such as thyroid problems.*
- *Is a night owl.*
- *Sleeps little and experiences frequent sleep interruptions.*
- *Has a sense of being psychic from birth.*

I possessed most of these traits, but I was not an only child. Although I no longer felt psychic—in fact, I felt rather cloddish in this arena—I recall as a child feeling that I had a unique attunement to animals. It frustrated me that with all of these traits going for me, I seemed unable to see a ghost. People tell me I'm trying too hard, but if ghosts want attention, as one theory suggests, then I would think I'm just the sort of person they would seek out.

Maybe things would be different in the city of moonlight and magnolias—Savannah.

—2—

By late morning, I had arrived in this charming, genteel place. Founded by James Oglethorpe in 1733 on the Savannah River in south-eastern Georgia, the City of Festivals was America's first planned city. For a while during the eighteenth century, it was Georgia's capital and became a shipping and cultural center for area planters. It still drips with Spanish moss and Old World grace. Its two-and-a-half-square-mile historic district is set up in a grid of squares in which one thousand historic buildings still stand.

I checked in at the 17Hundred90 Inn and then went straight to the first place I wanted to see: the redbrick Mercer House on Monterey Square, once owned by the infamous Jim Williams.

Millions know Williams as the slightly sinister character at the heart of John Berendt's "nonfiction novel," *Midnight in the Garden of Good and Evil.* He lived in the grand 1861 Mercer House on Monterey Square and ran an international business in antiques. Each year he threw *the* Christmas party of the season until 1981, when he shot Danny Hansford, a young man who lived with him. Claiming self-defense, Williams went through three separate trials, assured by his investment in voodoo magic that ultimately he would be acquitted. And he was—at least by the jury. He seems to have fared a little worse at the hands of Danny's ghost: He died of a heart attack in his home at the age of fifty-nine, falling to the very spot where he would have lain had Danny shot him as he claimed the young man meant to do. The voodoo practitioner whom he had consulted had warned Williams that Danny was angry and must be appeased. Apparently, he failed to take this seriously.

There is a better ghost story attached to Jim Williams than that of Danny Hansford. He was also a restoration entrepreneur who ended up owning what has been called the most haunted house in Savannah. This two-hundred-year-old, four-story frame structure sits at 507 East St. Julian Street. It even has a widow's walk. I heard a taped interview with him that focused on this place. Williams bought it in 1963 and moved it four blocks. At the time, he was thinking only of restoration, not of the sailor who once had hanged himself on a bed frame in the place, so he was puzzled when the workmen reported bizarre events.

They heard footsteps, voices, and furniture being thrown around, and they experienced feelings that others were present in the house. When this got to be too much, some walked off the job. One worker went upstairs to investigate a loud noise in a room that was supposed to be empty. When he failed to return, others went to find him and discovered him lying facedown on the floor. He said he'd walked into the room and felt as if he had plunged into ice-cold water. He seemed to lose control of his body, so he dropped to the floor to impede the force he had felt drawing him toward an open chimney, where a thirty-foot drop would have meant certain death.

All those people who have assured me that ghosts are benign or impotent apparently have not done their homework. That may be true of most, but this was not the last story I heard of someone experiencing a harmful force.

There were sightings at this house, too, of a tall man dressed in black with a silver cravat glaring through a third-floor bedroom. Some saw a gray-haired man wearing a silver morning robe, and neighbors often heard party noises and a woman singing or screaming. Once they reported seeing people dancing on the top floor when the house supposedly was empty. Williams dismissed the idea that his new house was haunted, although he did admit that an empty crypt had been found on the lot. He eventually moved in and found out more than he wanted to know. Several times he was awakened to the noise of footsteps in his room, like someone crunching broken glass underfoot. He was finally willing to acknowledge that at least something odd was happening.

Williams then called in an Episcopal priest to perform an exorcism. For nearly an hour, the holy man blessed the house and commanded the evil to leave. However, his rituals apparently failed because within a week the noises returned. Hans Holzer, a premier investigator of paranormal phenomena, looked through the place and assured Williams that it did indeed harbor something. Other psychics sensed a female presence, including one with children.

I took a look at both of Williams's houses and then headed out to the 130-year-old Bonaventure Cemetery. It was a few miles away, so I had to rent a car and drive. I recognized it at once from the movie that had been based on *Midnight in the Garden of Good and Evil.* It was here that the famous picture of the Bird Girl monument was taken for the cover of what Savannah residents now simply call "the Book." Having once been a great plantation, this cemetery now resembles a park more than a field of graves. Spanish moss drapes down over the numerous aging tombstones, while azalea bushes, moss-covered statuary, and a forest of huge oak trees line the wide avenues. Off to one side is a bluff that looks out over the Wilmington River. Apparently the ghost of a Confederate veteran appears here at midnight to run off vandals. Another legend tells of the party of people who witnessed the destruction by fire of the great mansion that once had stood on the site. One man had toasted to the party, requesting its eternal continuance, and he seems to have gotten his wish. According to the tale, one can still hear the shattering crystal glasses that the guests threw at a tree. Songwriter Johnny Mercer is buried here, as is the poet Conrad Aiken. His gravestone is a granite bench on which a person can sit and reflect on the slow-moving water below. I couldn't resist.

While there, I recalled a scene from the Book that took place in another cemetery farther away that had some relevance to my venture. It involved the midnight excursion of Jim Williams and John Berendt to meet Minerva, the voodoo practitioner. To understand the living, she told them, one must commune with the dead. She described "Dead Time," wherein the good spirits come around during the half hour before midnight and the bad spirits during the half hour after midnight. It was her job to make Danny Hansford's spirit loosen up on Williams. She had urged him to recall something that had made Danny happy, which Williams did, but she was unable to sense whether it had pleased the deceased. She'd shooed them away and continued with her incantations.

I thought a lot about what she said regarding the spirits of those people who were once cold or cruel are like—my thoughts always coming back to Christian. In fact, I had run across a quote in the Bible that made me think very hard about it. In the Book of Jude, it said,

"Woe to them! For they have gone the way of Cain . . . caring for themselves . . . doubly dead . . . wandering stars for whom the blackness of darkness has been reserved forever." That expression, "doubly dead," applied to those who murder people, rang true to me. Christian, if he was indeed the psychopath that Wraith had made him out to be, had already been dead in life. Now he was dead in death. Doubly dead. In other words, if there is any kind of spiritual enlightenment on the other side, it may be unavailable to his disconnected soul. But then what did that make him exactly?

I pulled out the papers I had from my conversation with Wraith about Christian's ghost. I would not have had to travel far to reach the spot where we first had met, and I was glad it was daylight as I sat there reading.

Wraith told me about how Christian had been found dead. After the funeral, he visited the place in the woods where they had discovered him, naked and bloody, on a large rock. Wraith found a note to himself indicating that this act had been by Christian's hand. He then saw an apparition. Racing to his car, he found Christian in spirit form, waiting for him. From that day, Christian had been his constant companion.

I remembered listening to this story with a fair amount of incredulity, yet had pursued it as if it were true, trying to see if Wraith would falter with the details. Now I was glad that I had.

"After Christian first showed himself and said he was going to be with you," I had asked, "what was his next appearance?"

"He returned the next night, in the same way, and thereafter for the next week," Wraith responded. "I was terrified . . . genuinely terrified. I thought about resistance, because what he proposed seemed unholy. In life he spurned the sacred, so I was not surprised that in death his desecration continued. But I was surprised at him inviting me—no, *insisting* on me joining him. He seduced me through my loneliness. I wanted him back. In life he would always eventually have his way with me . . . through gentle, creative persistence. He knew what I liked, what I craved."

He had told me how they had become a team, with Christian directing him in his choice of "prey." I had asked about their first episode together, and Wraith had responded, "Christian accompanied me to a beach party. I liked a blond, blue-eyed boy who was too young to be drinking. When I first saw him I felt a sharp stabbing pain in my groin, a shooting pain that quickly turned into pleasure. It was then that Christian was inside of me. I knew that a ghost can use a host's ectoplasm for entry, but I was not expecting him to enter like that. I could feel his hands move with my hands, and his fingers were inching inside of mine. I tingled all over and felt like I was going to exploded ... very, very hot, like a fever."

He went on to describe how "they" had attempted to seduce this young man, who had then witnessed an odd phenomenon. "He looked into my eyes," Wraith had explained, "and suddenly gasped and backed away, as though he'd just seen a ghost. He said, 'You're glowin', man, you're glowin' all over your face and head.'"

This disturbed and delighted him. It affirmed that he had this association with the spirit realm, and it made him feel powerful. Personally, I wondered if that's all it amounted to: He felt incomplete, so he invented a ghost that would give him courage and "make" him do things he could not do on his own. But had the boy really seen this thing, or was Wraith just making that up?

"Do you think you became addicted to his attentions?" I asked.

"Definitely. I become addicted to almost any attention and having a personal, passionate lover-ghost all my own—totally addicted."

I wondered if Christian was just some psychological projection. I wrote down my thoughts, still not quite sure what to make of what Wraith had told me. Perhaps I wasn't chasing a ghost at all. Maybe what Steve and Rosemary had told me was totally made up. Maybe ... but who had stacked the coins? That was the kicker. I still couldn't explain that.

I also had with me a book called *A Field Guide to Demons, Fairies, Fallen Angels, and Other Subversive Spirits*. It gave an overview of entities from all world cultures. In a section called "How to Identify a Basic Demon," I read how the demon will appear to you as something desirable, with the promise of giving you what you want. It will then lure you into a position of vulnerability and change its shape into the monster that it truly is. A demon may seem charming, but one must always regard it as feral. It can be destroyed, but only if you see your way through the illusion in time to save yourself. Some cultures have the idea that the demon was once a person who did not get fully developed and who will remain stuck in the dark unless he can inspire someone else to do what he did and thus take his place.

I smiled at that. I doubted there was much chance of Christian inspiring me to murder people. Even Wraith had not admitted to this sort of thing—Wraith, who would have done anything for Christian when he was alive. In any event, it was unlikely with me. I looked through the book to see if anything else might give me a sense of direction.

At that moment, I felt such a chill that I looked up from my reading. There was no one immediately at hand, but I sensed someone watching me. I glanced around at the stones. A few people at a distance were reading monument inscriptions, but the cemetery was pretty quiet. It had rained that morning, creating puddles, and another storm threatened, so people had probably stayed away.

I tried to continue reading, but again felt the intrusive presence of someone close by. It did not feel friendly. I took a deep breath to try to shake it. Then I tried to see from out of the corner of my eye so it wouldn't seem that I was trying to locate this person. Still nothing.

I got up to go to a different part of the cemetery. I felt eyes on my back but refrained from turning around until I got to a place where looking back would seem natural. I spotted an older man at a carved monument. He appeared to be studying the date. I didn't know him, so I doubted that he was the source of my weird feelings. Still, I walked farther away until I could no longer see him.

Finally, I just decided to leave. Whatever this feeling was, it was just too sinister. I knew that aboveground tombs can shield would-be muggers, so I decided to take no chances. In some cemeteries, there are worse things than demons.

—3—

It's easy to find a ghost tour in Savannah. There are at least five different evening excursions, including one in a horse-drawn carriage. I found most of them to be a mechanical rehashing of stories from Margaret DeBolt's *Savannah Spectres* book. Nevertheless, one tour guide stood out as someone who truly embraced the spirit world and had even done some investigations of his own. Harvey Ray's "Ghost Talk, Ghost Walk" tour, founded by Jack Richards, left at dusk from John Wesley's monument at Reynolds Square. His graying hair indicated his age. "I was born in Savannah," he later told me, "but not—as they say in the South—*reared* in Savannah." He spent twenty years up north in Yankee territory, in New York, before finally coming home. Talking to him reminded me that whenever you ask a true Southerner a question, you had better be prepared to listen to stories. He slowed my hurried Yankee stride to a pleasing stroll.

Harvey exuded strong enthusiasm for Savannah's spooky history. He was well rooted there and knew many of the people who had populated the Book. In fact, his talented cousin, Jack Leigh, had taken the photograph of the Bird Girl, spending two long nights in the cemetery seeking the perfect shot. A jazz player, stage actor, and director of film industry relations for the Savannah College of Art and Design, Harvey had the credentials to get him into a lot of parties.

He had a patient air as he delivered his ghost stories to the curious tourists. I sensed that he was aware that only a select few had much grasp of what he was talking about. Most of them were just waiting for some staged effect. As he spoke, pointing out this haunted building and that, I learned a few things about ghosts that surprised me. He told one story about how he had been with a group of people and had seen a figure on the steps of a house that no one else could see. He also said there was a ghost who appeared in one spot around three times a month but would never show himself to Harvey. That gave him the idea that ghosts appear selectively to people, which meant they possess a certain amount of intention. "These ghosts have been around for a long time," Harvey said, "so it stands to reason they would have an agenda. We may not know what it is, but they have one."

An agenda. I made a note to ask him about that after the tour. I recalled Wraith once telling me that Christian had picked me to tell his story. But perhaps it's not an agenda. It might simply be the case that some people can see them and others can't, just as some people have perfect vision and others are blind or need glasses.

As we walked through the quiet streets, we noticed the full moon overhead. Then as Harvey told us about the house that Jim Williams had once owned, a pure white owl flew over us. Harvey smiled, as if the owl had come on cue. He then took us to a tiny cottage, painted "haint blue," which legend says will ward off spirits. A bar owner whose husband had jilted her had once owned this house. Her experience with her husband had left her bitter against all men, and she was arrested for assault against one of her patrons. For the rest of her life, she refused to allow men into her house, and this apparently continued even after she died. Her cottage was left to an unmarried daughter, who left it to a niece, but somehow it was eventually rented out to a man. On his first night there, he felt a pair of small hands around his neck, trying to strangle him. He reported it, but the landlord had no idea what it was. The second night was peaceful, but on the third night, the same thing happened, so he moved out. He was quite shaken. Thereafter the landlord decided to rent only to women.

"Ha!" I thought. "Another mean ghost."

In front of my own hotel, I heard a new twist to the Anna story.

Apparently she dislikes newlyweds and will show her face in the mirror to scare them. I wondered if that was only in her former room—or in others, like mine. I was anxious to find out.

In Colonial Park Cemetery, which was shrouded in mist, Harvey told us about a young blond man who used to sit wordlessly at the bar in the tavern known as the Olde Pink House, back near Reynold's Square. Built in the eighteenth century by James Habersham Jr., it seems conducive to all kinds of spirits. One day a young woman who had fallen in love with the blond man from afar followed him when he left and tracked him all the way to the cemetery. There she saw him walk into the Habersham family plot and disappear. She ran to get a closer look, and although he had seemed as solid as any ordinary person, he simply was no longer there. She was so upset, she left Savannah for good.

The tour ended here. Most of the group departed quickly, giving me a chance to corner Harvey and ask him what he knew about ghosts—in particular about contacting them and learning their "agendas." It turned out that he once had owned a haunted house in Dawsonville, Maryland, a Victorian cottage.

"It was haunted by a single ghost named Darby," Harvey explained. "That's what everyone called him. He had built the house himself around 1870, when he was in his twenties. He raised his family there, but then later lost his mind. He was in his sixties or seventies at the time. He became pretty unbearable, so rather than put him into an asylum, which were terrible places back then, the family decided to lock him in the attic. He lived up there for about twenty years."

"Wow," I said. "You knew all that about your ghost?"

"He was a legend around there. Of course, he had the obligatory rocking chair with the obligatory ruts worn into it from his fingers digging into it as he rocked. That chair was still there when we moved in. And, of course, it rocked by itself."

I thought he was putting me on until he told me what happened on their first night in the house. As we walked together back to Reynolds Square, he described how when he and his family first moved in, they stacked about twenty boxes of papers and other items in the attic. They had visited the house several times prior to occupying it, but seeing no sign of a ghost, they had given the tales little thought. As they went to bed that night, they heard noises in the attic. The next morning, Harvey went to retrieve something from one of the boxes. When he opened the attic door, which was at the bottom of a set of stairs, he found the stairwell filled with papers. "I was literally thrown back against the wall from the weight of stuff that was against the door." The ghost apparently had emptied most of the boxes.

"So what was this ghost's agenda?" I asked.

"To scare the shit out of people. He succeeded nobly with several families who lived in the place before us. They moved out fairly quickly. And he did scare my wife. We'd hear him come down the attic steps, and our bedroom was the first door he'd have to pass. One night he hoisted all his banners. My wife woke up and saw a bluish glow go past, which really frightened her. I saw him, too, and when I said, 'Darby!' he disappeared. He met his match in my kids, though. They thought he was great."

"They weren't scared?"

"No. They had a ghost. They loved it. And they could perceive him in a room before we could. So could the dogs."

"Why is that?"

"Well, that's a question I've given a lot of thought to," Harvey said. He steered me out of the shadows toward a streetlight. "I think with dogs it's their lack of higher intelligence and preponderance of instinct. With kids, it's similar. Their intelligence isn't as cluttered as that of adults and their instincts are clearer."

That made some sense, and I was to think about it more in the days to come. But I wondered about Harvey. If his wife was afraid, why wasn't he? That's when I discovered that he'd had his share of paranormal experiences. For part of his life, he'd had precognitive abilities. "I'm attuned, Katherine," he said. "I don't know how else to put it. There have been people in my life with whom I've been able to communicate nonverbally. That's the way it's been musically for me, too. It's referred to among musicians as 'going outside.' My music is generally outside the traditional harmonic jazz. I can just move away from the normal way of playing and go somewhere else. That's how it is for me with these feelings. Ever since I owned that house, I've been fascinated with ghosts. I can now go to some house and know right away if it's haunted."

"How?"

"It's a feeling. I can't explain it. I just appreciate that it is what it is."

"But what's it like? Can you describe it?"

He shrugged and searched for words. "I just know that it's immediate. It's kind of clammy. I shift into another gear and there's a sense that I'm not alone in a room. I can focus at another level and get tuned into things. I know when they're there and I know when they're gone." He gave me a sort of strange look and seemed about to say something, but I cut in.

"And it doesn't scare you?"

He shook his head. "I've never really been afraid of ghosts."

"But you yourself tell stories about how a ghost has tried to harm someone."

"I know that. However, I think I attract benevolent spirits." He then told me about a time when he woke up from a dream and knew at once that something was there in the room with him. It stayed for about ten minutes and then left. "What works for me to bring them closer," he said, "is to hum. I make a very organic sound and that seems to keep them there. But the problem is, ghosts are like people. The same thing that will attract one might block or repel another. You can never be sure of any one approach. You just have to be as open and clear as you possibly can be."

That was helpful to know, except that it was still rather vague. I then asked him about his techniques for going out to find ghosts and whether he used any equipment. He said that he never had. He just relied on his attunement. Sometimes it gave him a specific feeling, such as whether a presence was benign or not, but most of the time it was just a general sense of having company close by. "What I think is that there is an opening, a channel, a clearance, a path into the mind and spirit of a living person. I think it's difficult to keep it uncluttered, but that's the way they use to get through."

As we parted company, I asked Harvey if I could call him with more questions, and he told me I was welcome to do so. He would help in any way he could. However, since he relied on an ability that he could not just teach me, I wondered if he could give me the kind of assistance I needed. I didn't even show him the ring, although in retrospect, I wish that I had.

−4−

To my relief (and disappointment), no ghost crawled into my bed that night—not Anna and not Christian. I was awake for a long time and I heard plenty of suspicious noises, but eventually I fell asleep. When I woke in the morning, the night images that had so disturbed me now seemed hollow. There was no sign of any disturbance. Nothing was moved and there were no images in the mirror. I could not imagine why I had been so nervous.

Then I remembered the dream. Mediums have said that ghosts will often communicate through dreams, and this one had been bad.

Very bad. I still felt the negative emotional tone. The gist of the dream was that I felt superfluous and alone. I had lost all of my work. I had nothing to support me. It was very disturbing, but was exactly what people had described feeling when they thought Anna was present. Sad, grieving, lost. Utterly disconnected.

Suggestibility. It had to be. People had told this to me, I'd been thinking about it, I'd been reading Wraith's incredible descriptions, and I'd listened to Harvey's stories. It was the most rational explanation.

Even so, I began to wonder if I really wanted to know Christian's story after all. If this was how I might end up feeling—if finding ghosts meant becoming some sort of emotional conductor—then I had to rethink this project. I didn't want to become manipulated by his anger or his despair. I remembered Wraith telling me that after Christian first appeared to him, he began to feel ill and depressed. I was not prepared to have my soul eroded.

I decided to call Harvey and ask him more about this. He told me that he, too, had had a dream like that once when he was in Hollywood. In the dream, he found himself in a theater, and when he woke up from the dream, he knew he was not alone. To his mind, a ghost had communicated through his dream. He did not think it unlikely that Anna had done the same with me. He went on to give me a few more examples of this type of communication.

I pressed him with more questions about his "attunement," but he insisted there was not much more to say. It was just a feeling and some people had it, while others didn't. He had tried to help a few people who were close to him to develop it but had succeeded only once, and only to a limited degree. The experience had been disappointing, and he had decided not to try it again. To him it was all a mystery.

Then I thought of something. "By any chance, did you sense anything around me?"

"Last night I did," he admitted. "While we were talking, I had a couple of moments with you when I felt quite definitely that someone had joined us. I was going to mention it, but went on to something else. In fact, it's happened just now while we've been talking on the phone."

"Like someone listening in?"

"Exactly that. Like someone listening in. It was kind of exciting, actually. That's part of the feeling. Ghosts excite me."

"But you didn't get a name, or if it was male or female?"

"No. It was just a sense that someone else was there."

This was frustrating. Vague feelings, fleeting ambiguous images, disturbing dreams. That wasn't much to go on.

By the time I left Savannah, I realized that if I were really going to pursue the question of whether I had a ghost, I needed a better way. I did not know then that what I sought was just around the corner on the most famous battlefield in America.

3   *High Tech and the Art of Ghost Hunting*

"GETTYSBURG MAY VERY WELL BE, ACRE FOR ACRE, THE MOST HAUNTED PLACE IN AMERICA."

—MARK NESBITT

—1—

In March, there was to be a ghost conference at the Civil War battlefield in Gettysburg, Pennsylvania, run by a couple from Oregon, Dave Oester and Sharon Gill, of the International Ghost Hunters Society (IGHS). They had a website where they posted ghost stories, sold ghost-detection equipment, offered weather forecasts conducive to ghost hunting, and promoted their own home-study ghost hunter's certification kit. In addition to all of this, the conference itself sounded interesting. There are so many reported hauntings in this area that the town has an official "Ghosts of Gettysburg" office, so it seemed like the perfect convergence between ghost and ghost hunter. As I sent in my application, I was unaware that this conference would change my entire approach to ghosts . . . and change me.

Initially, I saw it as an opportunity to find out more about a type of exploration that I'd only read about. What I knew of paranormal investigations to that point was that they required special equipment such as infrared devices, that the equipment is expensive and hard to find, and that people have to go through extensive paranormal training to be able to use it correctly. I'd always been interested but had never had time to pursue an entire program devoted to becoming a parapsychologist. I had been content to do my vigils and just read about what the ghost hunters were doing—which was getting photos of a filmy substance called ectoplasm, setting up devices to detect spirit movement, and operating surveillance equipment.

These people from Oregon seemed to be saying that ghost hunting doesn't have to be so inaccessible: It's easy, less expensive than one might imagine, and available to anyone who can find a Radio Shack. If that was true, I wanted to know more, because if I could buy and learn to use equipment that detected ghosts, I might be able to authenticate my own ghost. This could go way beyond Harvey's sense that we were not alone. I was eager to get over to Gettysburg.

I had been there many times before and was familiar with this town's history. Ghosts had been seen at each of the significant battle sites. Over 600,000 people died during the Civil War, and the three-day clash in July of 1863 between the Blue and the Gray in Gettysburg resulted in 51,000 causalities and 5,000 dead horses. General Robert E. Lee for the South, with 75,000 men, and the Union's General George Meade, with 97,000, faced off for what Lee hoped would be his army's supreme victory. Each commander searched for the most strategic ground.

The small town of Gettysburg is like the hub of a wheel, with many roads meeting there from all directions. Surrounded by hills and ridges, it provided both armies with some protective territory. On the first day of July, the front lines met just west of town. The rebels collapsed the Yankee line, sending the men in blue scurrying through town and southeast toward Cemetery Hill and Culp's Hill. Lee's army occupied the town itself and stretched out on Seminary Ridge, south and west of Gettysburg. Meade formed a line along Cemetery Ridge.

The next day was marked by fierce fighting around Devil's Den toward the Union-occupied hill, Little Round Top. Both armies fought intensely through the Peach Orchard and the Wheat Field nearby. Lee's attack on the two ends of the Union line found them solid and unyielding. There was only one plan left: Attack the middle.

On July 3, another stifling day, Lee ordered General George Pickett to lead over 12,000 troops across a mile-wide open field directly into Yankee guns stationed on the high ground. He was determined to drive a hole through the Yankee line. Many of the Confederates were slaughtered, but a few managed to break through at a spot called the

Angle. It is marked by a tree and a low rock wall. This isolated penetration was no victory, however, and Lee realized that he had made a grave miscalculation, as two-thirds of those troops that he had sent across the field were now casualties. His strategy had been defeated at a cost he could ill afford.

On July 4 it rained. The armies watched each other uneasily as they attended to their wounded. Many of the homes and buildings in town were turned into makeshift surgeries and morgues. Men were buried every which way in shallow graves, while dead horses were burned. By the end of the day, Lee ordered a disheartening retreat, leaving many corpses behind—and ghosts.

Michael Shaara claims to have had a transcendent experience at the High Water Mark before writing *Killer Angels,* a book about those four days in hell. By some accounts, he wrote in a heightened state, inspired by the spirits of Lee and Longstreet. The book won a Pulitzer and was eventually made into a movie, *Gettysburg.* While it was being filmed, the actors came off the field in the evenings with ghost stories to tell. One of the reenactors hired for a battle scene said that he and some other "soldiers" were standing around and out of thin air, they heard someone barking orders at them to fall into line. No one knew who it was, and no one was nearby. Others heard galloping horses but saw no animals within earshot. Mysterious campfires were reported that always burned out before anyone could approach, and strange lights were seen moving across open areas.

But the actors were not alone. Ever since the park opened, tourists going to the battlefield have been telling rangers about strange events—often repeating the same sightings. One of the eeriest is the Confederate sharpshooter who appears at dawn in Devil's Den atop Bloody Run and queries people about what they're wearing. Nearby is the Triangular Field, which plays havoc with even the most sophisticated camera equipment. There are numerous volumes of ghost stories for the area, including such tales as the one about the volunteer who dropped off a truckload of reenactors, saw in her rearview mirror that they were still in her truck, got out to ask why, and found no one back there! Many reports are associated with gruesome deaths. During one of my previous visits, a waiter told me about how he and some friends had camped out on the field for several evenings in late November. One day they saw a ghastly scene of hundreds of soldiers lying dead or dying on the ground. This waiter was convinced that he had experienced a time warp, complete with the sound, smells, and visual horror of the battle.

2

My sister Ruth agreed to drive from Michigan to join me only because she loves the Civil War stuff at Gettysburg. She was not so sure about the ghosts. We meet here on an annual basis, apart from tourist season, to explore the grounds. She went for the history, I went for the hauntings. She preferred to explore Chamberlain's former stronghold on Little Round Top or walk where Pickett had charged, but I always dragged her to some haunted site, assuring her that this would be *fun*.

"Why are you writing about ghosts?" she asked me. "You're scared of them."

"That's why," I said. She didn't understand that my intention was to go *toward* what scared me and see how dangerous it really was. Or maybe she didn't want to know.

I told her we had reservations at the Farnsworth House, a haunted B&B at 401 Baltimore Street. She was even less excited about sleeping with ghosts than looking for them, but she still agreed to come. On a prior trip, we had stayed at the nearby Cashtown Inn, which sported an eerie photo of a ghost looking out the window. I had insisted on leaving the door to our room open, to invite the ghost in. She wasn't about to let me do that again.

Patti O'Day runs the Farnsworth House, offering rooms in period furnishing in addition to a fabulous breakfast. They also offer tours, and in the basement each night, someone tells ghost stories. It seems that Jennie Wade, the only civilian killed during the battle, was shot by a Confederate sharpshooter from the attic of this house while she was making bread. (The Jennie Wade house is reputedly one of the most haunted in town.) It also has been conjectured that soldiers marching out of town stopped here for relief and possibly died. With great energy, Patti recounts what she has been told by staff about noises in the padlocked attic and of the apparitions of a soldier, midwife, and a civilian carrying a child. She's enthusiastic about her ghosts and always welcomes serious investigations. I also heard from one of the regular guests that four Yankee soldiers haunt the place. And then there's the story of a psychic named Karyol Kirkpatrick, who was featured on a live radio show from the Farnsworth. At one point the phone lines at the Inn went dead, but the phone rang anyway. She picked it up and told whoever was on the line that he was not welcome there and had to move on. I hope that she knew she was talking to a ghost. A prospective guest might not have been too pleased. Nevertheless, it seemed a perfect place for me to spend the night.

Just before the conference, I'd received a noticed from the IGHS that someone named Rick Fisher would be leading an investigation for members of the Inner Circle. I didn't know what the Inner Circle was, but I wanted to attend. I sent Rick an e-mail, explaining that I was a ghost hunter but didn't use equipment, and that I'd like to do the Friday evening expedition.

He e-mailed me right back. "How do you hunt for ghosts without equipment?"

Well, that put me on the spot. I didn't know how to explain this. I just go sit somewhere that's haunted, like I had just done in Savannah, and hope something happens. In other words, the vigil. I didn't want to tell him that, figuring he had special meters, infrared film, and gadgets of all sorts with blinking lights.

Rick told me that the Inner Circle was for members only. I was disappointed, but I figured that I could go out to Devil's Den and ghost-hunt in my own way.

The next day, to my surprise, Rick e-mailed me and asked if I was an author. He thought he had just seen me on a talk show. I told him that I was. He quickly said that not only was I invited on the Inner Circle expedition, but he would personally teach me how to use his equipment. I was pleased with his generosity. I accepted.

Little did I know that Rick and I would become fellow ghost hunters on numerous expeditions and fellow researchers in the effort to find convincing evidence of life after death. My interest in ghosts had been little more than a curiosity. It would soon turn into a search for answers.

Rick Fisher heads the Pennsylvania Ghost Hunters Society (PGHS), founded in 1997. He runs monthly meetings and two workshops a year for over two hundred members statewide. His organization goes out every Saturday night to investigate a purportedly haunted site, and had done over two hundred thus far. On the Friday before the conference, they were going to a place in Lancaster that dated back to 1794 called Rock Ford. Did I want to come a day early and join them?

Absolutely!

Before going, I decided to do some research so I'd know a little more about the history of ghost hunting. What I learned was that during the nineteenth century, spiritualist movements formed around the idea that people who died might return as ghosts. During that time, many people perpetuated frauds to bilk grieving people out of money. It was then that some people tried to establish scientifically whether anything paranormal was really at hand.

England's Society for Psychical Research (1882) established

guidelines for checking out mediums and for looking into haunted properties. In most cases, "ghost activity" could be traced to natural causes, or even to unconscious psychokinesis from a human agent. The SPR categorized possible ghost manifestations in terms of information received: noises, odors, physical contact, movement of an object, and appearances. They urged investigators to be open but skeptical, and to check everything. Sites had to be investigated under many conditions, during both the day and night. Maps are checked for things in the area that might be causing the apparent manifestation, and press histories are checked. Then eyewitness accounts are recorded.

Quite often in the past, investigators worked with psychics and mediums to see what kind of information they could provide by way of corroborating what witnesses had said. These days, lots of investigative groups avoid psychics altogether, perhaps because many psychics are little more than frauds. Some investigations involve séances to attempt communication, but that too appears to be a thing of the past. All investigations involve some sort of surveillance equipment, from spreading flour on the floor to getting ghostly footprints to making videotapes. Peter Underwood, former president of England's Ghost Club (1862), included black thread and black cotton, white tape, adhesive tape, gardening twine, sealing wax, and fuse wire. These are to seal rooms and passageways so they could try to localize a haunting and also rule out stray breezes. One might even use a bowl of mercury to detect slight tremors.

One of the first people to use technology in ghost investigations was Harry Price. He created a laboratory in an English rectory, a site where numerous appearances of a phantom nun had been reported, and over the course of nine years used every tool at his disposal. He claimed to have experienced numerous manifestations, but still could not prove anything.

Paranormal researchers eventually separated themselves from ghost hunters, concentrating on extraordinary human abilities like clairvoyance and psychokinesis, while ghost hunters continued to develop their instruments to find ghosts.

Ectoplasm seemed to be a key manifestation. Coined in 1894 by French physiologist Charles Richet to try to define the whitish substance that mysteriously emerged from mediums who went into a trance, ectoplasm is considered a lifelike substance that can be solid, liquid, or more like a fog. Also called a "pseudopod" in some of its forms, it appeared to mutate into faces, bodies, limbs, and other spectral shapes, including thin rods. On one woman, Madame d'Espérance, it took the form of a web, covering her face and body. It smells like ozone and can be different colors, but it is usually white and somewhat transparent. Contrary to what we might expect, some people who have touched it have said it seems warm, while others describe it as cold and rubbery. It can be vaporous or thick and sticky. When it comes from a medium—which was thought to be a requirement—it usually emanates from a body orifice. Apparently, the spirit is withdrawing "etheric energy-matter" from the medium, and it then manipulates the energy to move objects, make noises, speak words, or become a ball of light or an apparition. To fully manifest, it must disengage entirely from the medium's body, but the medium can still direct it. Ectoplasm can be caught on camera, but when a light is turned on, it disappears.

Baron A. von Schrenck Notzing, a German psychiatrist, conducted a number of experiments with mediums he considered genuine and managed to collect some of the cloudy fluid for analysis under a microscope. What made it up, he discovered, was "numerous skin discs, numerous granulates of the mucous membrane, numerous minute particles of flesh, traces of potash and cell detritus." As it dissolved, it left a white alkaline deposit and had no odor.

Unfortunately, as with everything else in the spiritualist movement, there were people who perpetuated fraud. Laboratory analysis of some pieces of ectoplasm obtained in a séance showed that it was made of chewed paper, soap, egg white, gauze, and animal tissue. One medium, Mina Crandon, who produced a long string of ectoplasm from her vagina that manifested as a hand, was examined by Harvard biologists. They found that her amazing manifestation of a ghost was merely an animal lung cleverly carved. Others hung material with luminescent paint from the ceiling.

Apart from mediums, however, investigators with infrared film have captured hazy clouds in haunted places, which they believe is the stage just prior to a spirit fully materializing as an apparition. It is variously theorized that ectoplasm is the residue that a spirit leaves behind, the decentralized energy a spirit needs to become a defined form, and an energy form emanating from certain areas of the earth.

I also looked up spirit photography, since Dave and Sharon's website had indicated that they post a lot of ghost photos. I looked at some but had not really seen what I'd expected. Just a lot of bright lights. I wasn't sure what to make of that, but I figured they would explain it at the conference.

During the late nineteenth and early twentieth centuries, spirit photography (also called psychic photography) came into its own, although in retrospect it seems that most of the effects could have been tricks of light or flaws in the film. The first known photographer was William Mumler, a jewelry engraver with no interest in spiritualism who lived in Boston, Massachusetts. In a self-portrait that he took, he noticed what he thought was the image of his cousin, whom he knew to be dead. More such images appeared in portraits he took of family members. News spread, and in the 1860s he produced many more portraits that included the floating forms and faces of transparent people (called "extras") who were deceased. He was tested every which way, and though he was actually arrested for fraud in New York, he was acquitted on the basis of the many photographers who vouched for him. His photos are still controversial today.

This kind of photography soon became a fad, and some unscrupulous photographers faked the effects to get more clients. The English photographer Frederick Hudson, for example, was exposed as a fraud in the 1870s when he used double exposure to create ghostly effects. However, he had also developed some likenesses that under investigative scrutiny appeared authentic, so his capers did not necessarily damage the spiritualist movement. This was not the case with Frenchman Edouard Buguet, who did photography in a partial trance. He too was arrested for fraud in 1875 and confessed that his photos were faked with dolls and masks. He also used assistants to obtain information about his subjects.

The serious psychic societies sent out investigators, and different people came to different conclusions. Even today, some people give more credibility to these early photographers than do others, so it's difficult to know what to think. For example, Hans Holzer met with American industrialist John Myers, who became a leading psychic photographer in the 1950s. He published several images of people he did not know in *Psychic News,* and soon readers wrote in to identify their deceased relatives. Professor Holzer performed a few controlled experiments and was duly impressed when he developed photographs of several deceased relatives. However, Peter Underwood, president of England's Ghost Club, seemed less convinced. He claims that Ghost Club members detected Myers in fraud, but offered no details. To his mind, very few ghost photos bear real scrutiny.

In 1937, in the Soviet Union, Semyon Kirlian developed what came to be known as Kirlian photography. This method used high-frequency electric currents that made it possible to capture on film invisible radiating halos around plants, people, and objects. It was called the Kirlian effect—a stream of subatomic particles that move in and out of living tissue. Some people believed that was evidence of an astral or etheric body. They thought that this type of photography held great promise for proving existence after death. While its utility for that purpose was never proven, Kirlian photography did yield psychological information about a living being. If a person is withdrawn or depressed, the aura shows up differently than if they feel in harmonious balance. However, no one has yet determined what the Kirlian effect actually is.

Then people like Ted Serios in Chicago began in the 1960s to produce photographs that he called "thought forms." He would stare at a camera for a period of time and make an imprint onto film. He could even project scenes and objects through his mind across great distances. Despite being examined under stringent conditions, he was never caught trying to fake anything. He remains an enigma.

During the 1970s, infrared-sensitive film became popular with ghost hunters because it responds to certain levels of light radiation that other film could not pick up; it could therefore capture images in darkness. Aside from psychic photography, it's used in forensic investigations, aerial surveys, and the restoration of paintings. Infrared is still in use today among some ghost hunters, but it is expensive and difficult to get processed. The streaks of light and strange shapes that appear remain unexplained.

So why doesn't everyone get these photos, particularly professionals who spend a lot of time at photography? Apparently some photographers are mediums, whether they realize it or not. They seem to draw on psychic energy that is available only to those who are sensitive. Perhaps that's why many so-called spirit photographers who were not mediums resorted to one of several possible effects: double exposure, underexposure, or the use of an accomplice. One person even sketched the "entity" onto a plain background with quinine sulphite made visible only with photographic emulsion. He would set the invisible sketch near the subject and it would seemingly "appear" in the photograph. A charwoman in Britain named Ada Emma Dean kept photographic plates close to her for "magnetizing." Some of her "spirit photos" were found to be copies from press photographs of famous people. Photographer William Hope, under cover of a cloth, sometimes flashed a lamp near the plate to get an ethereal effect.

Yet just because photos *could* be faked does not mean that all of them were fraudulent. In the history of psychic photography, there are some that cannot be dismissed so easily. Believers explain them as concentrations of psychic energy.

I had seen a few of these photos in books on ghosts and had

even noted ghostly streaks in one that were so similar to those in the photo of me at the L.A. County Library workshop (where I had talked about Christian) that I was a bit startled. So someone had actually taken a photo like this and had identified it as a spirit manifestation, namely "free ectoplasm." That spooked me a little. I had really thought it was just a camera effect. Still, I wanted to get something like this myself or be in the presence of someone who did. I was sure that real ghost photos could not be easy to get. How wrong I was.

—3—

When I packed, I grabbed Christian's ring, hoping I might run into someone who could tell me about him or about the ring itself. After all, you never know.

Rick gave me directions on how to meet him and Karl Silvius, his right-hand man, near the Intercourse exit (yes, really!) off Route 17. Rick was tall and stocky, with a bushy gray beard and hair. His intense brown eyes and focused gaze told me how serious he was about his activities. Although he refused to call himself an expert, since he felt more like an explorer, he clearly had aligned himself with the scientific method. The Thomas Edison of the ghost world in the guise of Grizzly Adams. As he spoke, it was obvious that he wanted to teach others to understand and do these things for themselves. He was patient and explicit about each step of the process. He also wanted everything to be documented, from the time and weather conditions to the history and geography of a particular area. It made no sense to him to be haphazard about such an important enterprise.

Karl was shorter in stature, with dark brown eyes and hair, and sporting a goatee. He was equally earnest, and the quickness with which he spoke revealed his enthusiasm. He readily told me that he had dismissed the idea of ghosts until Rick took him on an investigation. Now he was an eager participant, having mastered the equipment and become adept enough to teach others. Both were dressed casually and had an easygoing manner, although they were all business when it came to getting their equipment ready for the investigation.

One of the first things Rick explained to me, in the manner of a teacher with a new pupil, was the use of a digital camera. I had a vague sense of what this was: You could hook a digital camera to a computer and see your photos on the screen or e-mail them to friends. The great thing about a digital camera, Rick said, was that there is no wasted film. "If you get poor results, you can delete the photo and reuse the frame again and again. Also, you get instant results and you can

gHost

see them right there on the LCD screen. Sometimes when we're getting consistently good results on the digitals, we use a regular 35mm camera." I followed all of that, I acknowledged, but what did it have to do with ghosts?

"I'll show you," he said. Rick believed that experience would be more persuasive than anything he might say. Besides, it was time to be on our way.

Rock Ford wasn't far from where we had met in Lancaster. As we drove to our destination, I thought about how strange it seemed to be setting this up in the middle of the morning. That wasn't my idea of ghost hunting. It just didn't feel right. But I supposed if there was a ghost around, it could be present at any time.

I had learned a little about this place before coming. The house once belonged to General Edward Hand, a surgeon in the Revolutionary War. It was thought that his twenty-five-year-old son, John, had committed suicide there with a shotgun, and at various times tour guides had witnessed a floating mist. One psychic said that the place was filled with the presence of a demented spirit. The general himself had died there of cholera, and three years later his wife had followed him. An eleven-year-old girl had also died there.

We pulled into a large parking lot, and I saw the mansion. It sat at the end of a long brick walkway that passed through a white picket fence. The house itself was made of red brick, with white shutters on the ground-floor windows and a white front door. The wraparound porch made the first story appear much larger than the second story, like an apron around the hips of a large woman.

Waiting for us in the parking lot was a woman named Dorothy Fiedel, a local folklorist and author. She asked me to call her Dot. A slim, middle-aged brunette with a generous smile, she looked like a former beauty queen from Texas who had just jumped down from a horse. She was recently widowed and had written a book called *Living with Ghosts* about her experience with her husband's passing. She had also written several books about hauntings in the Lancaster area. She herself professed to be somewhat psychic.

We went into the building, and Rick introduced himself to the historical society team who cared for the place.

"Go ahead and walk around," an older woman told us. "The first tour is in half an hour."

The place was like most other restored colonial homes: off-white walls, a large staircase, a grand entrance hall. I looked into one of the roped-off rooms to the right on the first floor and glanced over the wooden desks, upholstered chairs, and printer draperies. I tried to imagine a young man killing himself there. Dot walked away to another area, while behind me Rick and Karl went across the hallway and started snapping photos. I watched them for a moment. They didn't aim and focus, which I thought was odd. They just held their cameras up in the air and pressed the button. Then they seemed to study the camera for a moment before going at it again. Rick had a Casio QV700, Karl an Olympus D340-R.

They also had other pieces of equipment in a large bag. Rick took out what he called an EMF meter and a thermal scanner. I asked him about them, and he explained that ghost hunters used electromagnetic field meters to find shifts in the electrostatic charges in the room. Sometimes the meter recorded man-made sources, like a microwave oven, but within a certain range of readings, the source was more likely paranormal—according to extensive experiments among these researchers.

They used the thermal scanner to see if there were any areas where the room temperature drastically dropped. Rick went on to describe how the infrared technology allowed them to measure the surface temperature of an area with pinpoint accuracy without being close to it. He just presses a button, points the device around the room, and monitors the readings. It was now about seventy-five degrees in the room. A sudden cold spot could drop it as much as sixty degrees. He asked me to watch for a dramatic change, handed over the instrument, and walked away.

I had no idea what to do with it except just keep my eye on the digital readings. The temperature changed quickly—seventy-five, seventy-three, seventy-six—but not excessively, for which I have to confess I was greatly relieved. What was I supposed to do if something happened?

"Got one," said Rick from across the hall. He was looking intently at the monitor on the back of his camera. He held it toward me to get a look.

I didn't see anything.

"There on the wall over the door," he said, pointing. "Do you see that whitish round object?"

I peered more closely and saw what he was talking about. "Yeah, so?"

"That's a ghost," he said.

I looked at him, deeply skeptical. A ghost? Since when? Ghosts to me were ectoplasm or apparitions.

That's not quite right, Rick explained. According to more recent ideas, ghosts appear in four shapes: these round things, called globes or orbs; a white tornadolike shape, known as a vortex; ectoplasm; and the least commonly seen—apparitions. Orbs were the most common to see and photograph. They can come in different colors, from white to yellow to rust, and different densities, sometimes transparent, sometimes opaque.

"They can read our thoughts and intentions," Rick went on. "If they don't want us there, we leave."

"How do you know that?"

"You just do. You get a feeling."

I listened with curious amusement. Although I'd studied ghost lore at length, I'd never heard of an orb or a vortex, and I wasn't happy that we were ghost hunting for dots on the wall.

"Just look," said Rick. "You get a picture, like this one, but with the naked eye you can't see that orb on the wall. It's not visible. That's how you know it's a spirit. The eye can't see it, but the camera is faster and more sensitive, and can capture it. The EMF meter shows a change in the field, too, and a thermal scanner captures a temperature drop. It's proof!"

Then Karl got an orb, and soon Rick got another upstairs. He gave me the camera so I could try my hand at it, but I got nothing. As usual. And the orbs were so faint, I wasn't quite sure I believed what my ghost-hunting friends were saying. It seemed to me that the orbs could just be some problem with the camera pixels, or the way the light hit the walls. I dropped back and watched as they huddled over their cameras and made exclamations of discovery. To me, they appeared to be excited over nothing, and I began to think I wasn't going to have a very good weekend.

I noticed that Dot walked around without saying much, so I had no idea if she was picking up anything. Nevertheless, following her through the house, I was forming a plan. She had said she was psychic, so when I had her alone, I would ask her about my ring.

The group soon finished, and they assured the historical society that the place was haunted (which I didn't believe). When we stepped out of the house, the bright steady sunlight made this expedition seem a little ridiculous. I wondered if I should even bother with the rest of the weekend. Pausing for a moment to try to decide what my next move should be, I instead found myself deep in conversation with Dot. She explained to me how her husband, Sam Fiedel, had been terminally ill and had made her promise that she would be very observant because he was going to give her "material" for her next book. He was not connected to the paranormal himself, but seemed to sense what lay ahead. He told her she had to pay attention and to begin her fourth book soon after he passed away. He raised the issue numerous times until she finally promised.

On a Sunday morning, just before sunrise, Sam weakened. As he lay in bed, his gaze followed something that Dot could not see. He then assured her that they had been given a little more time. He described two hooded figures that had looked at them both and then passed through the room. Later that day, he grew stronger. Not long after that, when he did die, Dot saw a luminescent glow near his mouth and nostrils. It increased in volume and formed tendrils. "What I saw was luminous, ethereal smoke that formed and fed a ball—a very dense, compact elliptical ball. The ball itself appeared so dense as it might have been palpable, like the clouds out the window of an airplane. The smoke I saw did not exit arbitrarily but fed the dense cloud formation . . . no wispy tendrils strayed from the shape . . . all fed the shape. So Sam's soul remained molecularly cohesive even after it had no vessel to contain it any longer."

Dot realized that Sam was allowing her to see his soul leaving his body. She wanted to touch it, embrace it, but knew she could not. The gift was to be observed, not hindered. She continued to watch as the ball floated above his head. It increased in density, and she asked if others present in the room could also see it. Only her son, Justin, acknowledged that it appeared to him as well. The round form hovered for a few minutes, unaffected by the breezes from the ceiling fan, and suddenly, it was gone. It did not float away. It was simply no longer there. For a woman who wrote about ghosts, it was profoundly moving, and as she had promised, she wrote *Living with Ghosts*.

It seemed to me that if she had been allowed such an intimate paranormal experience, she might well be sensitive enough to "read" my ring, so I approached her about it. Dorothy did not know much of anything about me. She'd heard my name only recently. She was interested in the fact that I was a writer, but didn't seem particularly intrigued by my vampire tale. I thought I had a ring with a unique history, I told her. Would she touch it?

She shrugged. "Yeah, I'll try it," she said. I pulled it out of my purse, still on its silver chain, and handed it to her.

Psychometry is a form of clairsentience (knowing by feeling); it is the ability to envision or sense things about prior events from touching people, places, or objects. I have also heard it called "soul measuring." If Christian, or anyone else, actually wore this ring, there should be some residual impressions that a clairsentient person could pick up. I was not optimistic that anything would really occur, but I wanted to give it a try, especially after Rosemary's impressions back in New York of someone named "Michael."

For a few seconds, Dot stood still, just holding it. Then her eyes widened, reddened, and instantly filled with tears. She started to tremble, and she almost threw the silver band back at me, saying, "What is this? It's the pit! It's terrible. You shouldn't have that. You should get rid of it. It's the pit!"

She was shaking. Tears were running down her cheeks. Rick and Karl watched her, astonished. She went on to describe the ring as being hot and just evil. I slipped it back in my purse.

"I'm sorry," I said. "I didn't realize it would affect you like that." I was a bit shaken myself.

"I've never experienced anything like that," she said. "Never. You shouldn't have that. Whose is it?"

I shrugged. It was too long of a story to be told here. After that, the conversation turned to other things, but I could not stop thinking about her reaction to the ring. It really disturbed me that someone would pick up such strong vibes when I felt nothing from it. Was "Christian" angry that I had handed it over to her? Or was he showing off in some way? Steve, the psychic in New York, had said I could use the ring like a phone, so maybe Dot had "called" him somehow. Maybe he wasn't always there, but would come when a sensitive person beckoned, or when he was able to use that person's energy. It was all quite puzzling.

—4—

The next stop was Gettysburg. On the way, I asked Rick more about himself. He told me that he was one of the first people to use scientific investigations relating to the existence of ghosts on the battlefield. He was also the person who first suggested the use of digital equipment, using cameras and recorders before anyone else had thought of doing so. He had been ghost hunting seriously for three years, but he had been interested in ghosts since he was seven years old. That was when he saw the figure of a man in the hallway of his home. Thinking it was his grandfather, he wasn't afraid, but then found out his grandfather was not in the house at that time. He saw the figure again in the night and became intrigued with what this could be. As an adult, he read Dorothy Fiedel's book on Lancaster's hauntings and thought that he'd love to try to investigate some of those tales. Along the way, he found the International Ghost Hunters Society—the same group I was about to meet—and went to their conference to learn how to do it.

"I'm fascinated with death and with whether life goes on," Rick said. "If that man I saw was a ghost, why was he there?" For him, it's simple: A ghost is the spirit of someone who once lived. Some remain earthbound, while some can actually choose to come back. Others have emotional baggage, or a desire to be close to a loved one.

After equipping himself, he went out to search for evidence of ghosts but got very little in the way of results. However, he discovered that the more one tries, the more sensitive one becomes, and then the spirits tend to come around more readily. "Every time I go out to the same place, I get better results than most people. My photos are outstanding, and I get more."

I wondered if that result had something to do with him—perhaps that he had some mediumistic ability like the psychic photographers from years before. He does not believe in using psychics on investigations, in part because he finds it difficult to authenticate what they say and also because he has found that when a psychic is in the room, the orbs tend not to be. However, that would not eliminate the possibility that he has some sort of sixth sense.

He explained to me that digital technology is more powerful than ghost-hunting equipment used in the past because it uses computer chips and gathers in more electromagnetic pulses than a film camera or a cassette recorder would. One can get results on either, but digitals are superior. The same was to be said for recorders. "If we're really picking up spirits," he says, "think of the possibilities."

"Picking up spirits?" I asked.

"On these recorders. They talk to us."

My mouth dropped open. "You get ghosts to say things to you?" I asked.

"Yes." He held up a tiny silver device that looked like a cigarette lighter. "It's called EVP, for electronic voice phenomena. We can actually pick up spirit voices on these things. It's amazing. If we can improve this technology, we'll be able to communicate with loved ones, solve unsolved murders, and find out what it's like over there. I have this feeling that they're around me, just waiting for me."

I felt a chill when he said that. If it was around him, then it was around me, too. It, or they, were around all of us. He claimed nothing had ever happened to him, but he and I had both heard stories of a supernatural force harming someone. I saw no reason to believe that ghosts wouldn't hurt anyone. Bad people die, too, and their spirits could very well have a malevolent agenda. In fact, if Christian was the kind of sociopath that Wraith had portrayed, I had every reason to believe he could—and would—hurt me. I'd heard of spirits choking people, pushing them down stairs, pinching them, and even hitting them. I thought Rick was dismissing these possibilities too easily.

I was interested in hearing more about these recorders. The promise of being able to achieve verbal contact with the other side was amazing—and here was Rick, claiming they were doing it. I wanted proof, of course, but this could be the very thing I was seeking in my quest to know more about my haunted ring. If Christian was really with me, I might be able to get him to communicate on a recorder—to actually tell me if he had been murdered. This could prove to be a huge opportunity. In fact, maybe he could tell me his side of the story. And if he wanted something specific from me, he could just spell it out. No guessing, no need for mediums. Now ghost hunting was getting exciting.

Our first stop on the way to the battlefield was an office supply store. That surprised me, but Karl and Rick assured me that ghost hunting involved ordinary devices found in places like this. In fact, they said it was time for me to invest in my first piece of equipment: a voice-activated digital recorder, like the one Rick had. Karl had one, too, and he told me to listen closely. He was going to play for me one of the ghost voices he had recorded on one of his expeditions. He held the recorder between us and pushed the button. With his left hand he gestured for me to be patient: It was coming. I listened to the crackling sound on the recorder and then heard what sounded like a gruff male voice. I couldn't make it out, so Karl backed up the recording and played it again, his eyes bright with expectation.

Then I heard it. Something like, "He beat me with the goddam chain." It was chilling. I stepped back and looked at him.

"Could you hear it?" he asked. He was grinning from ear to ear.

I nodded. I'm not sure I would have heard it had Karl not coached me a bit by hinting at what I would hear, but it was fairly clear nevertheless.

"I have another one," he said. He pressed the button again and another male voice seemed to mention a name, Jesse, and when he said that name, a third voice had quickly said, "You can't help him." Then another said, "Let's not kill him."

I just looked at Karl. I wasn't sure I'd be as pleased as he seemed to be to get such threatening stuff. He must have been close to the source to get those words, which meant he had potentially left himself open to violence.

But Karl was excited. He gripped the recorder and just beamed at me, so pleased with his spooky collection of recorded phrases. He assured me that one could get voices of all kinds.

Rick agreed with him, adding that he had used a recorder in the cemetery where his grandfather was buried, and upon playing the recording back, heard his name, "RRRick!" spoken quite clearly. At other places, he'd picked up whistling, laughing, and a man saying "Good-bye." As he talked about this, he grew animated. Obviously, they both felt that EVP was real and that it had all kinds of possibilities.

Could I get a recording myself? I was skeptical, to say the least.

We got into Gettysburg, a small town full of nineteenth-century homes that culminated in a strip of motels, T-shirt shops, stores full of Yankee and Rebel souvenirs, and fast-food restaurants crowding as close as possible to the battlefield. Directly across from it there are two fast-food restaurants, the National Civil War Wax Museum, the Lincoln Train Museum, the Dobbin House Tavern, and General Pickett's Buffet. Tour buses passed back and forth in front of these buildings, carrying scores of people to the visitor's center. The most interesting shop on Steinwehr Avenue, the main thoroughfare, was Servant & Company, which offered authentic uniforms of every size and color. Men who worked there or just hung out were dressed in period attire. If you were looking for Civil War ghosts, you might think you'd found them there.

I met up with my sister so we could get settled into the room. Ever the intrepid Gettysburg-ophile, she had driven nine hours to spend a day and a half on this historic ground. She looked tired, her long salt-and-pepper hair lying flat down her back, but she perked up when she saw our room at the Farnsworth. She just needed to clean up, she said. She could rest later.

We had dinner with Vicki, one of the Farnsworth storytellers. She assured me that most of the tales she told were true, although there was no way for me to ascertain this. Maybe she was supposed to say that. I saw Ruth watching her with the eye of a midwesterner who did not really buy much of what was said. To her credit, she patiently listened as Vicki told a long and dramatic account.

Tall and large-boned, with curly brown hair, Vicki had a face that spoke of deep suffering at some point in her life. She herself had had a unique experience when she was five years old. It was a time shift, she told me. She was near some railroad tracks when she saw a lady dressed in a purple satin gown standing with a man in uniform. She did not speak or move as she watched them, and she knew she was in another dimension. Years later, a psychologist helped her to use her "third eye" to be able to see paranormal phenomena more clearly. She seemed sincere, but I was not sure what to make of it. Harvey Ray in Savannah had said that children are more likely to have such experiences and to see and hear ghosts—perhaps because they have not been told that they can't—so maybe what she said was possible. Nothing like that had happened to me, so it was hard to say. But in any case, she was not to be the last such person I encountered.

It was fairly cold that night in March and I was tired. I gave some thought to canceling my lesson with Rick and Karl, and in fact, Ruth went right to bed. She did not really want to be left alone in a haunted room, but she figured she'd fall asleep quickly and never know what went on around her. I hesitated. Ruth looked so comfortable in bed. Still, I wanted to learn more about ghost photography.

"When I come back," I warned her, "I'm going to put on the digital recorder."

"Fine," she said. "Just don't wake me." In other words, *I don't want to know anything.*

So I bundled up in dark clothing. I don't know why this seemed appropriate for ghost hunting, it just did. Maybe I didn't want the ghosts to see me. I left the hotel and met Rick and Karl. We drove together to a place known as Sachs Bridge, and they were delighted to see that we were the only ones there. It was a popular ghosting spot, partly because it was not within the national park, so there were no time restrictions and it did not matter that we were there after hours. Only later did I learn its history. During the three days of the battle, both sides used the bridge at different times. It was a field hospital, and apparently two Confederate soldiers were hung there as well. For now, I just knew we were out in the cold on some historic covered bridge.

Rick and Karl set up their equipment, explaining it to me, piece by piece.

"These are motion detectors," Rick said. "You can pick one up at Radio Shack." They had tested this one in a building first, and each time it went off, they got a photo of an orb. "They won't go off just from a breeze or an insect, but really need something substantial going through the beam. If these go off, start taking pictures."

I didn't know why he thought a ghost would be substantial enough to set off a detector, but he was the expert. Later he explained that orbs were a form of energy that a detector could pick up.

Karl showed me the way a digital camera works and then went through a few of his photos on the LCD screen to make it clear what they were looking for. Again, I saw the little dots of light, sometimes one, sometimes a couple. How could anyone tell who they were? I mean, so what if you had balls of light if you didn't have a story? At least a female apparition appearing on a spot where a woman had died indicated a connection. This kind of ghost hunting I didn't get. Did this really excite them?

Rick told me that some of the ghost hunters were now switching to a videocam with night-vision capabilities. These cameras are usually set up and left in place, he explained, and the results reviewed later. Then he handed me the thermal scanner and reminded me to watch for dramatic shifts.

He and Karl also came equipped with electromagnetic field detectors. I learned that they used more than one type. The one he had shown me in Rock Ford had to be passed through the anomalous field to register shifts on the numbered meter, while devices like the Trifield Natural EM meter detect changes in an area the size of a large room from a stationary position. When spikes occur with either meter within the defined range for paranormal phenomena, it's time to start taking photographs. Inevitably, they said, when the detectors register the right degree of fluctuations in the field, the photos produce orbs or ectoplasm.

They also had infrared night-vision goggles. Invented for the military, you supposedly can see the orbs shoot right in front of you, unless as I did, you get confused and trip over a hole in the ground. An added disadvantage, even for the more coordinated user, is that many insects look like orbs, so I ended up agog over a June bug. I later found out that the second-generation models are recommended, but personally, I find them all disorienting.

"Always take a flashlight," Rick advised. "You need it to read dials and change batteries. And take plenty of extra batteries. Ghosts like the energy and you can run dry very quickly."

Rick also insisted on using notebooks to record the relationship between conditions and anomalous events, in order to learn which conditions are best. That way you can maximize your chances of seeing something and getting good photos. I can't say I stuck to the scientific method with his dogged determination, but I did learn the importance of keeping track of certain patterns.

That night, Rick handed me his camera, so I could get my own photos and become a real ghost hunter. I felt awkward with it, half certain I would somehow break it, sure I would not get the results that they did—but he and Karl left me alone while they went to the center of the bridge, halfway down, to place two motion detectors there.

I watched them walk into the darkness gathered under the shell of the bridge, their footsteps on the wooden bridge growing faint. Suddenly I felt alone, vulnerable. I looked around. I glanced over my shoulder, imagining that something was flitting around, coming closer. It got colder, although the scanner didn't "authenticate" that feeling. Pretending to be bold, I put on the night-vision goggles and stumbled around as I tried to watch for any motion in the thick greenish glare. Pretty soon I felt a bit seasick, so I took the goggles off and concentrated on taking pictures. I didn't dare to look because I was sure I would just see one black screen after another, with perhaps a few flashes off the red wood of the bridge railing. I kept it up, feeling foolish, absolutely certain that any efforts I made would fail. Finally, I stopped. I held the camera close to my face, looking for the button that Karl had told me would bring the last photo taken onto the LCD screen. I waited as it developed and then looked closely.

To my surprise, I got some reddish ectoplasm-looking stuff in the first frame. Maybe just mist reflecting the bridge. I went to the next frame. Nothing. The third one, too, showed no results. I felt discouraged. Then I pressed the button and watch a photo develop that took me completely by surprise. I got an orb! There it was, a round ball of light, right there in the picture, hovering over the water on the outside wall of the bridge. My own orb! I was amazed.

Just then, one of the motion detectors began to bleep, startling me. Rick went to turn it off, followed by Karl. While they were several yards away, bent over the device, I took photos, holding the camera high in the air and aiming it over their heads.

As the alarms were turned off and the guys rejoined me, I took a look through the four photos I had taken. I was excited now. I could do this and I wanted another orb. The picture came up and there they were, two of them, hovering in the air right over the men as they examined the detectors—just as they had predicted.

This was amazing! I was getting pictures of things that were otherwise invisible to me. There were things there, in the air! It seemed beyond belief.

Rick and Karl laughed at my amazement. To them, this was all commonplace. But it wasn't to me. I didn't even know if I believed that an orb was paranormal, but that night I did. I had a photo of a ghost! I'd worked all my life for this, and now I had achieved it. I was basking in the moment. The questions could come later.

When I returned to the room, Ruth was asleep, so I turned on the recorder. It was activated by sound, and the practice was to turn them on and leave them be. I crawled into bed and was soon asleep myself. I knew that Rick and Karl planned to stay up all night doing an investigation of the Farnsworth House. In fact, they were going to stay up all night for two nights in a row. To them, sleep was just time that could be better spent ghost hunting. I didn't agree. I wanted to be alert for the conference.

The next morning, I checked the recorder. To my surprise, I had fifty-two minutes of recordings. I wondered if Ruth had been talking in her sleep, but I had no time to listen just then. The proceedings were about to begin.

—5—

Dave Oester and Sharon Gill are from Crooked River Ranch, Oregon. In 1992, they began to collect local ghost stories, inspired by their own experiences, and four years later started the International Ghost Hunters Society. As of this writing, the organization has grown to more than twelve thousand members in some eighty-four countries. Dave has a strong background in electronics and radio, and knows how to apply all sorts of computer programs to ghost detecting, while Sharon has a degree from the New York Institute of Photography. She also has a master's in metaphysics, is an ordained minister, and has worked on a psychological profile of ghosts—at least as far as her interpretation of the evidence will allow.

They've been featured around the world in newspapers and magazines and have appeared on television and radio shows. They write a weekly newsletter and run a website on which they post thousands of photographs taken by their members. They also offer plenty of merchandise for the well-equipped ghost hunter. Their books, *Twilight Visitors* and *The Haunted Reality*, describe many of their adventures.

Dave and Sharon offer four workshops each year around the country, and I just happened to get into one of the best, in Gettysburg. Dave is a big guy with a trimmed gray beard, large glasses, and an easy laugh. He pulls his long hair into a ponytail and generally wears a baseball cap with a ghost logo. He's quite accessible, and you can tell that he thoroughly enjoys his work. After nearly every serious statement, he smiles, crinkling his entire face into a big grin. He also shows great affection for Sharon in small gestures, such as bringing her a cup of water. Sharon, with long reddish hair and sporting a ghost pin on her blazer, stays shyly in the background, although she's clearly as involved. She talks slowly, showing deep compassion for ghosts who are trapped or confused. She is uncomfortable at the microphone, but eagerly writes lengthy accounts of their ghost hunting trips in the newsletter. They seem to complement each other. Sharon makes it clear that they are not trying to force their ideas on anyone, but whatever they learn they share—albeit within their own frame of reference.

This couple was instrumental in introducing Rick to ghost-hunting techniques. At this conference, they had nearly one hundred attendees, some experienced, some novice. They were eager to train as many people as possible so that there would be more explorers out there with equipment who could advance the study of ghosts.

On the morning of the first day of the conference, over one hundred people gathered in a large mint-green auditorium in the Holiday Inn near the Gettysburg battlefield. Around the edges were display tables for books on ghosts, orb photos, ghost club information, and other paraphernalia. People ranged in age from a ten-year-old boy to a couple who appeared to be in their late sixties to early seventies. Many of them had camera bags and were already showing off photos they had gotten the night before. The familiar phrase, "Get any?" did not mean sex. It meant paranormal photos from Cashtown, the Farnsworth, Devil's Den, or Iverson's Pits.

At the podium, Dave launched into a speech about how ghosts are everywhere. He explained the approach of the IGHS and its attempt to free itself from religious superstition. He spoke about ghosts like they were his buddies. He's not nervous about going into cemeteries or having spirits in his own house. He likes telling stories about them, as if he's discovered a secret too sweet to keep. He seemed to get a real kick out of telling about the time when he bought a powerful infrared light to put on his videocam and thought he'd outwitted the ghosts, because they wouldn't have figured out yet that they were now within his range. He also thinks it's funny when they seem to trick him, as if this is all a game to see who is more clever.

He and Sharon believe that spirits have personalities, just like in life. They even believe that ghosts have a sense of humor. Rules for an investigation include not smoking, drinking, taking photos in the rain or snow, and no Ouija boards. Smoke, rain, and snow look too much like spirit photography, and alcohol generally produces a party atmosphere that hinders serious work. The Ouija board, they claimed, invites in negative spirits. I listened to Dave talk about portals, where orbs come through from some other dimension. These often occur in cemeteries, and if you stand close to one you might feel a sudden loss of energy or even a migraine headache. Ghosts are curious and thus are drawn to people, particularly people who do odd things, so Dave might wear a strobe light for joggers strapped around his arm while filming in a cemetery. According to these two, ghosts seem to be drawn to the same types of people they were in life—an idea that made me uncomfortable. What did Christian see in me?

I listened as the equipment was explained once again and wondered how people managed to do anything when they had to carry all of that stuff around. I looked around and got an answer: One guy had used twisty ties to attach his meters, extra batteries, flashlight, and motion detector to his camera. To bring along a videocam, he had a backpack. As funny as that seemed to me, it wasn't long before I was shopping for a backpack myself.

I was seated next to a plump blond woman in an oversized yellow T-shirt who raised her hand often to describe her experiences with ghosts. I couldn't see her name tag, but found out that her name was Meg. During the break I mentioned that she seemed to know what she was doing and asked what she got out of a conference like this. She shrugged and said, "This is something I can do without feeling self-conscious about being overweight. I'm accepted here. I'm with friends."

"You seem to have a lot of paranormal encounters," I noted.

"I go out of my way to look for ghosts. I go out as often as I can, so I'm likely to have more than most people. Mostly I smell odors that aren't really there, like tobacco smoke or campfires. But sometimes I feel things, too, and once I saw an apparition over by the monuments. I always get great pictures of orbs, especially after I explain what I'm doing so they can understand and then ask their permission. The pictures always turn out better." She had a photo album with her to prove it. She grabbed it from beneath her chair, opened it up to a spread of four-by-six color photos of all sizes of white blobs, and eagerly recounted the circumstances under which she had gotten each one. I noticed other people around me doing the same, like they were showing off their kids or grandkids.

In the light of day, I still was not altogether convinced that orbs were ghosts. Certainly they were *something*, but energy anomalies do not necessarily translate into spirits with personalities. Dot's experience with her husband notwithstanding, I wanted more evidence. (I was later to discover that Dot, too, wanted more evidence, since the orbs in these photos did not actually match what she had seen.)

The speakers at this conference included Rick and Karl on photography and EVP; Dorothy Fiedel on her new book; Mark Nesbitt, author of the *Ghosts of Gettysburg* series and coordinator of the local ghost tours; storyteller Ed Okonowicz; and Charlie Adams, a witty author of numerous ghost books. Each talked of his or her own ideas, and there were enough fresh stories about ghosts or ghost hunting to make the audience gasp. Dave opened the conference by reporting the apparent sighting by a member of a soldier in uniform the night before at the Cashtown Inn, along with the sound of a regiment marching past. I was glad that Ruth was not there to hear that, although I didn't quite believe it. When I was there, I'd heard heavy trucks all night that could easily be mistaken for a phantom regiment. I began to think that people here were so eager for *some* experience that whatever seemed out of the ordinary would automatically be attributed to ghosts.

I heard a lot that day about having the right attitude. If you're not open and interested, ghosts won't gather. Again, I had heard too many stories from people who not only don't look for ghosts but don't even want them around to believe that the right attitude was essential. If I were a ghost, I'd do whatever I wanted, regardless of what some mortal being thought of me—or didn't.

Someone mentioned that it was important to focus on what the ghost might feel. I wondered how we could even know. Rick had said that if they don't want you there, they'll find a way to make you aware of that fact: You sense their anger or you get the feeling that you're invading. How much of that, I wondered, might be anxious projection from us? I mean, if I were going into a graveyard alone at night, I'd be scared enough to be tempted to say, "Well, the ghosts sure don't want me here. I'm leaving."

I learned what the Inner Circle was, too: those members of the organization who were certified, had mastered the techniques, and had contributed photos to the website. I made a note to get myself through this process. That meant the home-study course.

Part of the point of the conference seemed to be shoring up members' beliefs. Theories that skeptics had submitted in hopes of debunking ghost photography were considered, and then refuted in turn. These orbs were not lens flare, poor pixelation, flash effects, insects, camera straps, spots on the lens, moisture, stars, headlights, or lights in the distance. The number and diversity of the photos proved that the skeptical "explanations" failed to address the evidence, such as the fact that three photos in a row showed something different—perhaps an orb changing positions. In successive photos, you might get one orb, then four, then none. A few people had sent their photos to camera companies to ensure that they weren't defective, and both Kodak and Sony had denied that they were the effect of a malfunctioning camera. They offered no explanation, aside from pixelation problems or a reflection of light from some source.

I wondered why the ghost hunters cared so much about the doubters. Most skeptics of that sort were just defending a piece of intellectual territory. They didn't want to actually learn that they could be wrong. Many of them were armchair philosophers uninterested in putting their own ideas to the test. I admit, I wasn't entirely convinced, but I was eager to learn what these people had discovered. If they had real evidence, I wanted to know about it. I liked Rick's approach: He believed, but fortified his activites with rigorous testing, not just accepting everything at face value, and searching first for the alternative natural explanation.

I was a little disconcerted by how much emphasis there was on doing things a certain way: Be respectful, ask the spirits if you can take their photo, say a prayer, believe in them, make a mental bond, thank them when you leave, avoid psychics. I doubted I'd remember all of that and it seemed rather narrow and restrictive, considering the number of sightings by people who never observed any of these courtesies. Besides, I'd never been one to follow the rules. If someone told me that I could get to Christian through an Ouija board or séance, I'd do it. I had no prejudices against people who could contact spirits apart from the use of devices. I was ready to try anything.

—6—

It wasn't long before another psychic offered to "read" the ring. I ran into her in the conference room as I was walking toward the door. She had been looking for me. Her name was Chanda and she was from Maryland. She was thin with long, curly auburn hair and a sort of New Age/Gypsy look. Her clothing was ordinary and casual, but I guessed she felt at home in more flamboyant attire as well. Her manner was bold and confident as she asked to examine my ring, which she had heard about from someone whom I had met the night before. I placed it in her hand. She held it and waited for an impression.

"There's a lot of pain," Chanda said as she looked intently into my eyes. "I just felt heat go down my right leg." Then her expression became more serious. "This was given to you in the woods by a tall, dark-haired man whose name you don't know. He wore this while doing the things he did. There are bodies buried there. You know what I mean. You can find where they are. You were lucky to get out of there alive. He was charmed by you, that's why you escaped."

Well, she was right, at least about Wraith and where I got it, but in fact the ring was not given to me. I had slipped it off his finger and then kept it. The other things she said made me think she was familiar with my story from the vampire book. It was just too close. I told Chanda about Dot's reaction, and she said, "I wanted to cry, but didn't."

She urged me to get a more complete reading. "We can contact him," she assured me. "I can help."

I figured that even if she had boned up on the details to impress me, it wouldn't take her very far in an actual séance. She'd really have to show her stuff. I made an appointment with her to do just that. If someone said they could get Christian to communicate, I was willing to try it. Chanda insisted that she could see him and that he was constantly talking to me. I was on my way to do a book signing but agreed to meet her later that night in her room. I then walked over to the Farnsworth bookstore.

It was there that I finally got the chance to listen to my recorder. I hadn't given it much thought because I didn't believe there would be anything on it. I had figured that while things were slow during my signing, I could check it.

Rick and Karl came in. They looked pretty haggard from being up for almost thirty-six hours, and yet it was the energized fatigue of those who believe their sacrifice is for a greater good. Even so, I expected them to collapse right there on the floor.

"We got some orbs in your room last evening," Karl told me.

"You did?" I hadn't heard that. I knew they had been in there at one point, but no one had told me my room was haunted. I looked around for Ruth and hoped she hadn't heard.

"Yes. And we were sitting in the lounge next door getting orbs most of the night."

That was disturbing. I also had heard from someone down the hall that her roommate, a young woman, had been accosted by something as she lay in bed in the Sarah Black room. "It was like a man was lying down on top of her, pressing his full body on her," the woman told me. "She ran to her aunt's room and stayed there the rest of the night."

So last night, while I slept, there was all that activity, with ghost hunters and spirits all over the Farnsworth, in the halls and rooms. A paranormal pajama party.

"Well, maybe I got some voices, then," I said. I waved my recorder in the air to emphasize the drama. While they watched, I slowly pressed the on button. At first there was a lot of static. Rick assured me that everyone got that kind of thing. It wasn't a voice. I sat back and let it run. I figured it would be fifty-two minutes of more of the same.

Then there came a noise that astonished me. It seemed to be a voice, all right, but like something out of *The Exorcist*. There were words—it even sounded like more than one person in conversation—but the voices were scratchy, deep, and gruff—almost angry sounding. A few loud, guttural sounds that were quite disturbing, that were, I'd venture to say, demonic. I glanced at Ruth across the bookstore, not sure whether I should let her know what seemed to have been in our room with us while we were sleeping. Here and there, I picked up a sense of urgency in the tone. I let the recorder run, getting what sounded like the inflections of a voice but failing to comprehend any of the words. I thought I heard "Hello," but wasn't sure.

Then a boy walked by the table. He had short blond hair and was maybe about twelve years old. "What's that?" he asked.

"Recordings of a man," I said with a shrug. "But I don't know what he's saying."

The kid picked up the device to listen. Recalling what Harvey had said about kids, I let him go ahead. Ruth moved a bit closer as he translated: "He's saying, 'Who are these new inhabitants of the room?'"

Ruth and I looked at each other in shock. "He" was talking about *us*. We were the new inhabitants of the room, sleeping, oblivious to this presence. I was chilled to think that someone had been watching us and talking about us, invisible and inaudible, but right there in the locked room with us, near us.

"What else?" I asked, almost afraid to know.

"Just something about going to the window. Oh, now he says he's going over to the bed. He's screaming that. He says, 'Hello? Hello? Why are they in this room?'"

I could have jumped out of my skin. He's going over to the

bed? Where we were *sleeping*? Wondering why we were there? Orbs were one thing, but this was truly alarming.

I grabbed the recorder. I wanted to hear it for myself. I listened and had to admit that it did kind of sound like that. Or maybe he was making it all up and this was another example of the power of suggestion.

"I just don't think he's very happy," the kid added. At that moment, his father came to get him and there went my translator. I started to write down what he had said, but Rick, who had been standing nearby, insisted, "Don't write that. It's not scientific. You don't know if what he said is right."

"It's the best I've got," I told him. "These are not voices from the hallway. This was in my room."

I listened to a few minutes more but could not make out what was said, so I gave up. There was always time to listen when I got home. I had a séance to attend.

-7-

That evening, Ruth and I went to the room where Chanda, the psychic, was staying. She told me that since she was a child she'd had special gifts and that she was clairaudient (she hears spirit voices). She told me how she'd once had a dream about being in a castle and then later met a woman who swore she had seen Chanda looking out the window of a haunted castle in Scotland. Since Chanda was of Scottish descent, this coincidence had startled her. She recalled that her mother had been tested for psychic abilities, but friends told her that she was merely crazy. For similar reasons, Chanda's grandmother had spent time in a mental institution.

She laid out a scarf with half-moons on it across a round table, and placed four chairs around it—one for a "guest." I tried to sit away from that. Then she lit a candle and got out her tarot deck. We turned out the lights and settled in. Nothing in here felt particularly spooky, but I was ready for anything. Chanda was certain she could get Christian to materialize, and I wanted to see that.

She warned me not to get too caught up with the man associated with the ring. "If you ask for an incubus," she said, "you'll get an incubus."

Then she took the ring again and held it in her hand. "It weighs a ton," she said. She was quiet for a moment, meditating. Then she laughed. "I see two nice-looking men having sex. That wasn't what I expected." She waited again before adding, "His friend was a violent person and this ring is a lock of some kind. You're the key to unlock it." She hesitated and then said, "But it serves some purpose for you not to unlock it."

She felt certain that Christian wanted me to help him to be better than he was, and he also appeared to be afraid to move on. Chanda proceeded to do a tarot reading, which revealed nothing related to my quest, so she linked hands with Ruth and me while she attempt to get Christian to rap on the table. She got no results.

"He's stubborn," she said. "He's possessive about whatever you're doing but isn't going to get involved with these activities." Ruth raised an eyebrow at me but said nothing. This wasn't her idea of a fun evening in Gettysburg. I didn't know what to make of Chanda's apparent inability to conjure up a ghost she claimed was visible and audible to her. I tried to be open, but I also felt silly. However, she said something that proved useful much later.

"Whatever you do," she said, "don't destroy the ring. Never throw it into a fire. There's something in it that you might release. If you have to get rid of it, bury it in black earth. Take it to where you got it. Make a sacred ceremony out of it."

And that was all. I was disappointed, but at least I'd tried and eliminated one more avenue of approach to Christian. He was not answering *this* phone.

For all intents and purposes, the conference was over. Ruth and I went out to the Angle that night with Rick and Karl so they could teach her about orbs. She actually had fun and thought that ghost hunting wasn't so bad after all. At one point I took a photo over her head, intending to scare her with the idea that they were hovering right over her. When I developed the picture, two orbs were right there next to her. That didn't bother her. In the course of one night, she went from a dubious and reluctant participant to an enthusiastic supporter of what I was doing.

So ghost hunting like that was fine. I wasn't scared. But I also wasn't alone. Nor was I entirely caught up in this new method. I wanted to put it to the test. As much fun as I was having, I wanted to know how much I'd really find out about ghosts this way—or if these things even were ghosts.

I did wonder how much of this might be something akin to a *folie a deux*—a sort of shared delusion induced by persuasion. I knew enough about the power of suggestion to be watchful. Which is not to say this *was* a delusion, but I wanted to try out things for myself without too much information influencing my experience.

Nevertheless, I left the ghost conference a changed woman. Orbs, voices, thermal scanners, night vision, and electromagnetic fields. This was a world I had never before encountered and I knew that my own ghost hunting was now going to be very different. I wanted to continue to find out about Christian and toward that end, I resolved to get equipped. The other ghost hunters would disapprove, because an implicit rule was to pay attention only to good spirits. However, I had a mystery to solve, and it did not involve Casper.

Next stop: New Orleans. One step closer to this devilish spirit and a very different way of trying to contact him.

4 The City That Loves the Dead

"I'M HALF INCLINED TO THINK WE ARE ALL GHOSTS."

—HENRIK IBSEN

—1—

I've spent a lot of time in New Orleans, Louisiana, and have heard it called the most haunted city in America. I wouldn't be surprised, since the South embraces its ghosts, and New Orleans is the epitome of southern charm and decadence. Ghosts are *fun* there. Ask almost anyone in this town about a ghost and you're bound to get a detailed account. While I was there once before, I got about as close to one as I ever have.

Down in the Big Easy, Mary Farrelly is my unpaid assistant. Slim, blond, and feisty, "Miss Mary" is ready to party. She can down four White Russians from one end of the French Quarter to the other, all the while insisting in her whiskey voice that "y'all need to have some fun down here." She had never given ghosts much thought, but she was more than willing to tour the local haunts.

Miss Mary came to pick me up one evening at the home of a friend, Corey, who was quite ill. I met her at the door, and as we got into her car, she asked, "Who was the guy at the dining-room table?"

I looked at the large window near the front door and realized that anyone outside could see into the house. I shrugged. "There's no one in the dining room."

"Yeah, a guy with red hair and sideburns. Just sitting there at the table."

"There's no one like that in the house."

She still seemed convinced she'd seen someone, but she let it go, and we drove down to the Quarter.

Ghost Expeditions was run by Larry Montz, who claims to have psychic abilities. Tall and beefy, with thinning brown hair, Larry presented himself as Louisiana's only parapsychologist. He told me that he was once Hugh Hefner's personal bodyguard, which made me wonder if he was really a parapsychologist or just a profiteer. He did tours of the French Quarter, orchestrated investigations, and even "cleared" haunted houses for homeowners at their wit's end. From him I learned of haunted restaurants like Antoine's and the Royal Café.

That evening, Montz took us to a pharmacy where he claimed that a physician had murdered several young women and to O'Flaherty's Irish pub. There a man named Joseph had killed his mistress and then his wife, and had buried them in the courtyard. His daughter got away. Larry assured us that many people experience Joseph's aggressive presence, as well as that of the dead women. I didn't feel any of the cold spots that he claimed were present, and the whole thing seemed fairly theatrical.

It was at Le Petit Théatre off Chartres Street, at 616 St. Peter, that I first encountered something odd. Founded in 1916, this is the oldest community theater in continuous operation in the country. The building was erected in 1797, and the outside patio is itself a landmark. Seven plays are produced each theater season, plus several children's plays. In fact, Montz said, many of the ghosts inhabiting the place are kids. He figures that during epidemics and fires many children died in the Quarter and that the theater's open spaces offer good places to play. He even knows them by name. Aside from the children there are actors, stagehands, and even a spectator.

Larry didn't suggest that we might experience something in this building, so when I felt a cold spot near my hand, it startled me. I looked down. My fingers were tingling.

"Oh, I see him!" Larry said. "A boy. He likes you. He's holding your hand."

The others in the group watched me, bemused. A couple of people backed away and left me standing by myself. I glanced around for an explanation—air-conditioning, an open door. Larry said the air-conditioning was off, and I couldn't find a clear source for a breeze. Besides, it was a humid night outside, and this was an icy chill.

Nevertheless, it seemed too easy. He'd seen me look down. He could have jumped on the opportunity for its entertainment value. As we moved on, however, the cold spot came with me, surrounding my hand as if some child really *was* grasping it. I wondered if "he" sensed my skepticism. When Larry suggested that this little boy wanted to come home with me, I thought it was time to move into another room. As I crossed the threshold, I lost the sensation.

Nothing else happened there to persuade me of all the spirit activity that Larry claimed for it, but I heard about things that occurred a few days later to people I knew.

Jana Marcus, a photographer, had come in from Santa Cruz. She's a vivacious woman with very dark eyes and dark, curly hair. One of her central interests is photo-documenting fetish subcultures.

I introduced her to Montz and she took the tour. Miss Mary went, too, with another friend, Barbara Trimmer. Barb, an educator with a pleasant round face and straight brown hair down to her hips, had begun a travel company that specialized in tours to supernaturally-charged areas. Afterward, they all told me of their experiences.

"I was there with my photo assistant, Eric," said Jana. "He's cynical. He has this constant flow of conversation about what's negative in some experience. So we went into the center theater room, on the floor area near the seats, and Larry told us to just be open. It was very stuffy in there. But at one point, near where I was standing, it just got freezing. The temperature dropped like forty degrees from the waist down. Larry told us there were now about ten or eleven child entities in this room."

That gave them all pause.

"We moved around," Jana reported, "and felt the cold sensation move with us. Mary and Barbara were up on the stage, laughing, and Eric was standing in the aisle by the seats, about a hundred feet away. He was babbling about what bullshit this all was. Then Mary let out a little yell and we turned and looked at her, and she burst into tears."

"Larry had explained to us," said Barb, "that people can be affected emotionally by these places. Some people feel sad, some happy. Mary had not heard this, but all of a sudden she just started to cry. It scared the heck out of me. She said she had this horrible feeling, just scared and sad."

"We were on the children's stage," Miss Mary recalled, "and I suddenly felt overwhelmed. Tears came to my eyes and I told Barb that I didn't know why I was doing this. I was sort of hyperventilating and upset, and I didn't know why."

At the same time Eric also felt something. "Within five seconds of Mary's reaction," Jana said, "Eric went absolutely silent. I looked at him and his whole face had drained of blood. I asked if he was okay, and he looked at me and burst into tears. I went up to him, but he put his hand out to indicate not to come near. Then he ran into the lobby. He sat there, crying uncontrollably. He'd felt a cold hand on the back of his neck and some woman speaking to him about love, a woman who was crying. He was completely overwhelmed with her sadness. I looked for Larry, but he was trying to figure out why Mary was crying, not realizing that whatever had hit her had gone in a diagonal line straight from her to Eric."

Barb brought Larry over to Mary. When he saw her crying, he said, "Oh, Katherine's here. I'm surprised because she usually stays in the attic."

That startled Mary, and she listened as he explained that Katherine had killed herself over a broken heart. Her spirit manifested in sadness, he said, and when her entity is near someone, they start to cry because they feel her sad energy. "He told me that back in the twenties Katherine had hung herself in the rafters and we were right by that spot. So I'm creeping out! Enough of this! And it was freezing cold in there but I was like, burning up."

Larry asked Mary to come back into the main theater. "Katherine wants to talk to you," he told her.

She wasn't interested: "I said, 'No, I don't want to.' I felt a pat on my back and I thought it was Barb, but when I turned around it wasn't her who was doing it. That scared me."

Larry thought that something was up because Katherine didn't generally come down. "There must be something up there that shouldn't be." He thought they should go up and see.

Those words weren't exactly enticing to Mary. "Don't ask me how, but he talked Barb and me into going up to the attic, where the spirits hung out. That was their place, Larry said, and there was a good bit of 'em. So we walked up these stairs and it was so dark we could not see our hands in front of our faces."

Larry went first, accompanied by one of his assistants. Barbara and Mary could barely see what was going on. Larry opened a door and they heard someone say, "Oh, my God!"

Then Larry yelled, "There's a lot of them in there!"

Mary saw a flicker of light, which was enough to send her back down the steps. "Me and Barb hauled ass down those stairs and Barb was going, 'Our Father, who art in heaven. . . .' We ran all the way down in the dark to get out of there."

But that was not the end of it. Larry saw what had happened to Eric, and since Jana was a professional photographer, he wanted her to come back to the theater that night to take pictures. He himself could never manage to get any, and he thought that with her experience and superior equipment, she might have more luck.

At around eleven o'clock that evening, Jana and Eric returned. Larry introduced them to Maria, a psychic. She had been in O'Flaherty's when "Joseph" had attacked her and thrown her on the ground, leaving imprints of his fingers on her throat. (I actually saw the photographs of these bruises.)

"Eric was already beside himself," Jana said. "He was crying before we even went in."

They went directly to the attic.

"I had a camera with fresh batteries and film," Jana recalled. "Everything worked fine before we went in. It was an expensive camera, brand new. Larry and the team started up the steps. Suddenly I got a sick feeling and I told Eric that I didn't want to go up there. Eric ran in front of me and I decided I wasn't staying behind all by myself."

The way Jana remembered it, as Larry opened the attic door, Maria screamed. Jana lifted her camera to snap some pictures and it jammed. "It wouldn't work. It would not flash, it would not advance, it wouldn't work on manual. Maria passed out into someone's arms and Larry was going through the door, yelling, 'Get back! Get back!' and everyone's screaming, and it was all chaotic, and then I saw this flash of light in the stairwell. Maria woke up and we headed down the stairs back into the main theater. Then she told us she'd seen a huge entity standing in front of the door that would not let them pass. She knew it wasn't a ghost. She thought it was an angelic spirit that was so eminent it literally knocked her back."

They decided to leave, and when they walked out into the street, Jana tried her camera again. It worked, but the batteries had been drained of energy. They were so weak they were nearly worthless. Montz told her that he believed the attic was a portal, or a place where spirits crossed from one dimension to another. Something very powerful was up there.

The following day, Jana and Eric returned to California. Then Maria called and told her more of the story: The spirit of Katherine claimed that she had killed herself because she was in love with a director, who was gay. "It seems," said Jana "that this spirit told Maria that Eric is the reincarnation of that man and that's why she went to him. She was calling him to come back. He never went back, but he was never the same."

Miss Mary, likewise, did not return for any ghost hunting in the theater, although each time she passes it, she gets a creepy feeling. She has the same experience regarding the house where my sick friend lived, because the day after she had picked me up, she got another shock.

I mentioned her comment about the red-haired man with sideburns to a woman who had known Corey for years. She showed me a photograph of a young man named Mark who had red hair with sideburns.

"He was Corey's lover," she said. "Maybe he's here to cross Corey over."

"What do you mean?" I asked.

"Three years ago, Mark died."

I asked Miss Mary to come over, and without explanation I showed her the photo. "Yeah," she said at once. "That was the guy I saw."

A month later, Corey died. And once again, I had been *that* close.

—2—

So that was my near-ghost experience in New Orleans. An entity in the next room that I never saw and a little boy who wanted to come home with me. I wished I had been with Jana that night, but I was with Corey in the hospital. Though I was ready to do more ghost hunting there after my experiences in Gettysburg, Montz had left town. As it turned out, I discovered that many of his stories could not be documented—including that of a woman named Katherine who had hanged herself in the theater—so I hunted around for a more credible guide. In particular, I wanted someone who might know about haunted objects, since I had brought Christian's ring with me. I had tried doing a bit of psychometry myself with it, but felt nothing—certainly not the fiery horror that Dot Fiedel had experienced.

I went to the rather dark and sinister Zombie's Voodoo Shop at 723 St. Peter Street to find out about the Haunted History Tours, run by Sidney Smith. They offer tours of cemeteries, architecture, vampire abodes, and haunted properties. Sidney was a friendly, dark-haired man with the kind of hospitable gentility that I have come to associate with the best of New Orleans. He offered me some beads that had been blessed to ward off evil, and he assured me the haunted sites were fully documented and all sources available if I wanted to see them. I knew the few he named were credible, so I decided to take the tour.

I learned that his wife, known as Kat, was a ghost historian and would be running a fetish party that night on the upper floor of a bar called the Fatted Calf, so I made plans to visit her after the tour. Though I already knew about most of the sites on the tour itinerary, such as the notorious LaLurie house where slaves had been tortured, I had never been in the seedy bar, Sin City, which was the location of the city's first mortuary. Women who used the rest room often lost their rings. On our tour that day, a young woman claimed that it had happened to her the evening before. I gripped the ring around my neck before I went in. I wasn't about to lose a ghost ring to a ghost.

After the tour, I killed time at the Pirate's Alley Café, because I had heard that there are frequent sightings of a pirate in that alley near the Saint Louis Cathedral. The notorious pirate Jean Lafitte had once sold goods here, and there had been plenty of duels nearby. At this point, darkness had settled all around. I sat at a table outside, apart from the tourists, and kept watch over the area, sipping coffee to keep awake for the party that night. After a while, I noticed a man standing in the shadows. I peered more closely, trying not to seem as if I were staring. I thought he looked familiar, but I couldn't see him well enough to tell. Then my blood froze.

Wraith!

I stood, nearly knocking over a chair. I grabbed it, distracted for a second, and then looked back to where I had seen the man.

He was gone.

I looked down the alley and saw only two couples drinking hurricanes in their portable plastic cups. I walked past them and realized I had lost him. There was no chance now of learning if Wraith was tailing me, or even if that person had been him at all. In New Orleans, people sometimes recognize me as the author of several books on Anne Rice's work, and I've noticed them watching me from a distance. But this was different. I thought for sure that the man I had just seen was the one from whom I had gotten my haunted ring. Did he know I was on this quest? Had he somehow heard that I was not satisfied merely to write his story as he told it but that I wanted to discover the truth about Christian's demise?

I walked up and down the alley and searched Jackson Square but saw no one who resembled the figure in the shadows. I was frustrated and a little nervous. It would have been easier to just walk up and confront him than to wonder where he was and whether he was following me.

Finally I had to leave. I found the Fatted Calf at 727 St. Peter Street, where Katherine Smith's party was supposed to be, and made my way to the upper room. This place was reputedly haunted by a man who back in the sixties accidentally hanged himself. It had been his intention to give Halloween trick-or-treaters a glimpse of a realistic body, and his friends thought he was faking it till they found him the following day still hanging from the ceiling.

Few people had arrived at the party; it was scheduled to begin quite late, and it was clear from the props that whoever came would be seriously into the fetish scene. There were cages and whips and other paraphernalia, including a full-size black coffin painted blood red inside that was leaning against one wall. Those few who were arranging the room wore historical costumes reminiscent of Romantic eras—men in puffy-sleeved white shirts and women in long, tight velvet dresses. I looked around for Katherine and recognized her from her photo on the book that her husband had given me.

Going up to her, I introduced myself, aware that she already knew who I was from my books. She seemed a bit harried from all that she still had to do for the evening's events, but I found her to be friendly and articulate. A large-busted woman in a tight black bustier, she looked a bit like Elvira, but much prettier. Her long straight black hair was polished and shiny, with straight cropped bangs, and her smile was warm. She talked loudly over some blaring music, speaking so quickly that it was difficult to keep track of what she said, but I was clearly in the presence of a woman who knew what she was doing.

We walked to a spot where the noise was less intense so that she could tell me about herself. She asked me to call her Kat. She made it clear that she was intent on documenting all ghost stories that she heard, and toward that end she used police reports, personal narratives, investigations, and the city's archives to make sure nothing got on the tour or in her book that was made up. She knew her subject well and proved to have a strong belief in the power of metaphysical forces. She and Sidney, it turned out, had thrown a vampire wedding and had spent their honeymoon ghost hunting at the Bourbon Orleans and the Place d'Arms Hotel. She even had an infrared photo, that she would show me later, of a hazy figure in a parking garage that appeared to be wearing a pirate's hat. We quickly made plans for what proved to be an extraordinary weekend.

3

Kat invited me to her Uptown home, which she believed was haunted by the spirit of a man wearing a brown suit, and I got to know her a bit. She showed me the infrared photo, and it certainly did look like a pirate's hat, but the shape was too blurred to be certain of anything. Kat set up a séance for us, along with several investigations. Upon entering her home, I was introduced to a large iguana (caged), two boa constrictors (also caged), and a cat and two frisky dogs (uncaged). I spent much of the afternoon learning more about the person into whose hands I was placing my mission. Her living room featured a blue cemetery painting and sculptures of nature deities, including a molded face and hands coming out of the red walls. There was also a large portrait of Kat in her black velvet vampire attire.

She told me that a psychic insisted that she would write a book, but since she had never written before, she thought it unlikely. Nonetheless, in 1998 her documentation of local haunted phenomena became *Journey into Darkness: Ghosts and Vampires of New Orleans.* Now she's writing a second one to complement the tours.

I was excited to learn that she had invited a woman whom she called a "ghost magnet" to join us, but no sooner had I learned of this woman's existence than it appeared that I wouldn't be meeting her after all. Mariah's car had broken down in Nebraska, which she had told Kat was a sure sign that "someone" did not want her there. She would still try, but was not sure she could come. Kat hoped to try to find someone else.

Then we settled down to talk. Kat was born in Uptown New Orleans and had grown up in River Ridge, a suburb. She had been married before and had two daughters and three grandchildren. With Sidney, she had a stepson. A student of healing and the martial arts, she is also the state coordinator for the Ghost Research Society. Currently she was studying to become a practitioner of "eclectic magic." She had first become interested in the paranormal as a child.

"At about age two, I remember seeing a dark shadowy being in the hallway of my parents' house," she said. "It frightened me, to say the least."

"Did you tell anyone?" I asked.

"I told my mother, but she assumed it was childhood imagination. My mother, the devout Catholic, told me that it was the devil, and that it would come back and get me if I wasn't good. That, of course, only added to my fears."

"Did you feel anything from it or hear anything? Did it approach you?"

"I was engulfed with fear, but looking back, it was not threatening at all, just there. It walked across the hall into a bedroom. I sensed it was male energy. At the time, it seemed horrible, but in hindsight, I doubt it even paid any attention to me. But because of my mother, I remembered this thing as a devil for the rest of my childhood. I spent years looking under beds and in closets. It was my 'monster.' "

I asked what her most dramatic paranormal encounter was like.

"Actually, there are two that come to mind: When I was twenty, my mother passed away. My father had died a couple of years before. I had inherited the house where I had grown up, and I would lie awake at night in bed and hear the front door open and footsteps coming down the hall. It terrified me. I eventually moved my one-year-old daughter and myself to an apartment, and I rented out the house. One evening, as I lay in bed trying to fall asleep, I heard a whispery voice of a woman calling my name. It seemed to come from my closet. She kept telling me 'Don't go to sleep.' Within only a couple minutes, I heard someone breaking through my front door. I had no alarm or even a deadbolt on the door. I literally sat on the floor and held the knob to keep the intruder out. When he gave up, I phoned the police. I believe that if it were not for that voice, the intruder would have broken into my apartment."

Her activity as a ghost historian, she told me, involves researching properties—as we were about to do. "When we started doing tours," she said, "we had little to go on for documentation. Nothing was solid. Other people were out there just making things up. I wanted to separate the facts from the folklore."

She used a Trimeter for electromagnetic fields and infrared film. "I have also used psychics and sensitives, backing it up with personal experiences."

"Have you ever done investigations in which you encountered malignant forces?" I asked this because supposedly my ghost was a malignant being and I wanted to know more about those entities.

"It has been my experience that most are not malevolent, but there have been a couple. One was in the 'St. Germaine' house from our vampire tour. I was literally attacked by what I believe was a Mara, or what's also known as a psychic vampire [someone who drains the life energy of a victim similar to the way a traditional vampire drains blood]. I also found a very negative male presence in the attic of Le Petit Théâtre. It's been my experience that what some people call a malevolent ghost may just be a spirit of someone who was in intense sickness, pain, or misery."

She had read about people with addictions who become entities and who then attach themselves to living people similarly addicted. I had read this, too, in *The Unquiet Dead*, aware of the idea that such people leave themselves open to possession. The attacking spirits supposedly find a weak point in the person's aura and move in. I was reasonably certain that Christian could not do that with me. Unless, of course, that was my weak spot.

Although Kat had read about my vampire adventures, she did not realize that my intention was to find some psychics who might "read" my haunted ring. It was her theory that Christian was a psychic vampire, anchored here and taking from those humans he was close to. I had read in the introduction to her book that according to local folklore, those who are murdered must remain earthbound until justice is done or their story gets properly told. That was my idea of what he wanted—unfinished business.

Kat explained to me her belief that one can make things happen in the world by "manifesting" them through meditation and a specific vision. She explained that she imagined something she wanted to have or achieve—mentally made it real—and focused on it with meditation until it happened. One example was the house in which we were sitting. She had envisioned exactly what she wanted and what she was willing to pay, and circumstances had delivered it to her in a synchronistic way. She was quite pleased by that and thought that, within reason, she could make almost anything happen.

"Can I 'manifest' to get Christian here?" I asked her.

She shrugged. "We could try."

"We could also manifest what we want for the weekend. If Mariah can't get here, then we could manifest another person."

—4—

Our first expedition that day to another haunted bar in the French Quarter produced no results, so Kat was determined to find a working psychic for our next outing. We went out to Jackson Square, the French Quarter gathering place of psychics in front of the Saint Louis Cathedral. All along the fence surrounding the park you have your pick of five-minute portraitists, plastered mimes who stand like statues, hot dog venders, tarot or palm readers, jewelry hawkers, and a few local artists of more serious stature. You can also find psychics here.

An elderly walleyed man with long gray hair and red suspenders called me over. I didn't want to spend money going from one to another, although there was really no other way to know who was genuine. This guy looked like an alcoholic, but he offered me a deal: $10 for a card reading. I sat down.

He said that he could see a place, somewhere out west. Then he named Flagstaff, Arizona. That startled me, because recently I'd been concerned about my college mentor, who was in a Flagstaff hospital. Still, my concerns were with Christian and the ring. This guy obviously did not pick that up. I asked him to touch the ring to see if that helped. He said a few inane things about getting what I wanted, that my future would be fine, and that I shouldn't worry. Blah, blah, blah. Then he sat up straight. A strange look came over his face and he said, "I just felt a cold wind pass through me. Someone out there, someone who matters, is dead. He's dead or he's out west."

Well, he was right, Christian was dead, but he was not out west. I paid the man his ten dollars and walked away, then stopped cold. Oh, no. It couldn't . . .

I ran to a street corner, found a phone booth, and called home for my messages. A chill went through me as I heard on tape the voice of a friend from Flagstaff telling me that early that morning, my mentor had passed away.

I just stood there. I was speechless. Somehow this old man had picked up on that. It seemed impossible, but this is exactly what happened. What other explanation was there? I began to give a little more credibility to the clairvoyant mind.

When one comes into this city, it seems like one passes into another realm. People talk so easily about ghosts that you believe them. Everyone's a psychic, and you're quickly drawn in to accepting just about everything. Rationality feels more like a mental disorder. But this was more than an example of the credulous atmosphere of the Big Easy, or of allowing myself to slide into the prevailing attitude about the supernatual. This had actually happened to me. This was—or at least seemed to be—real.

I went back to the square and a woman grabbed my arm. She looked at the ring that was hanging around my neck. "You shouldn't wear that," she warned. "Take it off."

I didn't know what to say. I wondered if she was just trying to get me to pay for her services. Scaring people, I knew, was one way to get business. Before I could decide which this was, legitimate or fraud, Kat beckoned to me to come. She had found someone to accompany us that afternoon on an investigation. Nora Natale, a palm and card reader, had agreed to come. I was only too happy to get away.

Nora turned out to be a beautiful, slim woman in her mid-forties, with long, wavy blond hair. She talked with a deep voice. She had grown up in Pittsburgh, working as a disc jockey, and had visited New Orleans on a vacation. "A feeling came over me," she said, "that I was finally home." She returned many times and then finally moved into the French Quarter. She thought perhaps that she had lived a past life there. Since she had moved, her psychic powers had increased, and that was how she now made a living. Her Irish grandmother had taught her how to read the tarot, and at times when her readings get intense, she feels completely drained.

In the car on the way to our next investigation, Nora agreed to hold the ring and tell me any impressions that she got. She closed her fingers around it and waited for something to come. After a while she said, "I feel a strong presence. An older man, maybe in his forties. It's been passed from one person to the next for a specific purpose."

Kat nodded as she drove us out of town, but said nothing. I did not know until later at the séance who she believed this person to be. At the moment, I was just tagging along on a ghost investigation. I had no idea that I was on my way to another significant encounter.

−5−

The person who allowed us to investigate the nineteenth-century plantation house that afternoon required that I not name it or give identifying information, but said that we were otherwise free to do as we liked. It was a Creole-style home with a raised living room, Gothic windows, and lots of porches. Ornate and colorful, it had once been a sugar plantation on the banks of the Mississippi and had been extensively renovated. As we walked toward it, Nora said she felt that we were being watched from the widow's walk platform on the roof. I didn't feel anything. Inside, Kat and Nora went from room to room while I looked around at the magnificent furnishings from a bygone era of luxury. In one room that featured a flowered bedspread and an elaborate ceiling medallion, both Kat and Nora said they sensed a child, then an adult reading to the child. Their impressions formed into the feeling of two children, a boy and a girl, along with an adult male.

When we were finished, the operations manager, Jacqueline, listened to what they found and said that over a century earlier a little boy had fallen into the sugar pots. His ghost had been seen, crying. She also confirmed that a little girl had fallen down the steps and died, and there was the spirit of an adult whose name was Charles. He had died at the age of thirty-five, and the plantation staff often saw the sudden, impossible impression left behind as his ghost paused to sit and rest for a moment on a mattress in the room that once had been his. Jacqueline shyly confessed to having seen him from time to time on the property, often dressed in a white suit and leaning against a tree outside, watching her. Once he even smiled. I sensed that there was more to her story, and she eventually admitted that, as a child, she had seen ghosts. She had thought that everyone did, but when she told her mother, she'd ended up the center of an exorcism that had badly frightened her. "I didn't stop seeing ghosts," she said, "but I stopped telling anyone."

The extent of her paranormal activities these days was a bit of automatic writing—a trancelike activity in which one allows a spirit to use one's hands to write a message. She would get up between three and six in the morning, sit at the computer, and "channel" poetry and other writings. She told us that she knew that Charles was around and had been watching us from the top of the building—where Nora had sensed his spirit, although he apparently preferred the attic. Jacqueline offered to take us there. When we got up to the stuffy place, she pointed to a ladder that went high up to the widow's walk.

"He's there," she said. "I can sense him."

Everyone else was nervous about heights, so I offered to go up. It was strange climbing the wooden steps with the idea that I was moving toward an invisible entity. I wondered whether I'd know if I passed right through him. I kept climbing and got all the way to the top without feeling anything. I looked down.

Jacqueline was smiling. "Back down about four steps," she said. "He's right behind you."

I looked back and saw nothing. I didn't know if I wanted to go down backwards, especially not if a ghost was standing there. In fact, right at that spot, the stairs stopped and went at a right angle. Only a flimsy railing would block a fall if I happened to go too far—or get pushed. The others were waiting, however, so I slowly walked backwards down several steps. Then I felt a chill go up my back and right arm, which turned into several rolling waves of chills. I stopped.

"He's hugging you," Jacqueline laughed. "He's right there. I can see light going up your arm."

I wasn't sure if he was hugging me or I was just getting chills from the idea that he was there. I waited until the sensation diminished, then went down, not entirely convinced. If she could see a light, why couldn't I?

After we returned to the front office, I asked Jacqueline if she did psychometry. "Not really," she said, "but if you have something, I'll try it."

I took the ring from around my neck and handed it to her. Casually, she put it on her finger. She was about to say something when her eyes widened and she immediately cried out, "What *is* this?" She took the ring off and shoved it back at me, saying, "I can't, I can't," and then her eyes began to water. We all saw the gooseflesh come up on her arms. She was trembling.

"Is that a man?" she asked. "He was evil, wasn't he? I just can't keep holding it. I felt it was hot, like it was going to burn my skin. I saw red, like blood! A lot of red. I just wanted to get it off. I saw violence, and a lot of anger and rage. It was furious, ferocious. It went up my arms and down to my toes. I didn't think I'd get anything, but I heard this voice that said, 'I'll make you *think* you won't feel anything.' It was like a whip. He's angry."

She also thought she had an image of a horse and buggy going fast, but it wasn't clear. What *was* clear was the emotional tone. She never wanted to see that ring again.

But that was not the last I heard from her on the subject . . . or from "Charles."

Upon returning to New Orleans, we knew we had to start getting ready for the big event. We visited Mimi Lansou, a practicing witch, in her shop, Esoterica. The walls were decorated with voodoo and witchcraft items, and a lot of floor space was devoted to freestanding shelves that held all kinds of exotic objects. I picked up a chicken foot and wondered if it was real. Then I looked through the shelves of books that offered everything from lessons in witchcraft to healing to herbal remedies.

Mimi was a petite young woman who dressed seductively in black and had short, styled black hair, cropped across the front. She wore bright red lipstick. Exuding competence in the magical arts by the way she efficiently dispensed advice to other customers, she listened to what I had in mind and then agreed to run the séance for us. First she examined the ring. Then she got to work. Selecting several different colors of candles for different purposes, she then put together separate bags of herbs that we needed to boil into a tea and pour into a bath. "Stay in it for ten to fifteen minutes," she instructed. I watched as she took three large glass containers from a wall of at least fifty of them, and carefully measured out the ingredients she would need: eyebright, for mental clarity; wormwood, for protection and power; and sea salt for spiritual cleansing. I noted labels on other jars like Bee Pollen, Lobelia, Burdock, and Lucky hands, which were voodoo charms. A large black-and-white Great Dane walked through the shop, and I noticed that it had one brown eye and one blue eye. His head was nearly even with mine. I hoped he was friendly.

"Expect to be a little woozy," Mimi said. "It's good for channeling." She instructed Kat to burn wormwood, sandalwood, and charcoal in a cauldron, and to purchase some surgical gloves and black ink. We would also need five tin plates on which to place the candles and a large shallow bowl or pan. For automatic writing, should the spirits care to communicate that way, we would need pads of paper and pens. She also included some sort of oil—I think it was orange, lily of the valley, and something else—and said I had to find a piece of plastic on which to float the ring, once she poured the ink into the pan full of water. Kat told her that Judy Garwood, the innkeeper at Southern Nights, had agreed to allow us to use the inn. The place itself was haunted and had a huge dining-room table, which would be perfect. Mimi said she would be ready and added that she would try to find a friend of hers, a voodoo medium.

If only Mariah the ghost magnet would get there, I thought, we'd have the perfect circle. How could Christian resist?

—6—

That night Kat and I decided to try to contact Christian ourselves with her psychic board. It's sort of like a Ouija board, only more colorful. There are two frames of mind on the Ouija phenomenon: Something supernatural is moving the planchette and needs a human agent to channel it, or the persons using the board have low-grade psychokinetic powers and are projecting their own ideas into the answers they get. Of those who opt for the first explanation, a percentage of them believe that malevolent entities use the open door to come through and plague the person contacting them. I've been warned numerous times not to go near them, but have yet to see any reason why.

The Q&A went as follows, with the small plastic circular planchette zipping along at a rapid pace as we sat cross-legged on the floor and touched it lightly. Kat closed her eyes and asked the first questions.

Is Christian real? "Yes."

Did he commit suicide? "No."

Was he murdered? "Yes."

Did Wraith murder Christian? "Yes."

Is Christian here? "Hello."

I nearly pulled away at the immediacy of that one, but Kat continued, her eyes closed. I asked the next set of questions.

Do you want something from me? "Yes."

Is this Christian's ring? "No." Then, "Yes."

Kat looked at me quizzically and then took out a pendulum with a dragon-shaped crystal. She held it on a string over the Yes/No options and asked the same question again. It confirmed that, yes, this was his ring.

Back to the board. Should I be afraid of Wraith? "Yes."

Do you want me to get your story? "Yes."

Were you and Wraith lovers? Confirmed.

Did you murder anyone? "No."

Okay, I didn't believe that. He may not have been the instigator in what he and Wraith did, but I felt sure he had a part. I figured he was lying. I wondered if we even had Christian. Perhaps this was all just a matter of minor psychokinetic powers of our own. Or maybe some demon was playing with our minds. On the other hand, maybe he was *not* a killer and Wraith had made up that story.

When the board failed to respond, we gave up and went to bed. I was in a room in which the air-conditioning was so loud I could hear nothing else. No outside sounds penetrated the place. I figured that would be good for recording any fragile spirit communications that might occur in this room, so I turned on my voice recorder, invited whoever wanted to speak to do so, and went to sleep.

—7—

The next morning, Kat announced that Mariah was coming after all and would be there very soon. She had felt compelled to come and had driven all night to arrive in time. I was delighted. I'd meet someone who attracts ghosts. I couldn't wait.

I went out to the pool in the backyard to listen to my recorder. With great anticipation, I looked at the digital display. To my surprise, I had recorded a whole hour of something. That seemed strange. These recorders are voice activated, so they come on only when stimulated by noise. They hold an hour's worth of messages, so if the sixty minutes is full, then whatever was talking could have been going much longer.

At this point, I did not know what kinds of things were possible. My experience had been serendipitous thus far. I didn't even know if

I'd get anything outside of Gettysburg, but I was hoping for some real results. It was not the best way to learn about EVP, but I didn't realize then that it had a long history and there were actual books on the subject or that there was even an international organization devoted to it.

I pressed the on button and listened. What I heard right away was the air conditioner. I couldn't believe it. A whole hour of monotonous noise. So much for the voice-activation function. I slumped in the chair in disappointment. What a waste. But then I decided to see if there might have been anything else recorded over the noise.

My instinct paid off. In three separate places, for about two minutes each time, I heard a very loud male voice. As in Gettysburg, I had a hard time deciphering it, but I knew I had picked up something. I thought there might also be a female voice, but I had no time to determine that, because just then Kat called to me to come and meet Mariah.

Her arrival was like opening the door to a hurricane. She's a big woman, tall and big-boned, and from the moment she entered she spoke in a loud, authoritative voice—the E. F. Hutton of spiritualists: When she talked, people listened. She absolutely filled the room. In her arms she carried three thick volumes of the works of Madame Blavatsky. Behind thick lenses, her eyes were intense.

Immediately upon meeting me, Mariah bent toward me and said, "There's a whole gang of spirits all around you. Maybe six or seven. They were all murder victims." She graphically described a woman with a slit throat and a man in agony. A bit daunted, I looked quickly behind me but saw nothing.

"They're talking to you," she said.

A chill ran up my spine. I could almost feel them back there, mouthing silent entreaties.

"Why me?" I asked. "I can't hear them."

"They think you can. They want to tell you their story."

That felt weird, the idea that all these wild-eyed spectral victims were focused on me. "I'd be happy to listen," I said, "but I really can't hear them."

"Yes, you can," Mariah assured me. "We all have the power. You're just blocking it."

I was blocking it. Right. In other words, if only I unblocked it, I'd start hearing and seeing ghosts. As simple as that. Before I had a chance to grasp how weird this all was, she changed the subject to something just as startling.

"I'm here," Mariah said, "because I was sent here. A spirit came to me in my home and said I was needed. He insisted I come. I think he was connected to you."

I was getting completely confused. I guess this is what it means to be a ghost magnet. You just live in that world as if it's your regular neighborhood.

Kat mentioned that she thought her house was haunted, and Mariah immediately said, "You have two ghosts here. One was on the property and one came here with you. They don't want me here. They think I'm here to get rid of them."

How could she know all of that? Was she just making it up? And if so, why?

"They are incomplete personalities," Mariah continued. "They're in the veil of illusion where there is no judgment. One here has no mind. He is residual, a shade. His existence is absolute repetition."

She looked at me and explained that there were many ghosts in her background. "I'm a Theosophy minister," she said. "I was born to it."

I recalled what I knew of that religion. The Russian-born Madame Helena Blavatsky founded the Theosophical Society back in the 1870s. By the age of four, she had reputedly developed the powers of clairvoyance, clairaudience, and telepathy, and she wanted to use them in the service of humanity. According to her tenets, the universe, which is conscious, derives from an immutable principle, the Supreme Existence, manifesting as both spirit and matter. That is, spiritual life seeks expression through matter, the lowest of which is the body, and evolves toward a more divine state. There is also an astral body, a mental body, and spiritual bodies that are known only to the most advanced beings. The abilities of clairvoyance, telepathy, and the like are manifestations of the more developed senses, and the soul unfolds through reincarnation, which proceeds by the law of karma. Eventually, a person is so evolved that he can move on and not return, unless he wants to help someone else. Blavatsky's idea was to form a universal brotherhood based on the inherent divinity of humankind. To her mind, we were not accidents, and it was important to fulfill out ultimate purpose. How all of this would play into our séance, I wasn't yet sure.

I told Mariah I had never seen a ghost.

"Oh," she said, "you need a doorway and some preparation to manifest a ghost. At least nine days of preparation, with three days of fasting. I wish I'd known. But let me know three weeks in advance next time you come and I'll guarantee that you'll see a ghost." Then she added, "Be careful what you hunt for. If they know you're looking for them, they'll come looking for you."

I was scheduled to return in a few months, and I made a mental note to call her. Anyone who could ensure that I would have this experience was worth checking out.

"You need to meditate and fast," she said, "and use some theosophical rituals. If a doorway opens on the right, don't accept that spirit. They are bound to the earth's core and they turn into pains in the ass. They're abominations. Put together a circle of people, seven or nine, and make a covenant. Say a prayer of cleansing nine times and do a cleansing with sea salt. Cover your body with it. Meditate for ten minutes, morning and night, always at the exact same time, and do it in secret."

As she spoke we moved toward the upper floor where Kat had all of her equipment. Mariah "listened" to the house and told Kat she had a female ghost from an older era, possibly pre–Civil War. The man was from the late 1930s and had grease in his hair. He was a businessman who had owned the house and did not wish to leave. He had suffered financial problems and he needed whoever lived in the house to succeed.

Overhead I heard thunder. It was about to rain. I wondered if that helped or hindered the conducting of spirits. We got to the top floor and sat down on the carpet. I asked Mariah to tell me about my ring.

"I haven't done psychometry in a long time," she said. "There's usually too much pain involved." Nevertheless she took the ring in her hand and went quiet for the first time since she'd entered the house. "I see murder," she said. It thundered again, and the lights went off and then back on. I tried not to laugh. This was too weird. Mariah was sweating, although Kat had the air-conditioning on.

"There's interest of a spirit attached to this ring," she said. "She's next to another woman. She's jealous."

She? When did a woman figure into this? A victim, perhaps? "Who are all these people you say are around me?" I asked.

"There's a teenage girl with a slit throat. I get the initials J. N. C. She's trying to talk to me. She's frustrated. So are the others. They think you can hear them."

"Well, tell them I can't." Then I remembered my tape. At that point, Kat had joined us, so I asked them both to listen to the points during my recording where I thought I'd picked up voices. I turned it on and they listened. Simultaneously they interpreted the voices, "I'm talking to you.... Get out.... Hear what I'm saying.... You think I can't hurt you? Listen to me."

I turned it off. "What?"

"That's what it says," Kat told me. "I can hear it."

"Do you think he's talking to me?"

"Maybe there's someone else in the room," Mariah said. This was getting weird. Spirits in conversation—angry conversation—over my sleeping form?

"You've dug up an elemental," Mariah said. "That's a spirit of earth that has been raised by some necromancer."

I played more. There was a long, loud scream that sounded male and furious.

"We've trespassed on their realm," Mariah pronounced. Then she looked around. "There is a man here who is saving you from retribution. He doesn't want you to see the others. He may want to hurt you. Be careful."

I looked at Kat, and she was looking back at me as if to say, *I agree.*

"If you draw this mass killer to you," Mariah continued, "he'll kill you. He's frustrated. He's warning you away. He's afraid for you and he wants you to quit. He's here with us now. He loves you. You're someone from his past life. He's murdered and wants to stop someone being in danger. He's fixated on you as that person." Mariah pointed to the ring. "At the bottom of that ring is a woman I know nothing about. The secret is in a woman's heart. She is frightened and childlike. Her death was shocking. All you can see is a red aura—red like dried blood, sheets of blood. He has a poisonous hate in his heart and desires to make something of it, to change it. You are the key, but you have to be careful."

Lightning and thunder cracked again, and rain began to pelt the roof.

Mariah went on, although I had no clue who she was talking about. Maybe Christian, maybe someone else. I didn't believe that Christian "loved" me. I had thought she might mean Corey, who had died in this city and who would want to protect me, but I couldn't see how he could have been involved in all of this.

"He wants you to pay attention," she insisted, leaning toward me. "He's trapped in the bottom ring of the spirit world. He needs to help *you,* not you him. He has only what he can recall, which will not be accurate. He says, 'I would be alive today if I had listened.' Possibly he was murdered, but the person who murdered him did so in self-defense. There was animosity and he can't get to the next level. His murder was a murder gone bad. He wanted to take another man's life."

So far that fit my idea, although I hadn't said it to anyone. I figured that he and Wraith had a fight of some sort and Wraith had killed him as a result. Not because he wanted to but because he felt he had to. I hadn't developed it beyond that. Mariah seemed to imply that Christian wanted to now save me from Wraith.

"He was snuffed from the sight of God," Mariah said, rocking back and forth, "and he will live out seven lifetimes in hell. He doesn't want you to be murdered. He has to save your life. He wants to protect you and he needed me to tell you that. That's why he brought me here."

I shrugged. "What should I do?"

"Don't make any lonely meetings. Don't be lured out someplace to speak to ghosts. When you start looking for ghosts, the ghosts will look for you. There is a man here who loves you and wants to protect you." She pointed again to the ring. "These murders had to do with love."

Mariah then asked Kat for her tarot deck and laid out some cards. The gist of it was the following: There was danger in what I was seeking, for something in one of my books had upset the one who was stalking me. I'm holding a secret that is important to him. The ring belongs to him. There's a person stopping him from coming, and all of this will be made clear within thirty days. However, I will lose something I love, and I may not get the story that I seek because there is no coherent story for this entity. I was not to become complacent, and eventually there would be a positive outcome. Those involved with the ring hate women.

"I'm getting the sense of five men and two women," Mariah said. "I think they were victims. They were all suckered and they want you to know that you're being suckered, too. The man with the giant red aura is the one who insisted I come here. I was going to cancel but he came to my living room at home and was all worked up. He was there for twenty minutes. All of these people are happy that you're involved because they want the truth to come out that this happens to people. They disappear."

That's all she had to say.

—8—

Kat and I decided that the optimal time for our separate baths in this wormwood tea would be thirteen minutes. Although everyone warned against it, we got a bottle of wine to help us relax. Like me, she was a little rebellious. I didn't think Christian would mind. Contrary to what I had heard that afternoon, I didn't really think he was there. Wraith was another matter, but we were safely locked into the Southern Nights B&B, awaiting the arrival of the others.

Southern Nights is a century-old, three-story Greek Revival Uptown mansion at 1827 South Carrollton Street. It is divided into two sides, one for the owner and the other for guests, although originally it had housed two brothers, the Cormiers. Pierre Cormier had a wife Cecelia, and a child, Katie. One day he accepted his brother's challenge to race their carriages on South Carrollton. There was a bad storm and they had an accident that killed Cecelia and crippled Katie. After the accident, she languished there in the house, where her mother's spirit was said to look after her.

Judy Garwood had welcomed us into the high-ceilinged living room and invited us to do whatever we wanted. She showed me a lovely suite for my overnight stay, up the grand staircase, and described the various sightings and sounds of Cecelia as she led me on a brief tour of the second floor. Apparently the smell of gardenia in my room was a sign of her presence, while people often heard the sound of swishing skirts in the hallway. Other manifestations included doors opening and the patter of footsteps. Judy talked with us for a few minutes and then said goodnight, wishing us well. It was time to prepare.

I ran hot bathwater into the tub in my bathroom and prepared the concoction that Mimi had given us. We'd made a tea of it, and I had part of that preparation while Kat had the rest. I knew that wormwood was the main ingredient of absinthe, which was hallucinogenic, and I wondered what the effects might be of absorbing such a potent substance through my skin. When the tub was filled, I emptied the magical liquid into it, watching the water turn a light yellowish brown, and then stepped in.

The water felt good. I knew I was supposed to meditate, which does not come easily to me, so I used the ring as a focal point. I held it out of the water and stared at it. Before long, I was distracted by other thoughts and tried to get myself refocused. I wasn't much of a meditator, and maybe that was my problem with seeing ghosts. I'd heard that the ghost receptor was in the right brain, which was best developed through meditational surrender. I once learned to read auras by making my vision diffuse rather than focused, so I tried that. You just stop looking at objects in the foreground and pay more attention to the larger picture. Everything blurred, and after a few minutes, I thought I saw some swirling red mist rising from the water. That made me focus again and I lost it. I had no idea if this was a ghostly visitation or the effects of steeping in a hallucinogenic. Then I realized that people who saw ghosts didn't have to go through this visual exercise, so it probably meant nothing at all. I returned my attention to the ring. When the time was up, I got out.

Donning a long black knit dress, I went downstairs to greet Mimi and her friend, Jeff. He was a voodoo practitioner who had spoken to spirits as a child and who possessed clairvoyant abilities. He asked at once that we give him a cup of coffee. This he placed in the rest room, "a gift for the spirits, because they like to take it in there. I don't know why. Maybe they like running water or maybe it's the place where things decompose. You can also use cigarettes." He was tall and thin, with dark hair and large beautiful eyes. I guessed that he might be gay, which I felt would be a good thing since Christian had been gay.

Sid, Kat's husband, came as the skeptic. He wanted to believe, but he wanted proof. The fact that he was in the house once when the cabinet doors mysteriously opened by themselves was not enough. But he was a sympathetic skeptic, open to possibilities, so it seemed fine to have him there.

Mimi was setting up candles on the large wooden dining-room table as Mariah made a dramatic entrance with her husband, "Fuzzy." He was a short, agreeable guy who seemed to go along with his wife's spiritualism and even claimed some psychic abilities of his own. Mariah said he was a terrific channel, but he just smiled modestly.

"Your ghost hasn't let up on me," Mariah told me in her booming voice. "He needs you to know you're in danger. He's been with me since I left and wants me to tell you that. You're not scared enough. He thinks you're not taking it seriously."

He was right about that; I wasn't. Not then, anyway. I wanted some proof that I should and so far, none was forthcoming.

Initially, there was some confusion as to who was going to run the séance, since both Mariah and Mimi were experienced in these things. In the end, they agreed on which of the materials to use and which to lay aside. Mariah was adamant that there be no black candles. Even the purple ones were too dark. She insisted that we use only pastels. We then placed a pan of water, as per Mimi's instructions, in the center of the table and emptied into it a container of black ink. I wasn't sure, but I thought this was to make the water more conducive to seeing images within it. Inside the pan, we placed a jar cap that floated, and in the center of that, Christian's ring. Then we lit the orange and white candles. We placed them on four tin plates on the table. We also put out the pens and tablets for whatever spirit might want to use this means to deliver a message.

Mimi handled everything with surgical gloves, which she said would be tossed out afterward. I asked her why and she said, "The gloves should be taken off very carefully, inside out so that the oil does not have any chance of contacting human skin. The oil is a blend that has the effect of creating a portal whereby all spirits can pass through, good and especially bad. That's why we keep a wash of salt water close by, in case of some accidental contact with the skin. If that happens, you wash the skin with the salt water to cleanse it completely and purify it so the negative cannot take advantage."

Kat placed two videocams at different angles to capture anything that might happen.

Then we dimmed the lights and all held hands as Mariah sat at the head of the table and said a prayer of protection. It was around 11:00 P.M. Mimi warned us not to let go, no matter what we felt or saw. I had Jeff to my right and Sid to my left. Mimi was on his right, with Kat next to her holding Fuzzy's hand. He was next to Mariah, who completed the link with Jeff. One chair remained empty to allow an entity to feel invited. That was next to me, and I had to reach across it to connect with Sid. My entire left side felt vulnerable.

I quickly explained to everyone present how I got the ring from a man I called Wraith, since only Kat had read the entire account. I said that my goal for the night was to discover if Christian had been murdered and if there was a way for him to communicate the details to me. Whoever got any impressions should report them, even if they did not seem relevant. Kat noted that Cecelia, the female spirit who inhabited the house, might also attend, but she thought we should concentrate on Christian.

"He's here," Mariah said right away. "I feel him. He's waiting."

I felt a chill but decided it was just my imagination or the air-conditioning.

"He's not so gay in death," Mariah said.

I perked up. "Really?" That was interesting. Hadn't Chanda said that if you called forth an incubus you'd get an incubus? Hmmm.

Then Mariah felt a woman's spirit, one that was much more evolved, and she figured this to be Cecelia. She thought Cecelia might want to protect us.

Although these initial impressions happened quickly, they seemed to drop off. Mariah and Mimi made several attempts to sense things, as did Jeff, but little took place. I was feeling tired, especially reaching across the empty space to hold on to Sid's hand. The three mediums seemed alert, but Fuzzy and Sid looked bored. It grew so quiet we could hear the candle wax pop as the candles burned about one third of the way down. I glanced at the pens on the table with the hope of seeing one move, but they remained as they were. If "Christian" was as worried about me as Mariah had claimed, why wasn't he using one of these gifted people to speak to me? Couldn't we even get a rap on the table?

As if reading my mind, Mimi warned us we would have to be patient. Sometimes these things took hours before real contact was made. Sid must have taken this to heart; he was so patient, he fell asleep. I shook him so he wouldn't accidentally let go and open up the circle. He was somewhat chagrinned. He didn't mind that by 12:30 he had to go relieve the baby-sitter. He was sure he wasn't going to miss anything. Carefully he joined my left hand to Mimi's right and then said goodnight to us all. Once he was gone, everything changed.

Mariah kept insisting that my spirit loved me and wanted to protect me. I wasn't sure I believed that. Wraith had told me that Christian had despised women—had even killed a couple of girls. I didn't know if that was true, but I also didn't feel the presence of a loving spirit who wanted to protect me.

"Isn't it possible this spirit is lying to you?" I asked.

"They don't lie. I've never had a spirit lie to me."

I wondered how she could possibly know, but I did not practice Theosophy; maybe they had some way to figure that out.

"This man who loves you is very solid," Mariah said. "I call him the Wall. He's like a wall." She described someone who looked nothing like Christian as Wraith had described him. I was annoyed. I told "the Wall" to leave. I wanted to contact Christian.

"He's not leaving," Mariah said. Her left arm jerked hard, shaking Jeff's. "See? He's pulling on my arm. He wants my attention."

At that moment I felt a mass of cold air between Jeff and me that seemed dense, as if it had form. He looked at me, and without my mentioning anything, he said, "I feel it, too." I looked at him with surprise. That was confirmation. We had both felt the same thing independent of each other. Maybe I was finally going to see a ghost. It sure felt like it, and I sensed that if Christian were going to "talk" to anyone here, it would be Jeff. Perhaps he was moving closer so he could communicate. The cold air remained right there between us. It felt at least twenty degrees colder than the air on my other side.

"What are you getting?" I asked Jeff.

Everyone looked at him expectantly. He was quiet a moment as he stared at the candle closest to him. Finally he said, "There's just one image I see, and I've been seeing it since we started. It won't go away. I don't know if it makes any sense. . . ."

"Just tell us," I encouraged him.

"It persists, so it must be important. It's a box. That's what I see."

"What kind of box?" I asked.

He struggled a little as if to get a clearer impression in his mind. "It's a gray or tan metal locked box. There's something in it that's about the truth."

I caught my breath. A gray metal box? Wraith had mentioned a box like that. He said he'd locked his diary into it—a journal about the murders. "What's in the box?" I asked. "Can you see?" My heart was pounding at this revelation.

Jeff shook his head a little before he said, "I think it's a book."

I couldn't believe this. I had never told anyone about that book. It was in my notes from my meeting with Wraith, but not published anywhere. I hadn't included it in my vampire book. No one knew about that except me . . . and Wraith. He had said that maybe one day he would send it to me. I had not given that box any thought in over a year, so I did not think that Jeff had picked up something telepathically from me. It seemed that someone else was communicating this image to him.

My eyes were wide as I listened. Jeff went on to say something about our cold spot. "He's standing here laughing. I can feel him. He's sarcastically amused. He doesn't care about you."

I nodded. Just as I had suspected—if he was there at all.

"He's working on your resistance. He's urging you to stay away from Wraith, knowing that you will go. He knows you're like that. But they're still a team. Wraith knows that Christian is here."

Suddenly, Mimi cried out. "My throat!" she yelled. "No! No! I can't breathe. No, I don't accept you. I will not allow it!" She let go of my hand to grab at her neck.

I stared at her. I didn't know if this was real or some performance. Then everything came too fast for me to analyze.

Mariah felt it, too. "I don't want you either!" she shouted. "Get away!"

"I've got a murder victim here," Kat added, "grabbing my wrist."

The cold spot to my right seemed to increase in density.

"He's right here," said Jeff, "right behind us."

"This person is angry that Christian is in the room," Kat said. "He or she was his victim. There are others here, too. They don't trust him."

"Christian's really pissed," said Jeff. "He's angry at someone not in this room."

"It was a suicide pact gone wrong," Mimi offered. "I see it. Wraith came up from behind. He took the opportunity to protect himself. He did not want to die. Christian's mad because Wraith isn't dead, too, and he himself doesn't have the strength now to take him down. He wants revenge." She looked at me. "He wants to use you to kill Wraith."

I laughed. "As if I would!"

"Don't be so certain," Mariah interjected. "It could be in self-defense."

"The Wall," Kat interrupted. "The Wall is Michael. He's here. He's been sitting there in that chair a long time."

I edged away. No one else knew whom she meant, but I did: Michael had been the vampire mentor to Wraith and Christian. He's been found murdered one day and Wraith had been a suspect, but he had told me that Christian had done it.

"It was his voice on the recorder," Kat continued. "The ring was his. He moved the coins in your room. He's in the blue light now. He wants this all to end. He's beyond it all and he's protecting you."

"They're going," said Mariah. "The murder victims are leaving." The others nodded in agreement.

"He's been communicating with you for some time now," said Jeff, "more than you realize. You're seeing things now. You're aware of things you otherwise wouldn't be. Now everything will change."

Mariah leaned toward me. "He was their mentor but now he's yours."

I felt a cold wave pass through me. I had come in here doubting I even had one ghost. Now I was told I had two and they were at odds over what they wanted from me. But why was I the only one at the table who had been told absolutely nothing directly? No one had an answer to that.

The séance seemed to come to a natural close around that time. It was 2:00 in the morning. We cleaned everything up, restored the table settings for breakfast, and I thanked everyone and bid them goodnight. In their minds, I had gotten my answers. In mine, I found only more questions.

I went up to my room, sniffed for phantom gardenia perfume, but smelled nothing. I went to bed. No ghosts visited that I was aware of. The next day I left New Orleans, but I was to find out that this haunting did not end when everyone walked out the door.

Voices in the Night

"THE DEAD ARE THE INVISIBLE ONES, BUT NOT THE
ABSENT ONES."

—VICTOR HUGO

—1—

The day I got back to my home
in Princeton, I received a strange e-mail
from Kat:

"I called Mariah to see how she's felt
since the séance. She said that she has had
choking feelings since she left us, and that
the girl with the slit throat has been following her, so she consulted with another spiritualist. Mariah noted that she never saw
Christian's face, so he could be a wandering
demon. She heard a voice say, 'You think it
has stopped, but it hasn't.' She wants to
come back next week and use the *Keys of
Solomon* to make a pentagram to draw the
demon into it, so we can literally exorcise my
house. She thinks we didn't protect ourselves enough—that we called in something
evil and that Christian is going to feed off
of our fear." She also noted that nothing
had come out on the videotapes.

I wasn't sure what to make of all
that. At the séance, I'd been bewildered that
everyone except me had been getting impressions, images, and messages from entities in the room. Aside from that one intense
cold spot, I'd gotten nothing. I couldn't help

but wonder if there wasn't some sort of psychological contagion happening—although the information about the locked box defied that explanation. Maybe I was just spiritually inept. None of the people involved had come across as charlatans—and I have met my share in the psychic world. They all had seemed sincere in their efforts to assist me. Yet why was I the only one who had no inkling of what had transpired? Even Fuzzy, who had said little, had agreed with the group's assessment of the situation. But I found that I couldn't even do that much. I just didn't know.

Kat had also included a postscript that read as follows:

"Last night, on the recorder, there was the deep growling voice and others whispering. It is really creepy. I swear this voice is saying 'Katherine.' And just for the record, I think he means you! Maybe you should put the recorder on in your room at night and see what you get."

Yeah, that's what I really wanted to do. Be there all by myself while some spirit growled at me. I thought about it and quickly responded:

"Wraith told me that Christian is a trickster and would make himself seem stronger than he really is, but all he has managed to do—if anything—is inspire a few bad dreams. I suppose it's possible that Christian was never quite human. Wraith implied that he thought that was the case. Nevertheless, I don't think you're in danger. I think perhaps Christian found someone in Mariah that he could make himself known to, so he's continuing to do that. But if we called in something evil, why isn't it coming for me?"

I was getting increasingly more confused about this ghost called Christian. I'd never really taken Wraith's haunting seriously, but I also hadn't expected to have two psychics who lived miles apart and did not know each other—or me—have the same violent reaction to the ring. And now I had a medium who told me quite specifically a piece of information about a locked box that I had believed to be secret. I recalled the group in Canada that had created their own spirit, Philip, who had rapped on and levitated tables. Either they had inadvertently called in a demon or their group efforts had created a powerful psychokinetic effect. Still, they made up those details and they had done it together, so they all knew what the details were. In this case, things were different. I had several accurate psychic episodes to sort through that had occurred at different times and places by unrelated people. It could be that we were taking small incidents and enlarging them together, but it could also be that my active search for the ghost in the

gHost

ring was conjuring up something. Maybe it was Christian, maybe not. Nevertheless, he seemed more real now than he had before I went to New Orleans.

I called Mariah to ask her what this was all about. She got right to the point.

"They want to see how far you can be driven," Mariah said.

"Driven?"

"This girl with the slit-open throat wants to stay here. I got quiet with her to see what she wants. She likes me. She's staying with me. She wants justice. Her story isn't over, she says, because the killing isn't over. I think Wraith is still out there, killing."

That had not really occurred to me. "What should I do? I don't want to leave a mess behind for all of you to have to deal with. That wasn't my intention."

"If you leave salt in a crystal bowl—preferably sea salt—and place it in the north corner of a room, that should help. If you put a mirror over it, that gives them a focal point away from you. It seems too simple, but if you have a haunting and you leave salt out, it will turn brown as the desert sand. And make sure that no mirror stands at right angles to wrought iron. That's a conductor."

I scribbled all this down, and asked, "So you think Christian is a demon?"

Mariah's response was immediate. "I'm wondering if he sought some sort of demonic possession. I don't think that's his name. I never saw his face, and with demons you have to see their face or call them by their name. I think Christian is having us call him that so we don't find out his real name. He keeps his power as long as we don't know his name. Demons come as black shapes, and his is of the lowest of souls. Minions own that soul completely. It's the soul that has given up all hope."

That certainly sounded like Wraith's description of Christian. But if he visited her for twenty minutes in her home, as she had originally told me, why had she never seen his face?

"Kat has some kind of scratching in the walls of her house," Mariah went on. "I heard them, and that signals the porthole of a minion."

I resisted the temptation to say, "Or mice." Instead I asked what I should do.

"You'll need the pentagrams of power. I'll look them up in the *Keys of Solomon* and get the right one. I need to try to get the demon's name."

We said good-bye. I hung up the phone and sat there wondering what to think of all this. I had set out to find a ghost, and now I was hearing all this talk of minions and demons. This wasn't anything like ghost hunting in Gettysburg. It was like the difference between chasing butterflies and tracking a tiger. One group thought that ghosts were benign, the other saw more predatory possibilities. Both methods seemed to get results that appeared to be supernatural, but neither had gotten me closer to knowing if Christian was real or what he wanted. Regardless, if he was around, I wanted him back with me. I was not about to lose him before I saw him for myself.

I soon found out that I was not the only one who wanted him back.

—2—

I decided to get out my notes from my clandestine meeting with Wraith that strange night down south and see if I had overlooked something. I had not paid much attention to the material on Christian as a ghost because I'd been more interested in what these two had done as a vampiric team. Even acquiring the ring had not inclined me to believe much of what Wraith had said on the subject. However, these warnings from Mariah and Kat, along with Jeff's startling image of the locked box, had made me rethink things. I wanted to get reacquainted with Christian's traits as a ghost. I went through pages and pages of notes detailing Wraith's sordid history with his sociopathic lover before I found what I was looking for.

The first one I wanted to read about was Michael. If he was indeed my protector in this spooky dispute, I wanted to know more about him. He had appeared fleetingly in *Piercing the Darkness* as the person who had introduced Wraith into a vampire coven, and the lavish descriptions of his home made me wonder if he'd been Wraith's imaginary creation. Wraith told me that Michael had been viciously murdered—a murder that was never solved. Wraith suspected that Christian had done it, but said that they'd never discussed it between themselves.

Wraith's initial story of how he met Michael had been a lie. I'd caught him in a contradiction, and he had then admitted the truth (or at least had given another version). He told me that at the age of sixteen, he'd met Michael while walking along a river, and they'd become constant companions.

"Michael began teaching me everything he knew about vampirism," Wraith had said. "He took me hunting with him and refined my capacity for charming people. Michael's principles of vampirism did not typically involve cruelty or murder. He preferred persuasion and charm. He was angry about Christian's brutality with kills. He didn't like the way Christian tortured his prey. 'He's a disgrace,' he once told me. I think Christian disliked Michael, used him for what he needed, and then killed him.

"Michael was flown overseas for burial. I never got to see his body. I was devastated. Then one evening, while walking on the shore near Michael's house, there he was ... standing in front of me. He told me not to approach him since he was speaking to me from the second world, a place he told me that vampires go when they leave earth."

I stopped reading for a minute. I had forgotten all about this. Michael, too, had come to Wraith as a ghost. I suppose I'd dismissed it at the time as sheer fantasy. And perhaps it was, but now it seemed more important. One thing I had to keep in mind was Wraith's persuasive powers. Like people who can make others sick by suggesting that they look ill, Wraith could easily have stimulated latent images in me that would come to the surface when I paid attention to them. With the help of this group in New Orleans, I was now very attentive. I know about collective narratives that develop when people grow anxious. Whole masses can develop common physical symptoms that are emotional in origin, and if they get promoted by journalists, therapists, physicians, and whoever else might have a stake in them, they become "real." I had to take care not to get caught up in having a stake in the existence of the ghosts of Michael and Christian. Yet I also did not want to dismiss the possibilities. It would be tricky finding the right line to walk.

I returned to Wraith's narrative about encountering Michael's ghost.

"I asked him if he was all right, if he was happy, but he was only interested in talking about one thing: Christian. He urged me to get rid of him and to do it immediately. He warned that Christian would destroy me. I asked him who had killed him, but he bowed his head and would not speak. I asked if Christian knew who did it. He looked at me and his eyes betrayed him. Then I knew."

So that established Michael as a spirit who appeared to Wraith to warn him. It seemed he was one of the good guys, so to speak. Or at least among those with more shades of gray (no pun intended). This situation was getting interesting.

Now it was time to look at what Wraith had told me about Christian as a spirit. To my mind, he was a trickster, a figure that simultaneously embodies creativity and destruction. Because he crosses boundaries, he "tricks" us past them, but offers no safety and can lead us toward our own destruction. The trickster is a chaos that seduces us when we feel stale but can wrap itself around us and destroy our center, like a water bug injecting bone-disintegrating venom. In world mythology, the trickster spirit, or imp, is an amoral, bisexual, demonic figure that blends beast, human, and god into an unpredictable shape-shifting entity. He is a thief of the soul, promising incredible stimulation while possessing and wounding at his whim. Erotic, greedy, and clever, he invites us toward great risk and may possibly reward us with transcendence . . . or not, as he pleases.

Wraith told me that after he got used to having Christian's ghost around, he became aware that Christian was there every day. "In a very real sense, he is not dead to me. I would be lying if I said I didn't prefer him to his ghost, but Christian *is* a part of my soul. I thought his ghost would go away, you know—after he settled things with me. But he didn't and I soon attached myself to his spirit presence."

Early on in our acquaintance, he told me that Christian had "picked" me to write their story. I had asked why he trusted me, and now I was even more interested in the response:

"He trusts you for the same reason that I trust you, Katherine," Wraith had said. "Your energy signature is very strong and reveals a kindred quest. You are very open to bizarre phenomena as genuine possibility."

Maybe too open.

I then looked at the response to a question I had asked about their relationship: If Christian had indeed committed suicide to join his spirit to Wraith's, hadn't he first discussed this with his lover?

"Christian did discuss with me his plans to die," Wraith had responded. "When he brought it up over coffee late one night I was terrified. I started to cry right there because I knew that once he got an idea worked out in his mind he would eventually make it happen. We are both very strong personalities, very determined to lead the dance. But when he revealed his plans to join with me away from his body, after months of periodic attempts to dissuade him, I acquiesced and began to trust him with it. After all this time I can see that this is what I did. I knew inside that I could not change his mind."

I noted, too, that while Christian had not admitted to Wraith that the ring he gave to him had not been his, Wraith had learned from someone else that it had been a gift to him. He never learned who it was from. I wondered about Michael.

Looking deeper into the stack of transcripts from that night, I was startled by several pages that Wraith had told me were from Christian himself. He had sent them to me, claiming that he had gotten them through automatic writing.

Now this kind of exercise is a strange thing. Supposedly the writing is done in a dissociated state and is attributed to some supernatural force that wants to send a message. Without a physical body, it can't, so it uses the body of a person who is willing to surrender to it. Spiritualists of the nineteenth century relied on this method to convince people that they were getting messages from their deceased loved ones. The writer remains unaware of the act and the content until he or she emerges from the trance. In fact, entire books have been written in this manner, allegedly channeled through the medium. In the old days, ghosts used chalk or pens. Now they've updated to computers.

Demonologists say that these messages are from satanic entities trying to possess the medium. Psychologists believe they come from the subconscious. That was my own reaction to what Wraith had sent me, although I did notice a dramatic change in tone. "Christian" was more brutal, direct, and nasty than was the more poetic Wraith. I had wondered if Wraith was a multiple personality, but little else about him was consistent with such a diagnosis.

Now I read these messages from Christian with a new eye. I soon realized they were not dissociated fragments but a chronicle of Christian's experience as a spirit bound to Wraith's body.

> Strange, staring from behind these eyes, typing these words. I feel as if I've come home again, to my lover's waiting arms. He has always waited for me, you know, never daring to venture out on his own. Without me, where would his life had gone?
>
> The world seems a better place now, I almost wish I hadn't left. Oh, the weak and pathetic creatures crawling around, their rusty red hearts ready to bleed. When I was in this place, it was an effort to bring them to blood. But now, with all the changes, children enjoy bleeding. I would thrive.
>
> So you want to know the memories I've stored with my lover, do you? True, I am more brutal then him—much more "a savage beast." His is a beautiful heart controlled by a restless

soul, I simply took advantage of the natural insanity buried there. He has been included in many of my most cherished blood hunts. Let me see . . . oh yes, I remember one very special exercise in terror.

He talked of how they picked up a young man and took him into the woods to abuse him. Christian hit him with a shovel and then cut a piece of flesh from his thigh as a souvenir.

I could not restrain my madness. I knew I should probably stop here and let him go, but I wanted a piece of him. I needed to bring back a portion of the lad. Wrapping the hot flesh around my jaw, I was able to smell the boy in the meat. It was delirious.

So this was now my ghost. Nasty. I read one more about how he had tricked a guy into his car and then had killed him.

The raw taste of freshly cut flesh is divine, at least as close as I'll ever get to God. Herein lies the power, the soul of experience: It rests within the secret. Secret longings and secret journeys into forbidden territory awakens the soul to its destiny. I am crazy. I confess. I enjoy the taste of blood, the sensation of quivering muscle and nerve between my teeth. Ripping into the bowels of a young boy brings me pleasure. . . . The art and texture of internals is transcendent.

I shoved the pile of papers away. That was enough for me.

—**4**—

However, it soon became apparent that Christian was not finished in New Orleans, and I was getting a little jealous at all the attention they were getting. By the end of the week, Kat wrote again. "A lot has come up down here. Perhaps the Summer Solstice helped makes us a little clearer or maybe because it is St. John's Eve, I don't know. The veil is very thin right now. Mimi saw Jeff tonight and she met me at the Calf with some strange news. Since shortly after the séance, Jeff has been experiencing Mara [psychic vampire] attacks each morning at 5:00 A.M. He is literally terrified, to the point, that lately he has stayed out all night just to avoid being awakened by this thing. Then at dawn he sleeps!

"Aside from that, this morning Mimi went to her office. When she turned her computer on it was in DOS on C prompt. She got distracted and turned away from the screen. When she returned this is what the screen had on it across the top:

'chchchais is an ass hole because i waas to bewithhim t'

"Then it ran out of room on the screen. It was spaced just like I have it and all in lowercase letters. Mimi doesn't have a computer with Internet access. She discussed this with Jeff and they both seem to think that perhaps, Wraith is Christian, and this person communicating with them, whoever it may be, is the one he killed."

I called Jeff right away to see if this was true and to find out how he was. He assured me that he was all right.

"What happened?" I asked.

"Well," he began, "this didn't happen right away, but a couple of nights after the séance. For several nights in a row, I would wake up at the same time each night feeling terrified. I couldn't move. I felt a malevolent presence in the room with me and I thought I must be psyching myself out. But at that moment, I was convinced there was someone else in the room with me, aware of me. I thought I was in danger."

"Did it stop or is he still there?"

"I put salt around the bed, just to cleanse the room, and after that it stopped happening. I haven't been waking up for the past two nights."

Nevertheless, toward the end of our conversation he asked me to please not use his real name in my book. He did not wish to be associated any further with this entity. If it was aware of what I was writing, it might retaliate again on him.

I understood, but I was bothered by the possibility that I had lost my ghost. I wouldn't blame him for preferring New Orleans to Yankee territory, but I wanted to contact him myself. Since I'd had a bit of luck with the recorder both in Gettysburg and New Orleans, I decided to try it in my own apartment. I had hoped to find out more about EVP first, but there wasn't time. I decided I knew enough to move ahead.

For several nights in a row, I let the recorder run, but I got no more than about six minutes of hazy stuff that sounded nothing like a voice. I began to wonder if there was really anything to it. Maybe what I'd heard before had been an anomaly, a one-time thing. I hadn't even listened to the entire tape from Gettysburg, mostly because I wasn't very good at making out what was said.

I already knew what the skeptics had to say about electronic voice phenomena: If you listen for a voice, you'll hear a voice. It's all about perception. Like seeing your mother's face in a Rorschach inkblot, you'll hear what you want to hear. On the other hand, I never really expected to get anything on my recorder in Gettysburg, so how could I have heard "what I wanted to hear?" And I especially wouldn't have expected two people to simultaneously interpret my EVP in exactly the same way, as Kat and Mariah did in New Orleans. So that skeptical response only convinced me that the people who take that position are just guessing at what it *must* be according to their worldview.

Critics have also claimed that EVP is just radio waves or some stray signal, anything but a ghost. I don't know about that. It sure didn't sound like a radio station, unless it was WDEMN. I just knew that I'd gotten something twice that sounded very much like a voice, and I might be able to get one again. If it all turned out to be nothing, that was fine, but there was no harm in trying.

—5—

It was time to get really serious. About ten days after I got back from New Orleans, I invited Stuart Lee Brown over to help me out. He had gone on one vampire adventure with me. Blond and lean, he was hyper-vigilant about any kind of threat. He even bought me a pepper spray because he was so nervous about my adventures. What pepper spray could do against ghosts, I had no idea, but it was sweet of him to help.

Stuart assured me that he had extrasensitive hearing and could help decipher some of my recordings. He even felt that he was a ghost-attractant. He told me about the time when he was twelve, about two years after his father had died, when he had a powerful encounter. He and a friend were in his home alone. The dog, Duffy, was gated in the kitchen, and the two boys were upstairs looking through Stuart's toys. Suddenly the other boy claimed that he had just heard a man's voice downstairs. Had they left the television on? Were the doors locked? Since the dog was not barking, Stuart assured him that there couldn't be anyone down there, but at the friend's insistence, he went down alone to check.

"When I got to the central hall downstairs," Stuart told me, "I heard a man's voice say, 'Duffy, I've been looking for Stuart everywhere. Do you know where he is?' I was surprised to find Duffy out of the kitchen and sitting in the hall. He was staring at the wall, oblivious to me, and wagging his tail like he was listening to someone. There was no one there, so I took Duffy back to kitchen and saw that the gate had been unlatched and opened all the way, which he couldn't do by himself. I told my mother and she said she had felt a presence in that hallway, too."

Stuart made himself comfortable in my office so he could listen to the part of the Gettysburg recording that I had not yet heard myself. It wasn't long before he came and got me.

"You have to hear this," he said.

I wondered what he could have heard. I sat next to him and listened as he played for me a very clear and plaintive male voice crying, "Help!" We looked at each other, startled. I listened to it again and was really surprised by how clear it was. And how creepy. Yet there was no mistake. He was begging for help. On another part of the recording, a little later, you could hear, "Help me." This was real and it wasn't any radio station.

"Okay, stop doing this one," I said. "I want you to listen to the recording from New Orleans. That's more important to me. See what you can hear on that."

For twenty minutes he worked on it and then told me he could hear the following phrases:

"I'm talking to you, I'm talking to you. Can you hear me? Are you listening to me?" Just what Kat and Mariah had heard. I hadn't told him anything that had happened in New Orleans, but he'd managed to come up with the same interpretation. Then next one was more disturbing.

"Very quietly," Stuart explained, "he says, 'Open your mind to me.' "

I pulled my sweater around me to ward off the sudden chill.

"Then there's something that sounds like an argument, and the voice of a child or a woman saying, 'Anything at all.' She's making utterances of distress like 'Oh!' and 'Oh, no!' Then I hear the male voice yell, 'Get the hell out of here!' "

He thought the long, extended noise that sounded like yelling was an attempt to interfere with the recorder, as if one were passing one's hand over it to create interference. He could hear another voice in the background. It seemed to him that the other voice was trying to influence the dominant one but he was resisting.

Stuart also thought that he was laughing a lot, a "deep and creepy kind of laugh."

Then he insisted that I listen to one particular voice myself. Clearly, it was that of a woman. All of a sudden she said (in an almost sexy displeased-but-faintly-interested manner), "What are you doing? Get off!"

I looked at Stuart. "This was where I was sleeping," I told him. "What was going on in there and who was doing what to whom?"

He shrugged. He was just the interpreter. I was alone with this enigma. I'd been asleep in a strange room while someone had been near me, speaking, arguing, yelling. I wondered if this activity was specific to Kat's house or whether these things had traveled to my home. How was I going to sleep at night?

Stuart continued to play some of the recording. A little later, right at the end, it sounded like the woman also said, "Get out of here." She tried to interject more remarks, but it was difficult to hear her over the male voice screaming as if he was trying to drown her out.

So there were two males, according to what Stuart believed he could hear, and a female. Kat thought that there was a female and male spirit in her home. If "Christian" were also there, that would make a trio—in particular one that was filled with stress over the entrance of a malevolent intruder. I decided I definitely had to look into this further.

After Stuart left, I decided to try the digital recorder in my room once again. (I had already put salt in a bowl as Mariah had suggested, but it didn't change color. After a week, I tossed it). The next morning I saw that I had gotten forty-three minutes of something. I listened to about ten before I realized it was all the same stuff: a pattern that sounded like a male voice and a lot of gruff growling stuff, but nothing I could understand. I remembered that Kat had recommended that I play it on slow speed and hold it to my ear. I did that, but it just sounded like the grunting pig in *The Amityville Horror*.

However, about thirty minutes in, something changed. I heard myself cough and I recalled that indeed I had coughed that night, right around 3:00 A.M. In fact, I had awoken myself with the need to cough and then had gone back to sleep fairly quickly. But almost immediately after my cough came a startling sound: an aggressive male voice coughing twice as if imitating me.

I stopped the recording and backed it up. I listened again.

There's me coughing . . .

. . . and two distinct but different coughs directly afterward.

I stopped the recorder.

No way, no way, I thought. That was not my voice. But there had been no one else in the room. I had been awake at that point and had heard nothing. What could it have been? To top it off, it was much louder than me, although I had been only two feet from the recorder.

And then I remembered that I had placed the recorder directly beneath Christian's ring, which hung from a black bed lamp. Could he/it have been that close to my head, coughing in mockery? Or was he trying to get my attention, attempting a form of communication like you see on fifties alien movies—imitation in an effort to communicate?

I played it again several times and then called Stuart to play it for him over the phone. He found it strange as well, and also described the cough as distinctly male. He thought it sounded mocking.

To me this was a significant EVP event, and I sent out a description of it to Kat, and also to the IGHS members, Rick, Karl, Sharon, and Dave. Rick and Karl urged me to keep gathering evidence. Dave Oester warned me that sometimes there are spikes that occur with digital recorders, implying that I ought not to get too excited about this just yet. I would have to find an example of a spike to compare, but it would have to be an odd spike that sounds like a cough for me to be convinced.

Then I asked Stuart to come back and listen to the entire tape with me, because I wanted him to hear the rest. He held the recorder to his ear and listened intently. I wrote what he dictated.

"He's giving a name," he said as he pressed the recorder near his ear. " 'I am something.' I can't make out the name, but it's two syllables. And your name keeps coming up."

That hit me like ice down my back. "My name?"

"He's talking to you or about you. There's someone else more faint. It's like a running conversation, but you can only hear his side. Oh, I heard him say, 'Can you hear me?' That was clear."

I grabbed the recorder and pressed the ten-second reverse button. I heard the same thing, but I wouldn't discount the influence of Stuart's suggestion.

"Now he says 'Katherine' again. He says that a lot, like he's trying to get you to wake up. Now it's, 'I'm talking to you, Katherine. . . . Help me to . . .' I don't know what he's saying there."

"Aghh! Help him to what?"

We played it back again but got no closer to a solution. At least I knew he wanted help with something. . . . but then, Mimi had said it was to help kill Wraith.

Stuart commented on the odd whistling that had started up in the background of the tape. It sounded to him like a high-pitched bird, as if Christian was using some other means to get my attention.

"Do you have anything in your apartment that makes that sort of noise?" he asked.

"Not that I recall. But if it was an audible sound, it would have woke me up."

"It's a ghost bell?"

"I don't know. I guess. It's on the tape for about five minutes, and then fades away. Then just a bunch of frustrated yelling."

"Yeah, that's hurting my ear," said Stuart. "Oh! He said your name again."

I backed it up and listened. Yes, he said my first name. It was pretty clear.

Then Stuart listened through to the end and heard the other voice, which was also male but of a different quality. "It's like some other spirit is trying to interfere, but it's too soft to hear much. But he says your name, too."

Then we heard quite distinctly, "Never!" and then a vocal pattern that sounded like a question. Then the recording cut off abruptly, as if I had shut it off in mid-conversation, although I had not.

I needed to try it again.

—6—

This time I decided to be a little bolder. It was the night before the full moon, and a storm was predicted to roll through in the early morning, which meant that the evening would be hot and humid, the kind of quiet sweltering heat that precedes summer storms. I had heard from the IGHS that these were optimum conditions for recording ghosts, because there were changes in the atmospheric energy. I didn't know what that meant, but if ghosts are related to energy fields, then it made sense that there might be more activity during the intensity preceding a storm.

It was around 12:30. I sat in bed, feeling somewhat foolish. Did I really want to try this while I was all alone? It had been one thing with my sister in the room or being asleep, but actually attempting a recording while I was alone and aware was altogether different. I didn't believe that anything would happen, but I wasn't sure I was prepared if something actually did. I breathed deeply a few times and listened. There was no noise. It was hot in my room because I'd left the air conditioner off. Nevertheless, I pulled the sheets closer around me. I thought again about those voices on my tape from New Orleans that seemed so confrontational, and I hoped that those spirits were still down there.

The ring was hanging from the black lamp on my bed table, about two feet away. I looked at it and wondered if Christian would respond. I thought again about that eerie cough. By day, it had not seemed quite so sinister as it did now. Finally, it was time to try this. I turned on a small flashlight so I could keep the room dark but also watch the indicators on the recorder. I said to the air, "Okay. I'm going to put on this recorder and you can tell me anything you want, but if you yell, I can't make out what you're saying. Just say it quietly and clearly. This is the only way I'll know what you want, because I cannot understand you otherwise."

I turned on the recorder. At first nothing happened. Then I noticed that the red indicator light went solid for several seconds. That meant that something was being recorded. I listened for stray sounds and heard nothing. Again, the light went solid. I was amazed. I waited a few more seconds until the VAS stopped and then turned it off.

Now it was time to listen to see what I had recorded. Did I really want to hear this? I took a breath and decided to go ahead. I pushed the play button.

To my shock, I got a huge, loud roar. It was worse than the one in New Orleans, and it even sounded like laughter. I dropped the recorder onto the bed as if it had burned me. What *was* that? And how could I have failed to hear something that loud? I looked at the recorder, breathing a little faster. Something was in here with me.

Now I really felt alone. This was just too weird. But then I thought that maybe it had just been a car or something. I hadn't actually heard words. I listened to it again and I just couldn't identify that loud roar as any normal sound. I noticed that my hand was trembling a little. Nevertheless, I had to try it again. I turned it to record.

"Okay, look," I said, trying to sound bold. "I'm not afraid of you and I don't know what you're saying when you do that. Let's start over. I'll ask you some questions and you answer them."

I waited, breathless. I strained to hear even the most distant remote sounds. There were none.

"What is your name?" I asked slowly so there could be no misunderstanding. Maybe we sounded as unintelligible to ghosts as they did to us. I waited for a moment, and then played back what I had thus far. This time I got a distinct two-syllable growl. I listened for "Christian," but could not hear that. Nor "Michael." Just "Rahrah."

"Okay, we almost have it," I said, growing excited. This time I asked a series of questions and watched the numbers move on the recorder as if in response. Three seconds, six seconds. Something was definitely happening. After about two minutes, I played this back and heard the following:

Me: "Let's try it again. What is your name?"

An angry roar.

Me: "What do you want?"

Two syllables, incomprehensible, almost like a knocking sound. (After listening several times, it could have been, "Your help." Or maybe not. A young woman later told me it was "Revenge.")

Me: "Are you Christian?"

"Yes!"

I stopped the recorder. My eyes were wide and my heart was pounding again. That was clear and distinct. And whatever it was, it was right there in the room with me, aware of me, possibly watching me. I couldn't see it, but it apparently could see me. I fought the urge to dive beneath the covers. I couldn't let it know that I was in my *not tonight please not tonight* mode. I took a deep breath and played this message again.

"Are you Christian?"

"Yes!" He yelled it. Yet clearly it was an affirmative response.

Now what? I wasn't really prepared for this. But I had to take advantage of this phenomenon—of getting responses directly to my questions. I certainly knew that it might very well *not* be Christian but some other spirit trying to take advantage of my desire to connect to him. But no matter who or what it was, it certainly was a voice and not a stray radio wave. I decided to assume for the moment that I was talking to my ghost of the ring.

"Were you murdered?" I asked.

No response. I asked again, and to make things easier, added, "Knock once for yes, twice for no."

No response.

"Did you kill yourself?"

No response.

I shut off the recorder to think of better questions, but I found it hard to focus. I felt as though I was on the verge of some amazing discovery. I couldn't believe that spirit communication was really this obvious. No one had told me about EVP in a Q&A format. Most of the people I'd met thus far who used these devices had told me that they just left their recorders running and walked away. I began to wonder if I'd lost whoever had been there. Maybe he only had enough energy for a short stay.

I asked again, "Were you murdered?"

The response this time was three syllables, but unintelligible. It sounded like he was trying to explain something, but it could have been anything from the identity of Deep Throat to a compliment on my decor. Obviously this was getting me nowhere. Couldn't he just say yes or no? I again explained that I couldn't understand him very well and asked my question again. I listened and the response did sound like a "yes," but I couldn't be sure.

Then I had an idea. I got up to get my magnetic tape recorder. I left the lights off to avoid disturbing the atmosphere, and only a few feet from my bed, I realized that was a mistake. I felt vulnerable in the dark. For all I knew, I was brushing right next to something that was in there watching me. I thought it might grab me at any moment. I ran barefoot into the other room, quickly searched through my bag, grabbed the recorder, and turned toward the bedroom. I stopped. There was some light in this room from outside, and that made the doorway to my bedroom look ominous. I thought I could feel the pulse of some creature in there waiting for me to return. But I had to get back to my other recorder. I decided to just do it. I sprang into action, rushing through the door and jumping quickly into bed before anything could get me. I was safe again.

I worked at setting up both recorders so I could play them together to see if I could get the same thing on tape that I was recording in digital format. Soon I was ready to ask another question.

"Is there something you want from me?"

Again, a long response, but unclear.

I tried once more with, "Are you Christian?"

Instead of a yes or no, it seemed that he was trying to explain something. It was an involved response, almost like a plea, and the name Christian and the word "me" was fairly clear in the middle of it.

Unlike the digital, the regular tape had picked up only my questions, nothing else. Well, at least that told me there were no extraneous sounds in the room, but why would the digital get it so clearly . . . and so loudly? I was stymied.

"What do you want?" I went on, with just the digital.

One syllable, a short roar.

"Will you hurt me?" That was a stupid question, stupid, stupid. Why invite it? I was stunned when I played it back and heard his answer, as clearly as when he had said he was Christian, and with some enthusiasm.

"Yes."

I was silent for a minute. I hadn't really expected that. He wanted to hurt me, but would he? *Could* he?

My next question got an even weirder reply. "What do you want to say?"

He gave a long statement, which I couldn't understand, and then a very long and loud roar. So much for communication.

Okay, I admitted to myself that I was rattled. I had hoped this spirit might be a little more charmingly malevolent. I had the fleeting idea that I should get some salt and put it around my bed, as Jeff had done, but decided I was not going to be intimidated. As often as he'd been around me—and for all I know, it had been two years already—he had never actually assaulted me. So maybe he couldn't. Maybe he could only try to scare me.

I decided to keep going.

"Do you have something to say?" I asked.

A rather grumpy response.

"I'm not afraid of you, so say what you want."

A roar. Okay, maybe I *was* afraid.

"Do you want your story retold?"

"Yes."

Ah, good. We were getting somewhere, although if he was going to tell it to me like this, I wouldn't get much of a story.

That response was followed by a sentence, which was too loud to comprehend. He didn't seem to understand that I couldn't hear his words when he yelled, but perhaps he had no control over the volume.

"Did the person I call Wraith kill you?"

A quiet response that sounded more affirmative than negative, though that was hardly conclusive.

"Do you want Wraith to die?"

No response.

"Does Wraith mean me harm?"

"Yes." Hmmm. I didn't want to know that.

"Will you let me know who murdered you?"

Again, not clear, but it sounded affirmative.

"Is there a female spirit with you?"

A roar that sounded like an animal in pain. I wish I knew why he persisted with such aggressive responses.

"Do you want me to get the diary?" I asked.

"Yes."

"Are you angry at me?"

A five-syllable response that sounded ominously affirmative.

"Do you want something from Wraith?"

"Yes."

"What do you want from Wraith?"

Sounded like "the diary," but I wouldn't swear to it.

"Did you murder people with Wraith?"

A long response, not intelligible.

"Did you kill Michael?"

Two syllables that could have been "No way."

"Did the ring belong to Michael?"

The answer to this question sounded like a yes, followed by a roar and then a three-word response that contained the word "I" and sounded defensive. None of this made any sense. I began to feel that I was getting nowhere. My original assessment that this was an obvious way to communicate with the other side had been naive.

"Will you help me tell your story?"

"Yes."

By now it was two o'clock in the morning and I was tired. I asked if he was still there and got no response. I said that I wanted to continue this tomorrow and asked if he would come back.

"Yes."

I left the recorder on the rest of the night and got mostly just dogs barking faintly in the background. Obviously, the moon was affecting them, too.

I wrote up my results and sent them to the various ghost hunters I knew. Rick Fisher came back with an interesting e-mail: "That is an amazing story. You need to ask more questions. Remember that spirits are not active every day, so some days there will be no results at all." Ever the scientist, he included, "I hope you are documenting these recordings with the dates and times and weather conditions. Also know that in my home on previous recordings, I had also gotten someone whistling so that is not uncommon. Knocking noises are quite common as well. I have been getting the loud roar and I believe that others are, too. We have to figure out what that is. The other night Karl and I were out and he had picked up two male voices telling us to get out of the cemetery we were in. Like everything else it takes time and an open mind to achieve the results that you get. Keep trying."

The next day I bought a second digital recorder, an Olympus, and this one recorded my own voice much more clearly, so I had some hope that I might get better results. At the very least, I wanted to see if I got different results with different recorders.

I had to work late on another project, and though I wasn't tired, I couldn't concentrate on the work. I felt sharply aware of the clock as it slowly advanced toward midnight, each minute that elapsed coinciding with a mounting anticipation in my chest. There was an electrical storm predicted for sometime that night in addition to a full moon. I felt certain the atmosphere was building toward another encounter with my spirit, whoever he was.

A friend had warned me not to be taken in just because the spirit claimed to be Christian. It could be another spirit trying to gain my confidence, masquerading as Christian. Not, I rationalized, that Christian could gain my confidence, necessarily, but I was aware that this might not be a genuine contact. Still, it was *something*, and that's more than I had imagined I'd get, especially on my first try.

To my chagrin, the promised electrical storm did not materialize, but the moon was bright and round. It was nearly one o'clock when I got into bed. This time I needed a brighter light because both digital recorders were a little tricky. In the dark, I wouldn't be able to see all the buttons. I sat up straight and held them, one in each hand.

I asked my questions again, trying to ascertain that the spirit was there and that it was the same one as the night before.

No response.

I asked again and thought I heard a quick "Hello" on the Panasonic. The Olympus picked up nothing.

And that, to my disappointment, was all I got. After fifteen minutes, I gave up. It was hot and I was tired. I decided to try it when I had more energy. Rick had warned me that one doesn't necessarily get consistently good results, and I decided to chalk this night up as a dud. I guess I hadn't actually asked him if he'd come back the next night, only if he'd come back. From a ghost maybe that meant twenty years from now.

—7—

The next day, I received an e-mail from Chanda, the psychic I met in Gettysburg. She had assured me that my spirit was fond of me and that one day I'd be able to hear him. Now that she had seen my e-mail about the EVP results, she had apparently had a change of heart.

"This is a bad turn, Katherine," she wrote. "You must be done with him and send him off! Your curiosity about him is great, but since he has decided you are part of the problem, you need him to leave! He probably blames you because you cannot hear what he says. Also remember, this man is basically evil and perhaps he misses killing. Also he envies that you have life. I fear he shall now contact the dark man and they will plot together against you. The dark man watches you also."

And speaking of the devil, the next e-mail, which I nearly deleted because it looked like SPAM from a porn site, was another warning.

> he told me it was a gift from him to me for all time. i should not have allowed you to take the ring. it was a mistake and i miscalculated the impact of its presence on your work—and in your life. A physical manifestation of his evil is with you all the time. I was selfish in letting you take it from me, thinking it would excise him from life. It has not done that, but instead increased the range of evil. i see and feel him as much as i used to and i don't even have the ring.

This was from Wraith. As usual, I could not send a return e-mail. The message was enigmatic, but I sensed that he knew what I was up to and didn't like it. The problem was, I didn't know what *he* was up to.

6 *Going Deeper*

—**1**—

I decided that I wouldn't tell anyone that I'd heard from Wraith. My friends were so worried that I'd even met a person like him, let alone was still in contact, and this would just make them more anxious. Not that I was in contact with him. I mean, I didn't know how to find him. Clearly he was annoyed, but did that mean he was coming after the ring? If the person I had seen in New Orleans was Wraith, he could have confronted me then. But maybe it hadn't been him.

In the meantime, I would continue to try and use it "as a phone."

I replied to Chanda that I believed I would be fine. To my mind, I was stronger than Christian, because try as he might to intimidate me, he had not managed to do anything that might physically harm me. It seemed to me that if a ghost wanted to hurt you and could, he would.

I called Rosemary, the exotic woman in New York who helped me get a tarot reading on Christian. We had discussed Christian several times already, and she had never felt moved to warn me.

This time it was a different story. When I told her about the EVP, she said that I was certainly not safe from spiritual hauntings. "If you call them, they will come to you. And you're opening yourself in order to use Christian as your channel." She pointed out that he needed me to continue to experience life. "When you messed with Pandora's box, then you began the adventure. And he will take you on the path of who knows what?"

"Is there any way to find out what he wants?" I asked.

She said that she had tried getting a tarot reading for me but her deck refused to accept his vibes. He was too dangerous. "Nevertheless," she said, "without you, he has nothing. With you, he has power. Wraith was only one person. With you, he has thousands. He's possessive. He's isolating you."

Okay, I considered myself warned. I still wasn't convinced (a) that I really had a ghost, (b) that he was truly dangerous, and (c) that any of these things would come just because I called them or went hunting for them. I needed to get some replicable results before I was willing to accept any of this.

That night I was ready to try again. This time I used a bowl of water as a conductor and candles instead of a flashlight. That seemed more inviting to a spirit. I turned on both recorders, prepared to be open. After a few minutes to experience the quiet, I began to ask questions.

I asked again if he was Christian, and his response seemed affirmative, though more low-key than before. I then decided to put a question to him to determine the authenticity of his identity—something only Christian would know.

"What is the name of the first person who went hunting with you and Wraith?"

I got an answer of some length but could not make out what was said. So much for a test. I decided to stick to yes-or-no questions.

"Do you wish to be freed?"

Sounded like a negative, or possibly "You can't."

"Do you want me to help you?"

"Yes."

"What can I do?"

The response was quiet and unintelligible. I asked again and could swear the response was, "Write."

"Is there someone who can help me to find out your story?"

Again I couldn't decipher his response, so I asked if the person who could help lived in New Orleans. I was thinking of Mariah. This produced an angry-sounding response.

"Do you want to be at rest?"

A quiet, affirmative response, almost as if he couldn't comprehend it. Then I decided to just go for it—ask what I really wanted to know. He'd said it before, but I wanted him to repeat it.

"Do you intend to hurt me?"

I got a less intense response than before, and one that wasn't that clear. Was he losing strength or sensing that I was not intimidated?

"Can you show me that you're here?"

"Yes," he said, but I didn't see any sign—at least nothing physical. Maybe he tried and failed. Or maybe that would come at some later time, when I was unprepared.

I asked a few more questions, but I could tell I was getting tired. The tedious process of record, listen, record, listen was hindering my focus. I decided to just leave both recorders on and let whoever was (or wasn't) there know that they could communicate if they cared to, but I was going to bed. I left some coins out, just in case. I also told Christian that he could try to communicate with me through dreams. Perhaps he was more comfortable with that medium.

"Just let me know what you want me to know."

In the morning, the coins were still as I had left them. I was disappointed, but only for a moment. Suddenly it came flooding back to me—the dream I'd had the night before. I still had a bad feeling from it. In the dream, I had been hit hard in the right shoulder, as if shot. The dream was about a murder, although it was maddeningly indistinct. But I vividly recalled feeling as if I were under attack.

I played back the Olympus and got two very short recordings. The first one definitely had caught the voice, but only faintly. Overshadowing it was a series of loud, rhythmic raps. I could tell from the internal clock that this had happened while I was still awake, and I had not heard any such noise. The second again contained raps. I also thought I heard a quiet male laugh. What was strange is that both digitals were on at the same time in nearly the same place, and they picked up different noises.

The other one went for twenty-three minutes, with much of the familiar male voice, but it sounded like he was in conversation with another male, whose voice was faint, as if he were at some distance. I found myself growing frustrated. I really did not understand any of this, and I had no idea how to get better at it.

I left off the EVP for the next few nights but had two more dreams. One was about an opera in which a woman and three men all ended up dead. The men floated down a river but told the woman that their spirits would wait for her. She was in a prison, and she broke out and ended up in the river as well. The impression I had was that she was going to slit her throat so she could join them. The memory of it chilled: It was a little too close to the images that Mimi and Mariah had gotten in New Orleans.

The third dream was about the missing reporter, Susan Walsh, whose disappearance had started me on my vampire escapade. I dreamed of a videotape that had been made in anticipation that I was going to end up missing, too.

The next night I woke up suddenly from a dream in which I definitely had died. The details of how it had happened escaped me, but it had been violent. My heart was still pounding. I felt that I was really in danger.

Okay, that was enough. No more dreams. This kind of communication was no better than the recorders. All I learned from it was . . .

I sat up. Is that what he wanted? I reached for the recorder on the bed table and turned it on. Trembling a little, I asked, "Do you want me to die?"

The EVP response was an emphatic, "Yes."

That scared me. He wanted me to die. Could he actually do it? Or was he just working on me psychologically? There was no doubt that I'd become depressed this week and was feeling depleted from having such terrible dreams every night. Wraith had said something about Christian's MO: that he would work on my mind until I grew physically ill. I had to gather my resources to defend myself.

"Well," I said to whatever hovered in the air, "I'm not going to die, so you can just stop giving me those dreams."

And I did not have another. Not immediately, anyway.

—2—

The International Ghost Hunters Society offered a home-study course for certification as a ghost hunter. It was based on over one thousand field investigations by Dave Oester and Sharon Gill, the couple I had met in Gettysburg who embraced ghosts as friends. The course included a CD of ghost photographs to help researchers tell the difference between good photos and bad. They made it clear that the IGHS does not judge a spirit to be a demon but views it as the surviving consciousness of a deceased human being. Ghosts, they said, want us to know about them and so in that sense appear to be purposeful. Otherwise, "we would never be aware of their presence here." The ghost phenomenon even included animal spirits, such as the soul of someone's pet. In the course, they make it clear that those spirits encountered by IGHS members have been consistently benevolent in nature. Nevertheless, they do note that there are spirits with negative attitudes, and those are the ones most likely to try and make contact through mediums like the Ouija board.

I sat down with the course, along with Dave and Sharon's book of true ghost stories, *The Haunted Reality*. I was immediately pleased to discover on their list of investigations one of my favorite ghost towns, Jerome, Arizona. Then I turned my attention to the course, which included a test that one would return for the determination of eligibility for certification. I remembered how amusing it had seemed to me when I first realized they had such a course. As if I could learn at home how to find ghosts. Little did I know then what I was in for.

The course also covers what people have traditionally believed about ghosts and why those beliefs often fail to match reality. They discuss hoaxes and Hollywood. To the IGHS, ghosts are composed of energy that has been transformed at the time of death from physical essence to spirit matter. They think that, as stated in the Law of the Conservation of Energy, no energy is destroyed. The soul, then, would be the sum of all of our energy patterns. In that case, whoever we were in life, we will continue to be in death. Our attitudes, emotions, intelligence, and beliefs don't become enlightened just because we die. As spirits, we still have to grow.

I noted especially the idea that if you were bitter, angry, or had unresolved issues in life, you will feel the same way after death. That is, someone like Christian, who was very angry in life, would still have the same anger as a ghost. Hmmm. I wondered how they could really know this. I could follow their logic but did not see the evidence—okay, aside from Christian wanting me to die. Nevertheless, it certainly made one think: If you aren't very happy with yourself as you are, you'd better make some changes, because death is no escape. I would have reason to revisit this idea as I continued to learn.

They discussed the concept that many ghosts are confused because they may not know they are dead. That's a common belief, especially among mediums and exorcists. If death is sudden, the person doesn't have time to think about it or comprehend that it is happening. Thus, he or she would not "get it." Though I would imagine just the fact that they can't make themselves heard would tip them off to something not being quite right. Still, I decided to be open to the idea that they might not accept that they're dead. At least, it offered one possible explanation for Christian.

The rest of the course dealt with IGHS protocol, equipment for ghost hunting, field investigations, and the psychology of earthbound spirits. They also offer suggestions for possible careers in the field. At this point, I accepted what they believed—that you'll find ghosts mostly in places where there has been a death, such as battlefields, murder and suicide sites, and scenes of accidents. I had no reason at that time to think otherwise.

One of the more interesting ideas—and one that I'd first heard about in New Orleans—was the notion of a portal from another dimension. Dave and Sharon thought that these wormholes could be found in cemeteries, and they even claimed to have examined photos in which the orbs appear to be emerging from a "black void," as they describe it. They also noted that cemeteries often have multiple orbs—sometimes more than there are gravestones in the place. What that means, I don't know, but apparently some ghosts can come and go as they please. Maybe those that are "exorcised" just slip into a dimensional "wormhole" and come out in some other place where they won't be bothered.

I looked through the protocol, which they said was based on field investigations and common sense. To some extent, directions like "Do not take photos from moving vehicles on dusty roads" made sense. So did the admonition to keep fingers, hair, and camera straps out of the way. If you were going to claim you had orbs, you had better eliminate the obvious. Other standards dictated behavioral etiquette. For example:

1. *Ask the spirits of the dead for permission to take their photos.*
2. *No smoking tobacco products during an investigation.*
3. *No alcohol before, during, or after an investigation.*
4. *Always conduct your investigations in a professional manner.*
6. *Respect posted property signs, ask permission, and do not trespass.*

They claimed that a positive mental attitude was important and that skeptical minds generate too much negativity. They warned those with pacemakers to avoid investigations. Ghosts like to suck the energy from batteries, and while that may not be so bad for a camera, it's not great for a heart.

They mostly spoke about orbs and vortices, but Dave mentioned that both he and Sharon have managed to capture an apparition in photos. It's rare, but it apparently happens. Sharon's was especially poignant—a transparent woman in a long blue dress. While this gave me some hope, I did not quite understand how they could be so certain about the nature of ghosts. For example, they stated that the brightness and magnitude of an orb will vary depending on how strong-willed the spirit is, how long it's been around, and what kinds of conditions exist for it to manifest. I couldn't figure out how anyone could tell from what an orb looks like in a photo how strong-willed it is, or how you would even be able to isolate that trait. I was willing to accept orbs as energy anomalies, and even tentatively to call them ghosts. To say anything about their personalities struck me as taking it a bit too far.

I moved on to the technical angles. They went through how to handle and interpret the various EMF meters, citing the "ideal paranormal" range versus the results that might appear in the presence of man-made energy fields. They made special note of the thermal scanner, which I had already used, particularly its added advantage of sweeping a room from a single location. The infrared beam emitted by the scanner bounces off a surface for a temperature reading, and when ghost anomalies reflect this beam, the scanner registers a sudden drop in temperature. Using either kind of instrument assists the ghost hunter in knowing when and where to point a camera.

What interested me most, however, was EVP. Since they did not say much about it beyond what devices to use, I took their test for the certificate, sent it in, and then looked around for some books on the subject. I learned that there was an American Association of EVP, run by Sarah Estep in Annapolis, Maryland. She had been experimenting with EVP since 1976, so I sent for her materials. Then I went on the Internet.

I found a site designed by a guy named Victor Zammit, who had done extensive work on all aspects of the paranormal. To my surprise, he said that EVP has been around for over fifty years and that the EVP community was composed of people from all over the world.

As far back as the 1920s, inventors like Thomas Edison had apparently attempted to develop some kind of electronic device for communicating with the dead. Pioneers of radio and television, like Marconi, Crookes, and Logie-Baird, had also attempted to engineer devices that would allow them to contact the other side. It wasn't until

1936, however, that Atilla von Szalay tried to record the voices that he had heard while in a dark room developing photos. He managed it in 1945 on a wire recorder, but the voices were too faint to prove anything. He resumed his recordings in 1956 with magnetic audiotape, and Raymond Bayless joined him. They published a paper in *The Journal of the American Society for Psychical Research,* but no one responded.

The person often credited with starting it all was Frederich Jurgenson. While taping birdsongs in 1959 in the woods, he happened to record a male voice discussing Norwegian nocturnal birdsongs. He worked at getting more and soon recorded voices that he identified as those of deceased friends and relatives—including his mother. He also introduced Church officials in the Vatican to his work. He published *Voices from the Universe* in 1964 and another book three years later, called *Radio Link with the Beyond.* In 1965, a Latvian named Konstantin Raudive, having read Jurgenson's first book, set out to discover just what this was all about. He wanted to show that there was a simple explanation that was not paranormal.

Although when he began his experiments he was a skeptic, and though he got no results for the first three months, he eventually became so obsessed with EVP that he devoted twelve hours a day to his experiments. By the time he published his own book, *The Inaudible Made Audible,* in 1968, he claimed to have recorded over seventy-two thousand messages in many different languages.

I made a note to try to find this book. I wanted to read it for myself.

Victor also made a distinction between EVP and ITC, or Instrumental Transcommunication. He defined this as voices communicating via a device other than a tape recorder, such as answering machines, or simply coming over the phone or the radio. I thought about a story I had heard from author Dean Koontz about how he'd received a call one day warning him to be careful. His number was unlisted, and the voice sounded very much like that of his mother, who had died years before. He did not know what to think. Nevertheless, he became a bit more vigilant, which turned out to possibly have saved him. That day his father attempted to kill him with a knife. Sounded like a good case of ITC to me.

I e-mailed Victor about his research and asked why he had put up such a detailed website. It turned out that he was from Australia, and he sent back the following response. "What inspired me to be so meticulous in my research? Someone was trying to contact me from the Other Side. I was then guided to visit the Inner Peace Movement in Sydney. They had the knowledge to explain to me what was happening, but I got the shock of my life when I made contact with an intelligence. I asked for proof that it was not my unconscious that was responding to my questions and got a powerful blow to my body from an invisible source, which nearly sent to me to the floor."

What? I'd asked for proof and got nothing. At this point, I'd even take a kick or a smack. Anything. How did he get this response?

"From then on," his note continued, "I had a drive to do objective research into the evidence for the existence of the afterlife. I have been communicating with intelligences from the afterlife for ten years. My deceased father visited me and after around two hundred questions about the family—and him getting them all correct—I was satisfied. Even the speech idiosyncrasy was identical to his. It was just amazing. And what he wanted was for me to forgive him for being such an incompetent father!"

I immediately went looking for the books he mentioned, planning to take them with me to Salem. On the eve of my departure, Dave let me know that I had passed the Ghost Hunter Certification test, and with the photos I had taken with Rick's camera, I was now a member of the Inner Circle. He promised to bring my diploma to Salem.

So now I was officially a ghost hunter, although I still felt very much the amateur. I didn't even have a camera yet, in part because I wanted to test Dave and Sharon's Sony Mavica before making my decision. I did have a recorder, however, and had gotten some interesting results. It was time to give it another test, and I had just the place.

—3—

On August 4, 1892, the bodies of Andrew Borden, seventy, and Abby Borden, sixty-five, were found in their home in Fall River, Massachusetts, just south of Boston. Andrew's corpse was in a semireclining position on the living-room couch, his face cut open and his feet still resting in his congress boots. There were blood spots on the floor, the wall, and the picture hanging over the sofa, but Andrew's clothing was not disturbed, nor was there injury other than to his face. His head was bent slightly to the right, and eleven fierce blows had cut his face. One eye was sliced in half and lay protruding from his face, and his nose had been severed. It appeared that, as he napped, he had been attacked from above and behind.

It was his daughter, Lizzie, who found him. She was thirty-two and living at home. The only other person in the house was the maid, Bridget Sullivan.

Lizzie sent Bridget for the doctor, claiming that she had been outside and left the door unlocked. Whoever had murdered her father must have come in that way.

A neighbor, Mrs. Churchill, arrived and asked Lizzie where her mother was. Lizzie recalled that Abby was out but mentioned that she'd heard her return. Mrs. Churchill got nearly to the landing of the second floor when she spotted the body. Abby Borden had been slain in the guest room with a sharp weapon, possibly a hatchet, inflicting upon her nineteen blows.

She had been found lying facedown, her skull crushed in the back. Her blood was dark and congealed, and crimson spots spattered the pillow shams that she had gone in to change. A thick bunch of artificial black hair, hacked off the body, lay nearby.

It soon became clear that Abby had been killed as long as an hour and a half before Andrew. That meant that the murderer had been lurking in the house all that time. That someone could have just come in and killed these two elderly people in the middle of the day is very odd, since it was the family practice to keep all doors on the first floor locked. Yet on that day, Lizzie claimed to have been in the barn, leaving the back screen door unlocked. She was in the loft for twenty minutes, she said, although there was no evidence that the thick dust on the floor had been disturbed. It was oppressively hot where she claimed to have been, leading many to speculate that she could not have been up there as long as she said and probably was not in the barn at all. (In fact, her first report was that she had been in the backyard.)

No footprints were found around the house on the grass, and no neighbor had seen strangers coming or going in the Borden yard. Theories about who did the ghastly deed ranged from sister Emma, who was visiting friends in another town, to Bridget, who had been told to wash windows when she was feeling ill; the brother of Andrew's first wife, John Morse, who had unexpectedly arrived the night before; Andrew's supposed illegitimate son; a wandering maniac; and, of course, Lizzie. She was the one arrested, and her contradictory answers at an inquest, coupled with a friend's grand jury testimony that she had burned a dress, resulted in a trial for murder. She was acquitted but spent the rest of her life in seclusion, ostracized by her former friends and neighbors.

Within six months, she sold the house at 92 Second Street with most of the furnishings, and through the years it was used as a rooming house, bookie joint, and Kewpie doll factory. Then in 1947 John and Josephine McGinn purchased it, signing the sales agreement on their wedding anniversary, August 4—also the anniversary of the murders. (In fact, Mr. McGinn died years later on July 19, Lizzie's birthday.) They didn't welcome tourists, wanting the place for their printing business, but when their granddaughter, Martha, inherited it, she and her partner, Ron Evans, wanted to do something special. They turned it into a bed-and-breakfast.

With help from crime-scene photos, the house was made to resemble its condition on that infamous August morning. For over a year they worked at duplicating the furnishings, floral wallpaper, dark woodwork, and patterned rugs of the era, right down to a replica of the sofa where Andrew was murdered, including even the painting that hung over his head. Much of the hardware, woodwork, and some of the windows are original. A display case in the dining room—furnished with Lizzie's own table and chairs—is filled with authentic items owned by the Bordens, and guests get to see the type of kitchen stove in which Lizzie burned the suspicious dress.

Those who spend the night get a special tour, and in the morning, there's a hearty breakfast similar to the one eaten by the Bordens on the morning they were hacked to death—except for the recycled mutton soup. (Their untimely deaths probably saved them from food poisoning.)

I was hoping to find out what type of person (besides a normal one like myself) opts to spend the night in such a darkly fascinating place, but discovered there were no other guests. I would be alone up there in the infamous John Morse Guest Room (where Abby was slaughtered), right next to Lizzie's former bedroom. I was surprised, because the place usually books up solid—but secretly delighted.

Before retiring to the bedroom (or putting it off?), I sat on the Victorian sofa in the spot where Andrew had been so mercilessly whacked, and read through what the Ouija board had delivered about the case. This record was included in the notes of the prosecutor at Lizzie's trial, which had only recently been published. According to the reading, using prussic acid was Lizzie's original intent. (In fact, she had tried to purchase some the day before but was turned away. Prussic acid is extremely lethal and was generally used for killing animals.) Lizzie wore trousers, according to the "forces," which she then buried in the yard. She also burned the handle of the hatchet that had broken off, and put the head in a box. John Morse assisted her with the cover-up. Dr. Bowen was also in on it, as was Emma. Lizzie had made up the story that Abby was called out, but she would never be found guilty of the crimes. Her motive? Money. She had overheard talk of an investment to be put into Abby's name. The board got the time of the murders pretty close, too: 9:30 and 10:45.

But were there any ghosts here? I'd heard that two psychics who had come to the house had insisted after reading the spiritual vibes that Andrew had been killed in the kitchen and dragged to the couch, and that one owner's dog had refused to go up the front staircase. A greeting placed in the rooms includes a note to guests: "If a door should open or close on its own, or a light go on or off, please take this in good humor, as we are mere mortals and cannot control our supernatural guests. They are generally well-behaved, but sometimes tend to get a bit mischievous."

Finally, I went upstairs to turn in. I glanced into Lizzie's room but saw nothing unusual. Then I went into the John Morse room. I hesitated about shutting the door, but once it was shut, I quickly locked it. As if that would keep out a spirit! When I was ready, I turned off the lights and got into the antique double bed with the towering dark wood frame, right next to where Abby had died, and turned on the recorder. In one corner, I could see the shadowy figure of a dress form that modeled an outfit Elizabeth Montgomery wore when she played Lizzie in a 1975 movie. It looked pretty ominous and ghostly on its own, and I reminded myself not to be spooked by it if I happened to wake up in the middle of the night. Staring at the ceiling, I listened for noises, both hoping to hear something and praying that I wouldn't. I then let my hand drop over the edge of the bed, almost touching where Abby had breathed her last. No cold spot.

While listening for unusual noises, I drifted off and actually did sleep, dreaming of a woman talking to me. In fact, I dreamed that the voice came from the recorder and was quite distinct. She seemed to be saying something urgent, and it was the voice of a youngish woman, not older, as Abby's would have been.

In the morning, I awoke and recalled the dream. With great excitement I sat up, reached for the recorder, and . . . *it was off!*

I couldn't believe it. Sometime during the night, for some reason unknown to me, I (or someone) had shut it off. And I had no recollection of what the woman had said in the dream. None at all. A few strange sounds on the recorder sounded like voices, but they were too faint to interpret. My ghost hunt, so rich with possibility, had failed, and I was leaving for Salem at noon. I was utterly crestfallen.

At breakfast I heard stories from Martha about guests who'd reported the ghostly figure of an elderly woman in the John Morse room who gently had tucked them in. There was also an old-fashioned sewing machine in the corner that reportedly had started up on its own, and people saw impressions of heads on the pillows. Martha even had two photos that showed something that looked very much like a spirit. She had waited to tell me this so as not to influence what I experienced. I loved these tales but was further disappointed by my own lack of results.

Then one of the tour guides, Amanda, who'd had doors mysteriously lock on her while showing people around, offered to take me into the cellar, where in 1892 the police had searched for the murder weapon and found a handleless hatchet rubbed in ashes. The cellar was dusty and cool, used mostly for storage, but I noticed that they had a defunct "voice printer" that Thomas Edison had invented—perhaps with the aspiration of getting spirit communications. We walked around a bit, keeping quiet and soaking up the eerie atmosphere. Then I turned on the recorder, let it run for a few minutes, and asked, "Is there anyone here with us?"

We could barely see each other, but Amanda watched, wide-eyed, as I waited a while longer for a potential response. We heard nothing as we stood there, although I could see that the recorder light indicated activity. Finally I stopped it, pressed the playback button, and heard my recorded voice ask, "Is there anyone here with us?"

That was followed by a resoundingly gruff "Yes!"

We both turned and shot up the steps.

I know, I know: A ghost hunter who's scared of ghosts is like a claustrophobic spelunker.

After her experience in the basement, Amanda wanted to listen to the voices I already had, so we went up to Lizzie's room. She wanted to avoid the room in which I had just slept because it gave her the creeps. I played my recordings of "Christian." Amanda turned out to be another young person who seemed able to hear the words clearly, and she did not hesitate to interpret what she believed she heard. Christian, she said, wanted "revenge." He did not kill himself. He had said, "Something happened to me." He did *not* want to hurt me, and at one point Amanda told me that I had turned off the recorder just as he said, "Wait!"

Then we listened to the brief recording I'd gotten the night before. Amanda was sure she heard a woman and she was trying to talk to a male. "She is telling him not to hurt you. He's talking to her but he wants only to talk to you. She wants you to turn it off." Amanda touched the ring and said, "Christian took it from someone he loved, but he was jealous." She picked up the ring to examine it, but then gave it back. "It makes me nervous."

Before I left, Martha gave me a brick from the chimney that had been searched for the murder weapon and insisted I come back when she could investigate with me. Too many guests had reported strange incidents to discount the possibility of a haunting here, although I couldn't say who it was. To me, it seemed most likely to be Abby, the woman who had been killed in the room where I'd slept. And there had been that voice in the basement—unless that was just Christian following me around. I hoped that the next time I came, I'd be an experienced ghost hunter with all the right equipment to give Martha some answers.

—4—

So on to Salem, once a thriving maritime trade center. The IGHS conference was booked in the Hawthorne Hotel in the center of the historic district. Salem is famous for its witch trials of the late 1600s, in which hysteria, prejudice, and malicious accusation led to the deaths of nineteen innocent people. While the ghosts of those who were falsely accused are reputedly seen on Gallows Hill as forewarning of some terrible calamity, and Giles Corey, who was crushed to death under boulders and who cursed the town, has appeared near the old jail on Howard Street, no one really knows where these people were buried.

Our hotel, near the Salem common, was named for the writer Nathaniel Hawthorne. He was the descendant of one of the witch judges, and his guilt over it produced some American masterpieces, including *The House of the Seven Gables*. In fact, the house that inspired that story is now a Salem museum, and it, too, is apparently haunted. Hawthorne himself spotted an apparition in the town's Athaeneum Library: For five days following the man's death, the Reverend Harris continued to sit in his favorite chair.

Salem played off the infamous trials with some fairly kitschy shops. Emblems of witches and witchy T-shirts served as constant reminders of what had happened there, and if that wasn't sufficient, there were reenactments and tours on the common every day. A select few of the tourist attractions were worthwhile, but most of them were more for kids. It seemed rather morbid to be having a lark at the expense of the people who had died so horribly, but the tourist income apparently was a great lure. I noticed that some people had set up witch shops like the one Mimi had in New Orleans. They mostly sold herbs, jewelry, New Age books, and divination devices.

I brought Christian's ring with me, hoping he might tag along. This was the kind of place that I thought would appeal to him, considering the degree of violence that had occurred here. I wasn't sure what I expected, but I thought perhaps he would acquire some energy that was more attuned to who he was and thus develop a better voice. Of course, the trick was to make sure he didn't pick up too much energy—I wanted him to find his bark, not his bite.

The first evening, I met Dave and Sharon in their room to let them hear some of my EVP. Sharon was again wearing a little piece of ghostly lapel jewelry, and Dave had on a black IGHS T-shirt and a baseball cap with an IGHS insignia. They were welcoming and jovial, while also quite serious about what we were doing. Their room was filled with equipment, as well as the books they would be selling at the conference. Dave had warned me about static on these recorders, so I wanted to be sure he knew exactly what I was hearing.

Before I was able to play my recorder, however, one of the conference attendees called from the lobby because she had gotten the most unusual photographs of an apparition. She needed an assessment right away. They invited her up, and it sure did seem as if she had something very unique. I'd never seen anything like it. She explained how she had just been taking photos outside and suddenly realized she had something unusual. On her LCD screen was the image of some legs and feet and a blurred, baglike object. She was amazed that she could have been that close to an apparition. Everyone looked closely, and then someone noticed the similarity between the bag and her fanny pack. It turned out that she had accidentally pointed her camera at her feet. Even the most honest and dedicated ghost hunters can fool themselves if they try too hard to find something. Once she had left, we got to the recordings.

I played what I had from when I had directly put questions to "Christian." I made sure they heard the yells. They both looked somewhat surprised.

"That's not a static blip," Dave admitted.

"He sounds frustrated," was Sharon's response. "Even desperate." She looked as if she would try to comfort this entity if she could. This contributed to my image of Sharon as a nurse to the paranormal. She wanted to bandage their wounds, heal their headaches, and help them reach a better state of ghostly health.

"He's probably a young spirit," Dave added. "He doesn't know how to break through to make himself understood."

He explained to me how I could analyze all of this for voice patterns on my computer by using software called Cool Edit to clean up background static. He also told me to get a passive trimeter to use in the room whenever I record and tell Christian to move around. They also thought I should take photographs of the ring.

"Can you see if he can ask some other spirit who's more advanced to help him communicate?" Dave asked. "He needs to be taught to refine how he speaks to you. Right now he sounds like a single radio band that's not altogether there."

I shrugged. "I can try."

They handed me my Inner Circle certificate and welcomed me into membership. They were impressed with my early efforts and urged me to keep working. I tried again that night with my recorder but had no results. I wondered if my ghost was even with me.

The next afternoon, I stopped at a bookstore on Derby Square to pick up some true crime books for research I was doing. As I walked back to the hotel, I pondered a statement that Dave had made during the conference that morning. "They radiate back to you what you give forth." Several times, Sharon had pointed out that spirits are governed by emotional stimuli and are attracted to like minds. I wondered what Christian saw in me. Sure, I could write his story (if he ever learned to communicate), but so could a lot of people. What was it that drew him to me?

Then I stopped in my tracks. I looked at the books I was carrying. One was *Murder in the Forties* by Colin Wilson and the other was *The Violence of Our Lives*. No wonder he was attracted to me. I had this strong desire to understand the rage and self-protective psychology often connected to psychopathy. I had just been to the scene of Lizzie Borden's outrageous crime, and I was working on a book with a criminal profiler. I brought Christian to where the citizens of Massachusetts had committed a number of cold-blooded murders. I guess it was pretty obvious why he might hang out with me. He was addicted to murder and so was I—just in a different way.

Sharon also mentioned something about not being able to remove spirits with exorcism, because the spirits could not just move on. They had to have some help with the change. In other words, they needed a therapist. That might be an interesting occupation—ghost therapist—except that they probably wouldn't pay their bills. I could just imagine sending a creditor after them. "Hey, go get this deadbeat— and I do mean dead."

I went to the Olde Burying Point Cemetery of Salem to meet the group for an investigation. I waited near the stone memorial benches, on each of which was carved a trial victim's name. The Giles Corey bench had the date of his death—September 19, 1692. I sat on it for a moment to contemplate how "righteous" people could crush a man to death. His curse certainly seemed to have played out in 1914 when a fire swept through the town for thirteen hours and razed nearly eighteen hundred buildings.

Somehow I had lost the others, so I wandered off deeper into the cemetery, walking among the numerous dark gray upright slabs until I found a grave marker near a tree. It said "Nathaniel Silsbee, 1748–1791." I sat down. After a few moments, I turned on my recorder, asking if anyone was here. Alongside it, I had the Olympus and a regular tape recorder, not set up for VAC.

I was far enough off the path that I was sure no one could overhear me. I asked a few more questions, such as "Do you like this place?" and "Do you know what happened here?"

I got results on the Panasonic again, but not the other two. They picked up a lot of background noise, like traffic, birds, and people talking, but nothing ghostly. However, I got both loud and subdued responses on the Panasonic.

I asked several times if Christian was there, but got nothing definitive. If some demon was imitating him, why didn't he do a better job of convincing me?

Recalling what Dave had said, I asked, "Can you find someone to help you speak to me more clearly?"

Immediately, I got that loud, angry, "Arrrrrrgggghhhh!"

I dropped the recorder as if I'd been burned. His aggression unnerved me. After a few moments, I reached for it tentatively. It pressed the button and asked the same question again, just to be sure.

The response was the same, and just as loud. I pressed the off button.

Okay, I guess he wanted to speak for himself. Or perhaps no one would help him and he did not want me to know that. Maybe he was supposed to be trapped right where he was because of who he was. Maybe there was some special afterlife place for those who cannot evolve.

Now it was bothering me that only the one model of recorder

seemed to be picking up on this. At Dave's urging, I tried his recorder, the same brand as mine, just to be sure this wasn't some anomaly in my instrument. We had tried it together in his hotel room but had no real success, although he'd gotten photos of orbs in there. I returned to my room in the Hawthorne and placed the recorders side by side. I made sure the settings matched for sensitivity, speed, and VAC. Then I asked, "Are you here with me?"

I watched as both gave indications they were recording. I asked other questions, each time waiting for a response. Then I played them back, one after the other. The responses were identical. Both machines had picked up this entity's noises.

Okay, that had been productive. It was a first step.

I needed a break and decided that it was time to read the research on EVP. I first picked up Konstantin Raudive's book, *Breakthrough*. At the same time, I set up the Panasonic and added a new machine that I'd bought online before I came, a Smith Corona digital. I invited Christian to speak while I read if he had something to say.

I opened the thick, old book to Peter Bander's preface, in which he explained how he had gotten involved with publishing Raudive's results in an English translation in Britain. What I read impressed me. At first, Bander had shown no real interest, not quite believing that spirits of the dead could be captured on tape. However, he had been impressed by the number of notable scientists and engineers who had worked on Raudive's team. Then his partner, Colin Smythe, had made a tape for him to listen to. For ten minutes he tried to hear something and was about to give up when he heard an odd pattern of noise. He played it several times, over and over, sensing something familiar. Then he realized that it was German phrasing. In fact, it sounded like his mother, who used to correspond with him by audiotape. She had died three years earlier, so it couldn't be her, but the voice now seemed unmistakable. He asked two assistants to listen and write down what they heard, and their conclusions agreed with his own. Now three people had confirmed the same thing. Bander was sufficiently convinced to look further into this phenomenon.

He decided to invite Raudive to his home for an experiment. The other participants included two electronics engineers, some professors, and a dignitary of the Catholic Church. They used a new tape recorder, operated by one of the engineers. New tapes were unsealed in front of them. Bander was excited, but when they did not get the expected results, the room grew tense with expectation. One person said that the only proof he would accept was if the voices named someone in the room, thus preventing the possibility that the voices were received from some radio station. After a while, the meeting broke up and some of the participants prepared to catch a train. Just as they were about to leave, the engineer played back two minutes of the tape and got "Raudive there." Everyone was astonished. The engineer declared that it was impossible.

As I read, I got confirmation on several things that had seemed odd to me. Those experimenters, too, got different things on different machines that were right next to each other. It's as if the spirits were selectively imprinting, similar to the way they seemed to selectively allow only one person in a group to see them. The researchers also mentioned that they got whistling or knocking noises. As Kat had noticed, sometimes they came at a speed different from that of normal human speech patterns and had to be slowed down or speeded up to be understood. They also responded to invitation. One of the funny incidents was when the researchers attempted to increase the length of the wire on the receiving diode, believing that longer is better. One spirit told them to cut the wire back.

These researchers, too, mentioned that there was often static that made the voices difficult to hear and that much of what was said seemed open to interpretation. One of the researchers learned that it was difficult for the spirits to generate the kind of energy necessary to communicate in this manner. Another got a spirit message that dusk was the best time to communicate.

Well, just at that moment, it was twilight in Salem. I stopped reading to listen to the tape. There was a very clear voice that sounded to me like a greeting. (Someone who listened to it later and who did not like what I was doing told me it sounded like, "I'm not going to talk to you anymore." I could never hear that and neither could anyone else.)

I decided to ask some questions. I got responses on the Panasonic, but not on the S-C. That frustrated me. The S-C was not voice activated, so I listened as it worked its way through dead space. This model keeps running the messages repeatedly until it is actively stopped. I came back to a prior message recorded at home just before I left that I had not listened to closely. I let it play. At the end of the message, oddly, I heard my earlier questions repeated in quick succession (this is not a tape that can loop back on itself). Where I had requested that someone "Say my name," I heard a quick, young male voice whisper, "Who are you?"

I sat up. The entire tone was different from what I'd heard on the Panasonic, and I wondered if this voice belonged to someone else or if this recorder just offered a clearer voice print. I listened again and again. There was definitely a whisper asking me who I was. Still, I got nothing else on that recorder the rest of the night.

By the end of my session—about an hour long—I was getting increasingly loud and long noises in response to my questions. In frustration, I said to the (apparently) empty room, "Look, I can't understand you if you're going to persist in communicating like this. Find a better way."

And with that, I stopped.

I decided to continue with Peter Bander's tale rather than delve into Raudive's theories and procedures. Bander wrote *Voices from the Tapes* to discuss his experiences after meeting Raudive. One tale he told involved the fact that he had not mentioned a specific person who had been at that original meeting because of his standing with the Church and the military: the Right Reverend Monsignor Stephen O'Connor, who had since died. O'Connor was strongly opposed to the experiment and throughout the evening remained unimpressed with the paltry results. He said that he wanted someone who was dead to address him by name, say where he was, speak to him personally, and confirm the authenticity of the procedure. He left that night without being satisfied. A recording was made that he was unaware of, but which was brought to his attention sometime after. The following words, in Russian, were heard: "Stefan is here. But you are Stefan. You do not believe me. It is not very difficult, we will teach Petrus."

O'Connor heard about the speech content and told the story of a young lieutenant of Russian descent whom he had visited in a military hospital for a serious neurotic disorder. Three months later, the young man, Stefan, tried to contact him and failing that, had killed himself. To O'Connor, this seemed to be a message from Stefan to him (Stephen), acknowledging his disbelief and referring to the Holy See. He later sent Bander a card that said, "You must come here and talk about *Breakthrough*." He died only a few weeks later.

Bander's book wrestled with the possibilities of this form of communication. Electronics experts immediately eliminated interference from radio waves. They had set up another experiment in which they used a soundproof booth to ensure that no stray sound could possibly be picked up. Nevertheless, they got voices—two hundred of them, including people whom participants knew to have passed on.

One man from the Society for Psychical Research wrote to them of his failed efforts. He suggested that the voices must come through incipient mediumship, in which case they were not generally available for anyone to experience. Colin Smythe urged him to try earphones to enhance the sounds, which he did, and he heard a message on his first attempt that he had not heard when listening without the phones.

Another theory, which was being considered by Dr. Hans Bender in Germany, was that the voices were some sort of projection of subconscious thought forms. His evidence seemed pretty solid, except that he could not explain how sometimes the voices spoke over the person as he addressed them, and often voices came from people the listener did not know and said things that were a puzzle. Other problems, such as defective tapes, voices already on the tapes, radio waves, and other random noises were effectively eliminated as explanations. That they might be extraterrestrials of some kind, or demons, was up to philosophers to figure out.

Bander offered a helpful suggestion in terms of ranking the quality of voices. "A" was the best, and usually the most difficult to obtain. It required fewer playbacks to understand. "B" and "C" voices were more common and were generally faint, scrambled, or polyglot. I decided to follow that hierarchy, with the hope of one day getting an "A" recording from Christian.

Everyone who experimented with the voices seemed to think that, despite how difficult they could be to understand, this method was an improvement over having to trust in what a spiritualist or medium said.

—5—

Running into Dave and Sharon on the pedestrian walkway near the hotel, we sat down and talked about the spirit world. Dave told me that he'd had a dream after we had spoken before about a German shepherd that had escorted me to a person who could help me. Some government people attempted to stop me because they wanted to cure me. The dog kept them away while I went to talk to the person I sought. "You were doing what you needed to do," he said. Unfortunately, he had no idea what the person told me.

Sharon described the time they spent in Sedona, Arizona, a spiritual energy center. For them, it had been transformative, and she believed that Dave was receiving a communication from a source other than himself. "He doesn't usually speak like this."

I admitted that I really had trouble feeling the things that others claimed to feel in haunted or spiritual places.

Since I'd once lived in Arizona, she asked me whether I had

contacts among Native Americans who might be able to assist me. That was a provocative suggestion. In fact, I did know someone, and this thing with Christian might interest him. I hadn't spoken to him in years, it but was worth approaching him.

It was Sharon's belief that we all have intuitive feelings, so we all have the ability to connect with the spirit world. "We help people," she explained, "to learn how to clear their minds and focus their thoughts on the spirits present or the events that took place at a site and to focus on the purpose for our being there. You can get some interesting impressions in different haunted areas."

"So different places hold different things."

"One place may hold negative energy, another sadness, love, joy, or happiness, and if you allow yourself, you can feel the emotions present and get some marvelous results on recorders or film. It comes down to attuning yourself with the energy around you. We do not evoke the spirits, we work with those already existing around us. We can get so caught up in our own routines and our own little worlds that we numb ourselves to what is around us. We tend to forget that those around us have feelings and needs because we become desensitized."

That evening, the group investigated a building in town that dated back to the 1600s and had been a church. Supposedly, it was haunted by the spirits of a pregnant woman who suffocated near the boiler room and a boy who had been deaf and retarded. In the building itself, not much happened, but when we went into the basement, I got to see what an orb in motion looked like on a videocam. Dave had his Sony videocam with night-shot capabilities. He explained that skeptics are quick to say that orbs are really bugs or dust. He took pains to show me that this was not the case.

"Orbs are defined by form and composition," he said. "With infrared lighting, we can clearly see this and it's easy to distinguish the difference between orbs and flying insects. The bug is highlighted as a glowing insect and it has spastic movements. As it comes into the beam, you can see the wings."

He was right. When I looked through his viewfinder as he held the camera toward a dark room at the end of a tunnel, I saw bright round shapes moving fast from ceiling to wall to floor. The insects had a definite insectile shape. Dust was just that: dust. It didn't move with the speed of an orb. I was a bit awed by the feeling that, unlike taking a photograph, I could see an orb at the very moment it was moving around and follow its path. This was like having the cold spot next to me in the New Orleans séance. I was present to this; if an orb was a ghost, we were in the same space.

"Many novices will film natural anomalies," said Dave, "and believe they've captured something paranormal, but we carefully examine all photos submitted to us and we reject over two thirds. We have very strict guidelines for ghost photography. True orbs are spirits, but clusters of orbs may not be spirits, just floating particles stirred up as you walk across a room. Learning to evaluate our own photos is the hardest aspect because we have to learn to disregard the natural orb patterns that are generated and look for the paranormal events. This is why we combine photography with using the thermal scanner and the EMF meter. We seek for a combination of physical changes to suggest the presence of a spirit."

As we walked over to the Howard Street cemetery to see what we could get over there on camera, Dave described "barrier oscillations." If an apparition has a small mass and enters our world from a higher dimension, he said, it will vibrate, producing the effect of multiple images or blurred edges. Someone else who was walking with us mentioned that it was this vibration that made the air colder in the presence of an apparition or an orb.

We reached the cemetery, which was closed for the night, and stood outside the walls so I could learn to use the videocam. Dave told me to ask Christian to show himself, which I did. While I was working the camcorder, Dave took a photograph and said that he got an orb hovering over me.

"That's significant," Dave later told me, "because very few people got anything that night out there."

Someone asked Dave about the sparkle effect they were getting— a spray of sparks that occurred as their camera flashed. Dave called them "sparklies."

"They're usually seen in areas that appear to be charged with spirit activity," he said. "However, despite their intensity, they almost never appear on the photograph." He thought that in some cases, it was just the flash reflecting off objects in the air. In other cases, they might be indicators of orbs in the area.

By Dave's assessment, Salem was not a very good place for "ghosting" (a word I had begun to use to encompass the range of activities in which I was now involved). He said that the whole place felt oppressive. They figured it was due to the religious bigotry that the tourist trade inadvertently promoted. "How can any spirits find rest," he asked, "when they are constantly reminded by daily reenactments of the foul deed done to them by religious leaders of the city?"

Personally, I had gotten what I came for: to see if I could get EVP with "Christian" away from my apartment and to get others to hear my results. I had also made a decision: I knew now which camera I wanted to buy.

—6—

I drove home and unpacked. I tried to get Christian to respond to a few questions, just to see if he'd picked up some energy, but had no luck. Exhausted, I went to bed. That night I woke up at 4:30 A.M. I felt wide awake, as if something had startled me. I reached for the recorder to ask if anyone was there. The three-syllable response was the loudest and most aggressive I had experienced to date. It scared me, so I laid the recorder on my bed table and pulled up the covers. Even the next day in broad daylight, listening to that one unnerved me. Yet the intensity of it told me that taking him to places with residual dark energy that he might resonate to could produce results.

Ghosts in My Neck of the Woods

"THE BUSINESS OF GHOSTS . . . IS TOTALLY AND INESCAPABLY LINKED WITH THE BUSINESS OF DEATH."

—DOROTHY FIEDEL

— 1 —

With the patient guidance of Rick and Karl, the two men from Lancaster who first taught me about ghost photography, I finally decided to purchase an Olympus D-340R digital camera. While the Sony Mavica had the advantage of putting the photos right on disc, it was bulky. I would be traveling, probably with a lot of equipment, so I decided to go with something more compact. This was the next step of my apprenticeship.

I started to research cameras and read the following note one day on a chat line, the latest communication between two people who had been discussing the technology of ghost research: "You [the other person] made some good points about the resolution of digital cameras versus film. Film is much higher resolution, but when I take a picture with digital it's almost the same quality, so I don't think the resolution argument has much value. I have seen pictures of the same orb taken with digital and film at the same time. They are virtually identical!"

I found that interesting. Rick had made a similar point. I then read the response:

"They may appear to be identical when you look at them normally. The problem arises when the analysis begins. Try a magnification beginning at eight hundred percent and keep increasing it. Then compare the two images. The digital image will be pixelated to the point of not being able to perform the first stage of analysis at a level that will be acceptable as credible analysis or identification. It is on this point that the resolution is imperative, as magnification is a key element in photo analysis. There are many different types of energy and wavelengths involved in paranormal patterns. Binary and film handle these energy patterns in different ways. The human eye sees up to about 720mm [apparently a color frequency range]. Anything over this will not be seen. It is in the areas exceeding these levels [that film captures] where the mysteries lie. But I don't really care what the skeptics say, as you can't convince them anyway."

That was certainly true. I was to learn, despite the many photos I got, that a skeptic would always try to counter them by saying I had manipulated the computer imaging or that the orbs were dust particles, water drops, points of natural light, or whatever. It seemed to me that one had to be there doing it to be convinced. I was already aware of people who were using digital imagery to fake these photos, although to someone like Dave Oester, fakes were pretty obvious. Nevertheless, the fact that photos of orbs and apparitions *could* be faked did not mean they all were frauds. What differentiated the lazy skeptic, who dismissed everything based on what could be done with technological effects, from the diligent skeptic, was that the latter made an honest effort to look at genuine results and review all the possibilities.

Once my Olympus arrived, I walked out to the memorial field where George Washington had led the continental army in the battle of Princeton, in what is now called Princeton Battlefield State Park. People had fought and died out there, so like Gettysburg, there should be some orbs.

Along with the Battle of Trenton, the Battle of Princeton was part of Washington's campaign against the British forces in New Jersey during the winter of 1776–77. After Washington had been defeated on Long Island, he crossed into New Jersey late in the fall. On December 1, the troops moved into Princeton, and then Trenton as the British and Hessians (hired German mercenaries) advanced. The American army at this point was badly demoralized, pockmarked by deserters, in poor health, and badly equipped. They moved across the Delaware River into Pennsylvania. The British stopped in Trenton, Princeton, and places north and east. The rebellion looked to be fizzling out, and they assumed they did not have to push too hard to make an end of it. Washington felt the pressure to make a dramatic move, and thus began the "Ten Crucial Days."

With less than five-thousand men in his army, he decided to launch a surprise attack He waited while the Hessians partied on Christmas Day and then crossed the Delaware in a snowstorm and marched into Trenton. It was so cold it was feared that the muskets would not fire, but it turned out that they didn't really need them. The Hessians had decided not to send a patrol out into the storm, so they were taken by surprise and quickly captured. Many ran away. The fighting lasted only ninety minutes.

Humiliated, the British marched on Trenton, leaving a rear guard at Princeton. They fought with the Americans until nightfall, at which time Washington moved his men around the enemy and into Princeton. General Hugh Mercer guarded the American left flank, and when he met up with the British, he was mortally wounded. Washington came up from behind with more troops and led a successful charge that scattered the redcoats. The fighting continued through town, driving the British toward Nassau Hall, the main college building. Those inside surrendered. It was Washington's first victory against the British regulars on an open field. By the time the British came back from Trenton, the Americans had moved north.

Not far from where I lived were common graves for those who were killed in this battle. A small sign marks the British grave, but the Americans have a distinctive set of tall, white columns. People today get married on that monument. On the other side of the road, a huge oak tree stands in an open field. Mercer rested under its branches from the wound that eventually ended his life in a small house nearby.

I went first to the marble columns. It was dusk, but still a bit light out. I took numerous photos, quickly checking them out on the LCD screen, and was disappointed to see that I was getting nothing. I also placed the recorder on the grave marker but heard no voices. That was strange. I had expected this to be a very fruitful place. I knew that this model of camera worked because I had used one in Gettysburg to good effect. I hoped I had not bought a defective one (although I suppose some people would say it was defective if they were *getting* blobs of light in the photos). I continued to walk around, shooting here and there without aiming, as the ghost hunters had taught me to do. I kept in mind Rick's admonition not to expect results the first time out. Sometimes it took a while for the ghosts to find you.

I wandered down to the woods near the Institute for Advanced Study—my familiar exercise paths. I walked them every day, and that was where I got my first orb. I had to look closely because it appeared to be roosting in the branches of a tree. But there it was, a small white circle where no circle belonged. That made me smile. I went on to take more photos of the battlefield and again got nothing, except for a few deer. Still, I had gotten my first orb on film on my own camera, and I knew now that I could. I walked by the Mercer Oak and took a few shots. By the time I left the field and stood near a very old bridge that predated the Revolution, I had a number of photos to look at. I went through one after another, seeing nothing. That was to be expected. Someone had mentioned that only a small percentage of photos would be "positive"—capture paranormal phenomena. Maybe I had just the one. Then I stopped.

What was this? Oddly, there was a long, shiny stemlike thing in one of the photos, stretching from the bottom of the shot and going toward the bridge in the middle. I hadn't been near anything that would look like that, and there were no weeds or branches on the bridge. I examined it from several angles and simply could not say what it was. I nearly erased it, but at the last minute decided to keep it.

Then I went around to another open field where I knew that General Washington had set up his field hospital. Numerous amputations and other surgeries had been done there, and many men had died. It was right behind where I once had owned a house. In fact, in that very house, I had been telling a ghost story to the guy installing my cable when a wineglass shattered on the table. He'd left in a hurry. I'd thought little of the incident until sometime later when I laughingly described it at a brunch I'd served. Right there on the table, in front of everyone, a second wineglass shattered.

So as I stood at the edge of the field, holding my camera high over my head, I was confident that I would get something here. The moon was behind me, barely a sliver. No streetlights were in sight, and the place was dark and spooky. I pressed the shutter button. The camera flashed, illuminating the weeds. I closed the lens, pressed the LCD screen button, and took a look. There it was, dim but large and perfectly round. An orb. This was my first really good one. And my instincts had paid off.

Clearly this camera worked. It was time now to go see if Christian was home. I walked into my apartment in the dark, keeping quiet (as if he couldn't see me). I crept up the wooden steps and rounded a corner, taking pictures all around as quickly as the recharging battery allowed, and then stepped into the bedroom. Flash, flash, flash. He could run—he could even go through walls—but he couldn't hide from the digital eye.

I was not disappointed. Although it was small and showed up in only one frame, there was definitely an orb in the bedroom near the window. I had several shots of that same spot, and only one of them showed a small circle of light. There was nothing in the room that might have reflected the flash, and it was in here that I had gotten my EVP. If an orb was really a ghost, I had him. Or had someone, anyway.

Then it occurred to me that I hadn't exactly followed IGHS protocol. I hadn't shown respect or asked permission. Oh, well. I didn't think that Christian and I stood much on manners. I had the feeling that we were both predators and each was the other's prey.

—**2**—

Few people would suspect that Princeton, New Jersey, harbors ghosts. Few residents, anyway. On one side of town is the medieval ivy-covered Princeton University campus and on the other side are stores that cater to the upper middle class. Talbot's, Laura Ashley, LaVake Jewelers, Starbucks, and numerous banks. There was a bookstore that that refused to carry any of my books because they weren't "serious." Palmer Square, the town center, is a beautiful green surrounded by boutiques, along with Anne Taylor, Banana Republic, and the Nassau Inn. You almost have to dress up just to cross the street. Even a date for coffee requires a bit of polish.

Before living in this town, I'd never been to a place where people actually seem offended by the idea that anything there could be haunted. Whenever I asked, I had the feeling I was prying into some family secret that was none of my business. Someone else told me there were no police files of any reports of paranormal events—very strange. It's generally the case that the police get called into homes where people believe they have an intruder—even a paranormal intruder. One cop whom I asked about this agreed that it seemed unusual. However, I'd spoken to a couple of people, who declined to be named, who had stories to tell, and I knew of the one famous story of the Hessian soldier in the "Barracks" on Edgehill Street that was repeated every Halloween in the local newspaper. Apparently he had been wounded in the nearby battle and had died in the kitchen. Every Christmas Eve he would appear near the fireplace in the kitchen. A woman who had lived in the house had told me that as a child she had seen him in the living room while she was playing hide-and-seek. He was pacing back and forth, dressed in his shiny helmet and uniform with striped trousers. Supposedly, during the 1940s, an Episcopal priest had exorcised him.

A friend of mine went to a house on Snowden Lane that once had been the residence of one of the signers of the Declaration of Independence. At the time, the place was vacant. He had seen the glowing white figure of a woman standing on her toes on the balcony. She wore a dress from the 1920s, and her right hand shaded her eyes as she looked out toward the field. As he watched, he experienced a heavy feeling, as if he'd been sedated.

There was also Cleveland Tower on the graduate campus, where students had taken suicidal leaps and workers had called in security to check out numerous odd incidents. I had heard as well that a ghost stole people's jewelry on Mercer Street (that's a trick), and a glowing nun has been reported near Our Lady of Princeton, which purportedly has a crypt in the basement.

I soon discovered that one of the early ESP research centers, Psychophysical Research Laboratories, had been developed in Princeton, on Forrestal campus. For about ten years, it had been one of the most productive institutes in the country until it lost its funding in 1989. In 1979, researchers at the university began investigating psi phenomena in the Princeton Engineering Anomalies Research Laboratory, and they made numerous contributions to the field of consciousness and person–machine interaction. They were still going strong, although they had been unable to assist me with my questions about EVP.

I decided to start in the rather prominent cemetery on Witherspoon Street. I was less interested in going where phenomena had already been reported than in trying to find some haunted places on my own. To some groups, that's the difference between a ghost hunter and a ghost investigator: The ghost hunter hopes to break new ground, while the investigator may return repeatedly to the same place to see if the phenomenon repeats itself. (Neither is a ghostbuster.)

With my recorder and camera in hand, I met my friend Stuart Lee Brown outside the Greenview Avenue gate at 11:40 P.M. This is a guy with acute hearing and an intolerance of environmental disorder. He rushed up and told me that he'd had some dreams since listening to my EVP. He wanted to tell them to me.

"The first one was *I Love Lucy* meets *Rosemary's Baby*," he said rather breathlessly. "A man gets his wife to drink a potion, and his father-in-law helps. It tastes sweet and she's lured into a stupor, and together they sacrifice her."

He pointed out that this involved two males, possibly symbolizing Wraith and Christian, and a female—me. The implication was that they were luring me with their dangerous beauty and charm. I nodded. I was used to Stuart's dramatic interpretations.

"The second dream," he went on, "also involves two men. They're like brothers but they're not related." He raised his eyebrows to emphasize the significance. "They were in prison together, in a dungeon, waiting for judgment. They're both guilty of the same thing, but they wonder who will face the judge first. One of them had a dream and he knows who it will be. They are pressed together against a board and someone in a black robe who has no face or hands comes forward with a blade. He slips it into the one who is first to be judged, and he is bled quickly and efficiently."

"Geez, Stuart," I said. "You're making it sound like Christian is telling you what happened to him."

"Maybe he is. Anyway, the figure in black looks at the other guy accusingly and the guy says, 'No, wait, he did it all, not me.' And he gets spared."

I looked at him. That was pretty weird. It was almost identical to the notion that Kat and Mariah had raised in the séance—that it had been a suicide pact in which one of them got out. "And how did you feel afterward?" I asked. As a dream therapist, I had always asked clients to report the emotional tone of their dreams.

"Terrible," Stuart said. "They were really dark. And one got away when he shouldn't have."

I had nothing to say to that. Maybe the dreams came from just being part of this, or maybe Christian was conveying the truth, or maybe he was lying, or maybe they were just random dreams that only appeared to be part of the pattern. It was cute that Stuart hoped they would help, but they only raised more questions for me.

"Let's go in," I said.

We entered the quiet grounds without speaking. It was a coolish night in July, around seventy degrees, with low humidity, following a four-day heat wave. A thunderstorm had rolled through the day before, but there was no mist. The moon was about a quarter full but hidden behind clouds. I took some preliminary photos across a crowd of silent headstones, which yielded nothing, and then we looked at the map. A lot of famous authors, scientists, and presidents were buried there, but they lay mostly in the opposite direction.

My goal was to find the stone for the Menendez grave, where Kitty and José were buried together after being brutally slaughtered in California by their sons, Erik and Lyle. Few people knew that they had been brought back to Princeton. It wasn't on the official map, but I had insider information.

We walked in a loop and a tried a few more photos. Once again I'd forgotten to ask permission, but when I examined the shots, I had orbs. One photo in particular showed several, so we retraced our steps.

Stuart, ever polite, introduced us. "We intend you no harm," he said to the air. "We'd just like to take some photographs."

Despite his observance of propriety, I felt sure that the best photos were already achieved, and I was right. I took a lot of photos, but there were no more orbs to be detected in that area.

"Hey, I thought you attracted ghosts," I complained to him.

"I usually do," he insisted.

"Well, we have time."

We came upon a fresh grave, less than a year old. Stuart felt sure there would be activity here, but I got nothing. I even felt a bit invasive. For me, spirit activity was more interesting with those who chose to be there or clung to the spot rather than those who were confused and hanging around for no particular reason. The residual hauntings where some figure went repetitively through the same routine were equally uninspiring. I guess I wanted a story as much as I wanted a spirit, some interesting motive for being there. An unsolved murder or suicide was more captivating than just someone who had passed away.

Finally, we found the grave marker we sought, and right in front of it was a gravestone in the form of a bench, so we sat on it while we examined the site. Of the dozen or so photos I took, none came out, so I place my voice recorder on the gravestone and we sat talking about how this was like Conrad Aiken's grave bench in *Midnight in the Garden of Good and Evil*, except without the river view—or the champagne.

After about five minutes, I went over and checked the recorder. Forty seconds were registered. We played it back. There was a voice on it, and Stuart was certain that the first word spoken was my name.

I listened several times and *could* hear my name in that weird rhythm but wasn't positive. (I later discovered that EVP researchers often experienced their own names called repeatedly.)

I asked, "Is it okay for us to be here?"

Two syllables came back. Stuart thought they were "Get out," and that made him nervous. He said we should go.

"We just got here." I ignored his fidgeting and continued. "Do you know who I am?"

Then came an odd sound, like a clarinet, and some further talking that neither of us could decipher. I urged Stuart to ask some questions.

In his usual lengthy narrative (his phone messages generally last five minutes), he addressed the spirits: "We do not mean you any harm. We just want to communicate with you. May we speak with you? Please?" Then within a few seconds, he said, "We're going to play back on the machine to hear what you say and then respond to it."

I resisted this because I usually gave them much longer to respond. I felt we were rushing it. As I suspected, we got no rejoinder, so I held my hand up for him to be quiet and tried again.

"We want to respect your wishes. Will you communicate with us?"

The reaction was a loud monosyllable, which I heard as "Yes" and Stuart heard as "No." I was beginning to see how this activity had a projective side to it. Stuart, who wanted to leave, heard consistently negative things, while I, who wanted to stay, interpreted mostly positive responses.

"Are you buried here?" I asked, because I wasn't going to assume anything. There came what I felt was an attempt to say something, but it wasn't clear. Stuart was sure it was "Get out of here."

I rolled my eyes. Just to placate him, I rephrased the question. "Do you want us to leave?"

"Yes!" That was echoed on the recorder by two more emphatic responses that both sounded like "Yes."

I grabbed Stuart's arm, suddenly aware that here we were on the far side of the cemetery with no quick escape and with some angry voice insisting that we leave. I should have listened to him.

We got up and left. I snapped a few pictures on the way out, since I had heard they often come up from behind, but got no orbs. We waited until we were in the safety of the town before listening again to be sure we had gotten those messages right. They sounded pretty clear. I noted the time, as Rick Fisher would insist I do: It was 1:00 A.M.

I drove Stuart home. On the way, he pointed out a Catholic cemetery that we could drive through, so we went into the center, stopped the car, and each snapped some photos. We got a couple of orbs—nice, clear shots. Then we used the recorder to see about our status.

"Is there anyone here with us?" My typical starting question.

"Yes."

"Is it okay for us to be here?"

Four syllables that, in our frame of mind, sounded like "Get out of here." We left.

I got home at 2:00 A.M. and went right to bed, a bit shaken by the feeling that I had invaded someone's space. When I was a kid, I always believed that if you stepped on someone's grave, the spirit attached to you and followed you home. I had that same feeling now. Despite what I believed about ghosts going for those who act scared, I pulled my covers over my head.

When I listened the next morning to the recorder, it didn't sound as threatening as it had in the cemetery. Nevertheless, for an initial venture, it had been productive. I had four more photos of orbs and some EVP from Princeton burial grounds.

Of course, it could be the case that my own hitchhiker spirit was answering all my questions. Stuart believed the voice was different, but no matter how carefully I listened, I couldn't tell.

—3—

It was time now for me to look at some of my photos. I didn't have many yet, but I hadn't forgotten about that odd one at the bridge with the stemlike image. And I needed to face the fact that I had to learn how to use the camera in conjunction with the computer if I was ever going to print these out.

To my shock, when they downloaded, they all appeared to be black. I was in despair, thinking I'd never be able to print these as I saw them on the screen. I sent messages to Rick, Karl, and Dave, asking anyone for help. I was frantic. Was this some trick of my ghost—that I could get photos but couldn't do anything with them?

Dave was the first to respond. He patiently explained how photo programs work, helping me through my frustration like a trained therapist, and soon I was fine-tuning my photos like a pro. Even so, I was still puzzled by the tubular thing I'd gotten in my second anomalous photo, out by the old bridge. I didn't recognize it as being anything that I had been near. I sent it to Dave to have a look.

"Wow!" he wrote back. "This is a terrific photo of a vortex." He had worked on the gamma qualities and had sent it back to show me how one could make out the line of orbs stretching from the bottom of the photo, near where I was shooting it, to some distance away. I was stunned. My second photo and it was a vortex. I'd nearly erased it.

Quickly, I inserted the CD that came with the home-study course so I could better learn the difference between authentic photos and mistakes. I noted what lens flare looked like, as well as someone's thumb and camera strap, although I didn't think they had accurately portrayed how much like a vortex a camera strap can look. I'd seen an article in *The Skeptical Inquirer,* that fanatical magazine that tripped over itself to disprove practically everything that made life interesting, where they had shown several photos of camera straps that did appear quite ghostly. Nevertheless, to use that as an argument to dismiss all ghost photos was attacking a straw man. Not once did they mention orbs, ectoplasm, or photos of apparitions. Just camera straps.

I had already photographed my own thumb and knew what that looked like. At a later time, I would photograph my own breath on a cold day, nearly mistaking it for ectoplasm. I soon learned from experience why you don't take photos in rain, dust, snow, or around cigarette smoke. I was surprised at how similar a cloud of dust looked to a pack of orbs. Lens flare doesn't look like much of anything but lens flare. It's not even round, so I doubted that anyone could mistake it for orbs (although there was that girl who photographed her own feet and thought she had an apparition). The point was, one had to be careful. Still, I'd already gotten some pretty good shots and I was only just beginning.

Rick told me that the more you go out on investigations, the better results you get. He had implied that the ghosts get used to you, which leads to more success. In addition, he felt experience had helped develop his own intuitive powers and these gave him a better sense of where to take photos.

That was my weakness. I wasn't very good at intuiting ghosts. I could work with these devices, but left on my own, I was like a nearsighted person without her glasses. Practically every psychic and medium I know has insisted that everyone has some degree of psychic ability. However, the research labs for psi phenomena dispute this. I didn't think psychics had actual evidence, only logic or intuition, and I could devise an argument just as logical against their position. It could be, for example, that psychic ability had to do with brain waves or the ability to use a part of the brain not accessible to everyone, depending on their genetic makeup. I did not think it followed that just because

I was alive and human I was psychic. Still, I had once learned how to read auras—perhaps that ability was associated with the ability to see ghosts?

—4—

What I was doing soon got around to people who knew me, and I had several requests to investigate private homes where people had reported odd experiences. I knew enough about reactions to the paranormal to realize that not all people who claimed they wanted to know really did. After going into one house and getting a couple of photos of orbs, for example, I heard from the owner, who shall remain anonymous:

> I was totally freaked out Saturday night. I woke up suddenly around 2 A.M. and was overcome with panic. I could not even move my arm to touch my husband who was sound asleep next to me. Then my dog, who sleeps out in the hallway, came into my room and started to whimper. I went around the house turning on every light with my dog in tow, but when I went back upstairs, she refused to follow me. I jumped into bed and pulled the covers up. This morning, after I'd finished showering, the detachable showerhead came flying off its perch and scared the hell out of me. I immediately bellowed, "cut that out, I'm not impressed," while praying nothing else would happen. So far, all is quiet. However, whenever I mention "the ghost" to anyone via the telephone, loud static suddenly appears and gradually gets louder until I change the topic. I swear to you, this is true.

I had learned a lesson in the power of suggestibility. Once one believes one has a ghost, every incident becomes a matter of paranormal cause and effect. So when I was invited to a three-hundred-year-old horse farm out near Hopewell, New Jersey, I talked at length with Liza, the owner, before going out.

Her place was situated only a few miles from where one of the most notorious crimes of the century was committed: the Lindbergh kidnapping. Across the street from her farm is Lindbergh Road, which takes you right to the former Lindbergh property. American hero Charles Lindbergh had chosen the Sourland Mountains, the largest contiguous forest in central Jersey, for building his country home because he believed his family would have privacy. The area is known as the

Sourlands because it won't support crops, and legend has it that a black man warned Lindbergh not to go there because the land was cursed. A native of the Sourlands who had been interviewed by the press said about the area, "Queer things are seen, queer things are heard and queer things happen." He pointed out that ghosts, murders, headless forms, luminous shapes, and crying voices can all be found in what he called "the Devil's own stomping ground." Even today there is a legend of "knitting Betty," the headless ghost. Supposedly a cannonball that fell from the sky killed her as she sat on a rock knitting and waiting for her husband. During Prohibition, government agents looking for moonshiners vanished without a trace.

Lindbergh's house was not even finished when, on the night of March 1, 1932, Charles Lindbergh Jr., twenty months old, was kidnapped. The police arrived and found footprints in the wet ground below the nursery window, along with two deep impressions. One hundred yards away, three sections of a rough-hewn ladder were discovered, the bottom section broken. On the windowsill in the nursery was a ransom note.

Jake Lakamont, an Indian tracker, predicted that the baby would be found in the woods only if he were dead.

On April 10, the child's body was found in the woods about four miles from the estate, face downward, covered with leaves. It was little more than a skeleton, the outline of a form in a murky heap of rotting vegetation. The left leg was missing from the knee down, as were the left hand and right arm. The cause of death was a massive fracture of the skull. The remains were cremated. Two years later, in 1934, Bruno Richard Hauptmann was tried and convicted of murder and sent to the electric chair. Whether he was guilty or railroaded is a question that still remains unresolved.

Although Liza's house is on the other side of the mountain from the former Lindbergh home, one cannot escape the aura of a famous family's violation. There's also a feeling of vulnerability from the dense woods where a witch, Silvia Dubois, was once said to live. She had been a slave and was reputed to have survived to the age of 115. She saw supernatural forces at work in every wood and swamp, and she liked to frighten children with her tales of what could happen in those woods.

Before the seven-hundred-acre estate had come to Liza, it had been passed down through the Wert family until one Wert bet the farm on a horse race—and lost. Stories were passed around about suicides that had been committed there, the appearance of a ghostly little boy, and strange cold spots that occurred in several of the rooms. A previous owner, who had broken up with one woman to marry another, also experienced a "message" from the other side. On his wedding day, his jilted girlfriend died in the hospital, and after that everything seemed to go wrong for the guy. His wife bankrupted him and then left. Finally he had to sell the estate.

The oldest room in Liza's house is made of stone, with wooden rafters on the ceiling. I opted to spend the night in there. Initial photos showed numerous orbs in the place, all up around the ceiling, which was puzzling, since Liza believed there was only one ghost—a male. She mentioned that this room had once been a slaughterhouse, which brought to mind a story I'd heard in New Hope, a town not far away. A rock band had been practicing in an old warehouse, but they claimed that whenever they played back what they had recorded, they could hear the sound of pigs squealing. That place, too, had once been a slaughterhouse. I wondered if some of these orbs were animals.

By now I'd added two meters to my ghost kit: The first one was the electromagnetic field radiation tester, which Dave and Sharon had supplied. They had included instructions for recognizing the typical energy magnetic field readings for paranormal activity, anything between the numbers 2 and 7 on a meter that registered from 0.1m to 199.9m gauss. Man-made sources of radiation typically registered higher, and normal levels fall below 2. The spirits supposedly move out of range fast, so even a quick spike can indicate activity. (For those who want a simpler device, a compass will often do the trick. If the needle skews erratically, spins, or points away from where it should be pointing, it may be attracted to a concentration of paranormal energy.)

I had also purchased the Trifield Natural EM meter for using inside. It registered any moving magnetic field, including that produced by a human body—it can even detect a person through a wall. Indoor transient phenomena are easier to detect during calm weather. The meter also measures electrical changes and has the capacity to read those two forces together. It also reads radio waves. The nice thing is that if something approaches within ten feet, it signals with both a needle and a high-pitched tone. I was now pretty well equipped for an amateur ghost hunter.

At Liza's house, I used the Trifield meter, which fluctuated, but not dramatically. The other EMF meter went as high as 5 near the bed. I took more photos and only got one positive out of thirty or so, but it was a nice, glowing orb that was not present in the photos taken of the same spot directly before and after.

I went to bed that night without much fear, perhaps because others were in the house. It struck me that I had grown less afraid since I'd learned how to use the equipment. I wasn't sure why and I didn't know if I liked this development. Being scared was what made ghosting fun.

In the morning, I had fifty minutes' worth of EVP from the room. I heard lots of static and growling-type noises, as well as what sounded like a greeting: "Hi!" That was said after I turned over in bed. Liza and I both had difficulty making out the other words, but then her daughter Pam came in. With John, her boyfriend, she claimed to hear phrases like "What are you doing?" "Hey. I'm here," and "I want to tell you something."

It was another example of younger people having an easier time than I hearing what was said. Even so, I had no context for understanding these phrases, or even for knowing if they were directed at me.

—5—

On February 26, 2000, the chief benefactor of the Princeton Battlefield Area Preservation Society died. A memorial service was held on March 2. Less than twenty-four hours later, the centuries-old Mercer Oak on the Princeton battlefield split in two and toppled over. This was the tree where General Mercer had sat after being wounded in the Battle of Princeton. It seemed a weird coincidence that the ancient tree would give up the ghost upon the passing of someone who had fought hard against its removal. I decided to go over and have a look. It was nearing dusk when I got there. I was shocked at how empty the field looked without that majestic oak. It would be even worse when summer rolled in.

To my surprise, I encountered a guy who was equipped as only a ghost hunter would be. Cameras, tripod, meters, binoculars. There weren't many around the Princeton area, and the few I knew were frustrated by the lack of information about haunted sites or support for paranormal investigations. I figured this guy was from out of town. I went over to what was left of the tree stump and introduced myself, noting that he had a Sony camcorder set up, ready to roll. I'd brought along my Olympus camera and a digital recorder, but nothing else. I felt naked.

"I'm Bobby," he said, "from Arkansas. I was just rollin' in when I heard about the tree. I had to get a look. What a tragedy."

He stood with his feet apart as if at military rest, which is not really a rest at all. I sensed that he'd served in some type of service. In fact, his black hair was shaved up the sides but thick on top, about an inch long. When he talked, he leaned his head back and looked at me through a pair of small, intense blue eyes. His nose had the most extreme ski-slope shape I'd ever seen, and when he spoke, his lips jutted forward. He wore tight jeans over cowboy boots, and his plaid blue shirt, perfectly pressed, was tucked in tight. In fact, everything about him was stiff and taut, from his posture to the muscles in his jaw to the skin over his temples. I sensed a man about to explode.

"You don't look quite ready for the proper reconnaissance," he noted, nodding at my camera.

"No, I'm not," I admitted. "You can't stay long after dusk here. They run you off the property like they think you're gonna steal something. It didn't seem worthwhile to bring a lot of equipment here this close to dark."

"That's too bad. I was fixing to spend the night here, maybe. Get a good feel for the body count. Hope to see a phantom." He walked over and looked though the viewfinder on his camcorder. I could see he had the infrared going already and even had a slave unit with a light that extended the infrared range about sixty-five feet.

"See anything?" I asked. I couldn't very well take any flash photos while he had the infrared on.

"Naw, just bugs, I think." His face wore a perpetual worried expression.

"Why would you come to Princeton?" I asked. "There are lots of better places for ghost hunting."

He looked up. "I was here."

I waited for an explanation and then realized what he meant. It's a phrase I'd heard in Gettysburg a few times by men in some sort of military transport. "I was here" meant "I was here *then*." In another life, they had served there or more likely had died there. It haunted them into other lives.

"At the battle?" I asked. He nodded. "Don't ask me how I know, I just do. The first time I ever came here, I knew it. I resonated. I've been a lot of places but nothing gets me like this place. I come back when I can, about every three years. I hate that this old tree went down. I think I must've been near it when I was killed. Y'unnerstand?"

I suddenly felt like a therapist in a room with an alien abductee. At such times, it's difficult to know what to say. I said nothing.

Bobby squinted at me. He stood up, putting his hands in his back pockets. "I always need a bit of stress debriefing after I've been here," he commented. "It's such an impact. I don't really expect to see anything, but what I'm doing is getting prepared."

"Prepared?"

"I go through the drills so if I actually face a critical incident situation, I can go on automatic pilot." He grinned and ran his hands over his bristly hair. "Like a fire drill for kids. They have to go through it over and over so in a panic situation, they don't panic. Their bodies know what to do. Course, if I ever saw a ghost here, y'unnerstand, there'd probably be a quick mobilization of legs and a trail of unnecessary fluids. This place is pretty high on my phobic scale response. That's partly how I know I was here. It scared the shit out of me then and it scares the shit out of me now."

I never quite know how to talk to someone who lives simultaneously in two time periods. I was relieved that he didn't seem to expect a response. Gallantly, he shut off his infrared light so I could get a few quick digital photos, but nothing showed up. I guess the ghost of General Mercer went with the tree.

Just then a light hit us from the road. The ranger patrol. It was time to head out. I'd been warned before, and I didn't relish running into any trouble. Bobby gave me his card and told me to look him up if I got down south. He planned to stay a while and take the consequences. I thanked him and meant it. He alerted me to something that had escaped me until that point: the idea of being so adept at "the drill" that you can go through the motions no matter what is happening around you. It's a combat preparation exercise that has a lot of relevance to ghosting. If you see something that flusters you, you can keep filming, despite how scared you might get. And when you make all that effort to go out, but nothing happens, you can at least comfort yourself with the idea that you're just practicing to be in top form for the real thing.

At this point, it was time to assess where I was at. I had a camera, a recorder, a few meters, and more confidence in my ability to go out ghosting on my own. I still did not know what to think about my haunted ring. Thus far, several psychics had reacted negatively to it, and others had warned me not to go any further with my investigation. Even Wraith had sent a note saying it was evil. However, nothing had happened to me yet. Despite all the assurances that if I called to them or looked for them, I'd get ghosts in spades, I didn't think I'd gotten much. A few orbs, some strange voices. I wasn't satisfied. I mean, if Victor Zammit could say, "Hey, I want proof," and get kicked in the side, why couldn't I get something that clear? I hadn't yet tried humming, as Harvey Ray had suggested, or using the ring as a phone, so perhaps there were still some avenues open to me.

Then an unexpected note from Kat led me in an entirely new direction.

"SOME ARE BORN TO SWEET DELIGHT
SOME ARE BORN TO ENDLESS NIGHT."
—WILLIAM BLAKE

—1—

"I just got a call from Jacqueline," Kat wrote. That was the woman at the plantation who had so strongly reacted to the ring. "She was awakened in the middle of the night by Charles [the ghost she sees]. He's been warning her about Christian!"

I called to see what this was all about, and Kat said that after we met with Jacqueline, Charles had made it clear that he was unhappy. "He was upset about Christian. Evidently, these ghosts know each other on their plane."

Know each other? How could that be? "I guess I'd better call Jacqueline."

I tried several times but could not get her on the phone. Since Dot Fiedel had had the same reaction to Christian's ring back in Lancaster, I asked her what she thought about the possibility that some spirit in New Orleans could know Christian. And if so, what could he be so upset about? This wasn't making sense to me.

Dot told me about George Anderson, a psychic who acquired his ability in the aftermath of a childhood bout with encephalitis. Because he saw people and heard voices, he ended up being treated by a psychiatrist. Yet when he described a man standing in the room with them and the doctor realized the "visitor" was his own dead relative about whom Anderson could not possibly have known what he revealed, the psychiatrist was convinced this visitation was real. He then put Anderson through a battery of tests and found that the frontal area of his brain, where there usually is little activity except during REM sleep, was lit up during a trance state.

"This guy," Dot went on about Anderson, "mentioned that he's selective about who he lets through. Not every spirit is 'in the light' and there is indeed a hell. He only asks that those who dwell in the light be permitted to speak. So if that's all true, then possibly your ring completes a circuit between spiritual dimensions and serves as a conduit to the living. As such it allows Christian's spirit to 'jump floors.' If Charles is on a level occupied by the enlightened souls, it stands to reason he might consider Christian an unwelcome intrusion—a contamination. In that case, Charles's reluctance to contact his living lady friend seems reasonable since she completed the circuit and precipitated Christian's ability to jump floors. Supposing ghosts experience emotion, Charles was probably shocked and dismayed."

That the spirits were on different levels was new to me. Obviously, ghost hunting could become a very complicated pastime. It wasn't long before Jacqueline returned my call and further astonished me.

"After you guys left," she said, referring to my visit several weeks earlier, "I was working late here and I heard this loud clump on the front porch. I went out to look and found a large branch, about three feet long, lying there. It wasn't a windy day, so I couldn't figure out why that would happen."

"What did you think it was?" I asked.

"Charles. He wasn't happy. I knew that at once."

When she had touched the ring, she reminded me, she'd gotten the image of a man who had looked at her with an evil smirk, as if to say, "I'll make you *think* nothing will happen." That image had remained with her, she now told me, and had greatly disturbed her. She asked if Christian had dark hair, and I said, "No."

"Was he about five foot nine?"

"I really don't know, I never met . . . *wait a minute*. Wraith had dark hair."

"Well, I wrote something one night in a trance. I'll send it to you."

After explaining that when she types like this, she doesn't turn on the lights or look at the computer screen, she faxed to me the following. First she explained herself, and then included the communication from the other side.

You asked me to let you know if Charles reacted to your visit. Yes, he did. Approximately an hour after you left, he threw a branch onto the porch of my office. This has never happened before with him. I went out onto the porch, and while not seeing him, knew he was there. Like you suggested, I spoke to him, rather than just observing him. He smiled and walked right through me. I could smell him—amaretta is the only thing that comes to mind to describe it. It is an awesome feeling. Remember your first real kiss? Not the peck, but the moisture and softness of another's lips. I swear your head is in another time zone and all you know is you don't want it to stop.

Back to Charles. I did not feel him again for approximately two weeks. Then it was to talk about the ring, and he left again for a few weeks. Then he wanted me to write.

This was like many nights when I was close to being asleep but not ready to dream. Not at peace but my breath ready to slow down and the lights of my subconscious or daily activities seem to pass through my soul and I heard him or someone say, "It is now. You must do it now." At first I hesitated, weary from the day's activity. I almost said no. Almost missed the call to create something. I am worried no one will want to read our words.

The first time I saw him was in August hot and humid like now, like breathing water. He has touched my soul. Why . . . how can I know or say why he brings my heart to tears. I feel his presence. I am afraid of him now, afraid I won't understand and the opportunity will fade.

"His name is Charles. Don't worry, he says, I guide you. Tell the story and I help you. . . . Charles said to be careful with the ring because he thinks Christian can come back. He is desperate. He thinks he can return, and isn't believing half the battle? Charles warned me not to touch the ring again. Since your visit, I have thought of it and the images many times when I least expected to, and I have had the desire to touch it again. Craving really. He firmly relayed to me, 'No, don't touch.' "

That was it. The end of the message. I called Jacqueline back and pressed her to tell me about the image she had of Christian.

"He's a brat."

"Did you by any chance have any unusual dreams?"

I heard her catch her breath. "I *did* have a dream. Shortly after I touched the ring, I had a dream, but it was about a dark-haired man, not a blond. There were a lot of disjointed elements to it, which is not like dreams I normally have, and I remember that I cut off someone's head."

That image again—slit throats, cutting people open. It was becoming a common theme. "Did you think," I pressed, "that Christian wants to come back through you? Like he senses your receptivity? Maybe he thinks you're a better channel for him than me."

"That's possible, I guess. But the dark-haired one, he's dangerous. The blond was not the instigator. He just went along. The dark-haired one was using him."

That was certainly my own suspicion.

"If he's weak," I said, "maybe he's trying to take substance from other spirits, like Charles."

"Maybe."

I wasn't sure what I really thought about this. I had to admit, it bothered me that everyone but me seemed to be getting some kind of contact from Christian. Did I really have a major block to the spirit world? Despite these communications, I was still in some doubt that Christian was even a ghost. Perhaps not as much as when I first started all of this, but it seemed to me that if he really wanted to contact me, he could. Surely he knew from my conversations with Wraith that I'm not inclined just to accept someone else's word. I wanted proof. Clear, unambiguous proof.

In the meantime, just in case, I would extend to him a certain amount of credibility and respect.

I related all of this to Kat, and she came back with the possibility that things had indeed happened to or around me, but I had not noticed them the way she or Jacqueline might. "She's definitely sensitive and she pays more attention to the subtle hints that someone on a less ethereal plane might disregard. Particularly if you are busy and preoccupied with left-brain activities. If a ghost were to warn you, would you really recognize it as a sign or would you be more likely to rationalize it away? You have to be in a different space in yourself to really tune in. If you get some time to meditate and ground yourself, then you should shift to that right intuitive side. See what happens."

I had to admit I wasn't very good at that.

Then Jacqueline wrote another note to let me know that she had experienced a second disturbing dream that she believed was connected. "I had a dream about some folks that have been making my life miserable and all of a sudden the dark-haired man was there, saying I should take care of them. Then he helped me kill a person with a knife. The killing was not fast; it was brutal and very slow. I awoke terrified of myself. You know what the Bible says about what we think; it's as if we actually did the act. He laughed all the way through the ordeal, quietly and with malice yet feeding the rage. He said, 'Why are you angry with me? I didn't make you do it.' I said, 'You encouraged it.' He sat and watched just off to the side. I told him he was a coward. For some reason he was furious. He said, 'Well you're the one that wanted revenge and you felt relief, didn't you? I just wanted you to be happy.' "

She went on to suggest, "Perhaps he needs others to do his dirty work. Having power to control or influence someone on this level must be extremely exciting to him. He was almost laughing with glee as he instructed me."

Yet another dream like the others. Could it really be coincidence?

<h2 style="text-align:center">—2—</h2>

I was frustrated over the difficulty I was having understanding what "my" ghost—or any other—was saying. Tired and wondering where to go from here, I went to the movies and watched *The Muse*. It was about a screenwriter who'd lost his edge and was sent to try to coax a mythological muse to take him on as a client. His first mistake was to neglect to bring her a gift. Once he did that, he had a break.

It got me to thinking: Should I give Christian a gift? Would that coax him out or get better results? Might it even change the nature of these brutal dreams?

I used to teach dream workshops, and one of the exercises was a technique called Active Imagination. People selected an image from some dream that disturbed them or regularly recurred, and by mentally interacting with the image, they were able to get some control over it. I would then instruct them to ask the image for a gift. The results were often surprising and usually enlightening.

So the question was whether I should ask Christian for a gift . . . or give one to him? In other words, was he my muse or was he my recurring (and disturbing) dream image? And in the event that I decided

I should be the gift giver, I was stuck with a further dilemma: What exactly does one give to a ghost?

I had been reading books by mediums who all seemed in accord in the belief that spirits continued to evolve in the afterlife and were very happy there. I doubted there was much a spirit might need from one of us. I thought about asking the experts, but realized that those who took a more scientific approach might find this question confusing. Considering who Christian was, they might also find it offensive.

Sharon Gill from the IGHS, who had shown compassion toward Christian's frustration, might be the person to ask, but what if she suggested something that would be difficult for me to do, like the way people on fairy tale quests were tested? Then there might be no turning back: If I was given the answer, I had to act on it.

The idea nagged at me, so finally I sent Sharon a note. I thought she'd have an insightful response, and I was right.

"I would think when offering a gift to Christian," she responded, "you would want to consider something that was meaningful to him in life. A special scent, a candle lit on a special occasion, or maybe something that he had a special feeling for in life. I feel like there is something that will soften his anger for a time. Almost on the order of a token of peace. Katherine, I don't know where that's coming from, but I just started feeling a strong sensation that you already know what it is."

As with everything else in this realm, the bottom line was my own instinct. I "knew" him, so I should find a way to discern what he would want.

Then I had an idea. Why not put the question to him? Not as EVP, but through another medium. I decided to look up the instructions to the Ouija board. I'd tried it before, with poor results, but that could have been because I don't read instructions.

Right away I discovered that I'd done things wrong, more or less. The book said I should have a window open somewhere and insisted on other conditions that I had not met. Typical of me to just guess at what ought to be done rather than follow the ritual.

So I decided to try it again and see if Christian might let me know what kind of gift I should offer to a ghost to coax him to tell me just what it was he wanted me to know or do. (Just a side note here: I realize that some people will say that he already told me at the séance, but I wanted to hear it directly, not through a medium. I wasn't convinced that he wanted me to actually go kill his former partner. If he did, he'd have to tell me that himself.)

I waited until nearly midnight and cleared off a round antique table. On it I set a red candle and the board. Next to the board, I placed Christian's silver ring. I sat in a chair and worked to clear my mind. I was a little worried because a friend had used a ritual to discover that while all of my physical energy points were in balance, my "third eye" chakra was not working. In other words, I would have a hard time contacting spirits. I became as meditative as I know how to be and stayed that way for about twenty minutes, concentrating only on Christian. Everything was quiet. The window was open a few inches. The night was clear. The room around me was dark.

I breathed deeply a few times and then placed my hand on the planchette. Recently I'd read that several people had turned communications they'd received through the Ouija into best-selling books. While I didn't quite have that much time, I hoped that some spirit might see fit to send inspiration my way.

The planchette didn't budge. I waited, trying not to push it. Sometimes things just need a start and they go by themselves. I refrained. I waited until my arm nearly fell off and still got no results. Okay, back to meditation. Think myself through the chakras. Ohm, ohm, ohm. . . .

Now back to the board. Nothing.

This time I did push it, just a little. And that's how far it went.

I tried to blur my vision the way one reads auras, hoping I might see something in the room. I only saw a blur.

I grabbed the recorder and asked a few questions. Also nothing. Then I wondered if Christian was gone. Perhaps he was with Wraith again. Maybe I hadn't given him enough attention. Maybe he'd grown bored with the whole enterprise.

I'd heard about the "Decline Effect" in psychical research. That's when an investigator probes too closely and the phenomenon recedes, as if something prohibits full contact. I wondered if that might be happening here. I'd once viewed his haunting me as psychological trespass. Perhaps that's how he viewed this attempt to reach him. Maybe I should see his absence as a blessing.

Maybe . . .

But . . .

I was beginning to feel I had a situation like in *The Ghost and Mrs. Muir*. In that movie, a woman acquires the ghost of a sexy sea captain when she moves into his former residence. She comes to think of him as hers, the way Christian was *my* ghost. He was becoming a companion. I expected him to be around. But on the other hand, the sea captain had left Mrs. Muir alone for many years. When she wanted him back, she didn't get him—not till she died.

I wondered if I had offended him. I thought perhaps he'd found someone else who could see him and be more receptive. He liked attention. Maybe he liked it better from someone who had an active third eye.

So here I was, feeling jealous and abandoned by a ghost I didn't even believe in. What was happening to me? I'd started this quest in the hope of using the ring as a point of entrée so I could learn about the ghost world. Obviously something else was going on.

I picked up the ring, holding it tight, and tried the recorder again.

"Christian, are you here? Are you with me? Just let me know." Nothing.

I shoved the board away. Feeling silly about all this ritual, I blew out the candle and put everything away. So much for my right-brain access.

I went to bed. Then just before I feel asleep, I reached for the recorder and tried it again. "Are you here?"

"YES!" Loud and clear.

My mouth dropped open. "Oh . . . you . . . !"

He'd been playing with me. All that ritual nonsense. The mediums can use it if they want. It didn't work for me.

Nevertheless, I still did not know what to offer as a gift.

The next afternoon, I decided to see if I could get some EVP during the day. Obviously, there was no reason why ghosts should talk only at night—although I'd heard that the earth's energy shifts at certain dark hours to enhance communication. Anyway, I got out the recorder to give it a try.

I asked if this was the best way to communicate and got no response. Then I said, "Is there something you want to talk about?"

"Murder."

It was that clear. I had no doubt about the response.

Tentatively I asked, "Am I talking to Christian?" No response. "Is there someone else here?"

"Yes." This was a deep male voice. Michael?

"Do you want to talk about how you died?"

"Yes."

Okay, that was a good start. I didn't have to waste time trying to figure out whether or not to mention that uncomfortable fact. I got right to the point by asking if he was murdered. Blank.

gHost

"Were you betrayed?"

"Yes."

I ventured onto another troublesome topic by asking if he had killed himself. The response was strong, whatever it was, but not clearly a yes or no. I asked if he wanted to answer some questions about his death. He said yes, but try though I might, I got nothing further. I guessed he had found an open "window" of communication and that window had now closed.

Later that day, while I was mindlessly vacuuming (right brain?), I suddenly realized what Christian's gift should be. It was so obvious! Christian's favorite song. I went out in search of it and came back with a CD of Gordon Lightfoot's music. I put it on and pressed the "skip" button until I had the right selection: "The Wreck of the Edmund Fitzgerald." Wraith had told me that Christian would play this song over and over while he lay on the bed with his arms crossed over his chest and meditated. If ghosts had any kind of sensory apparatus, which it seemed they did if they could respond to questions, then Christian must be missing this song. I was sure he'd be pleased.

I listened to it once. The lyrics were eerie. The song was about the 1975 disappearance of an ore carrier on Lake Superior in Michigan. The lake never gives up her dead, the song says, when the winds of November overtake them. God, I felt *cold*.

An odd thing to meditate on—the slow awareness of a captain and his crew that they're soon going down into the icy water. But that was Christian. The thing about him that had hooked me was his embrace of death. To me it showed a great sense of vulnerability. That it had joined his rage to become a murderous inclination was abhorrent, but what he had displayed during his less aggressive periods was an abiding loneliness. A song like that, so persistently rehearsed and absorbed, spoke of his longing to go down with them. Maybe it *had* been suicide.

Anyway, it seemed to me that if he could get me to actually do something for him—besides murder Wraith—it was to play this tune that he had loved in life. So that's what I did, pressing the button that stayed on that one song, repeating it over and over.

After a while, I used the recorder to ask whether this was a good gift. I received no answer, not even the mumbling that sometimes serves as a response.

I was puzzled. "Is there something else you want?" I asked.

I thought there was a faint response, but could not tell if it was affirmative.

I asked these questions again, sensing that this might *not* be the gift he wanted but that he would not respond until I figured it out on my own. He didn't respond. I didn't know what else to do.

The next evening, I had dinner with a friend, Sue, who suggested that Christian ought to go to the families of his victims and serve as a guide, in order to get redemption. I couldn't convince her that this was no soul seeking salvation, not as long as revenge was an issue. He wasn't interested in crossing over.

"Look, just be careful," she said. "Don't let him get too close. He might want to possess you."

I was surprised. Possess me. I couldn't even imagine why. I mean, I was a woman and he'd been a gay man. Why would he want *my* experiences? On the other hand, Wraith had told me that Christian had wanted to be a writer. There certainly were gay writers around he could possess. But perhaps they were not receptive to him or they were uninterested in the darkness of psychopathology.

I recalled the weird sensation I'd had in bed a few nights. I'd had chills all over my scalp and a weird feeling of transport, as if someone was trying to get inside my mind. I had chalked it up to being tired, but now I wondered.

"Don't worry," I said to Sue. "I'm not even remotely curious about that."

But I was. I had seen a movie called *Kissed* about a woman who worked in a morgue. She'd use her body as a channel to help the spirits of the dead cross over. It was her observation that love is the craving for transformation, a desire to defy boundaries, and she was happy to free them. I'd been enchanted with the idea that a person could provide such a service. Of course, she only did it for beautiful young men.

That night I once again asked whoever was behind the EVP if this music was the gift he wanted, and again there was no response. I was getting frustrated. I put the recorder down and told him he could say whatever he wanted. I was just going to read.

Well, he was talkative enough in a rather indeciperhable way, so he was there. I asked again about the music. Nothing. So I went to bed.

The next night, I put the music on and allowed it to play through the Lightfoot song several times. I turned out the lights and got into a state of meditation, letting the music penetrate until I had a feeling for the rhythm. Once more, I asked about my gift.

Once more, the ghost was silent.

Damn! I'd spent $14.95 for nothing.

Exasperated, recalling Sue's fears, I asked, "Well what do you want, then? Do you want to *possess* me?"

I stopped the recorder and hit the playback. The response was clear.

"Yes."

Oh, Lord. Why had I asked *that*?

No, I'd heard that wrong. I had to put that differently. Slowly, carefully, I asked, "Am I to understand that the music is not the gift you want, I am?"

"Yes." It was loud and surrounded by static, but it was clear.

I sat there in the dark. My apartment suddenly felt threatening. Something was in there with me—something that was seeking a way in. I suddenly had the sensation of a big black cloud floating around me, watching me, just waiting to close around and suffocate me. *He thinks he can return, and isn't believing half the battle?* That's what Jacqueline had said. Maybe I *was* getting in over my head. Maybe he was stronger than I thought. I recalled Wraith warning me that whatever Christian wants, he gets. At that moment, I felt very much alone with this entity.

"Okay," I said quietly as I turned off the music. Hoping to hide my fear, I stood and looked at a dark corner, because I did not know where he—it—was. I felt completely defenseless and a little anxious, but also quite clear.

"This is going to be a test of wills," I told whomever, "because that's a gift I'm not willing to give." I turned off the lights and went to bed.

—**3**—

Recalling what Dave Oester and Sharon Gill said about finding a shaman, it seemed now that I should take that more seriously. I sent word to some friends from college to see if anyone knew where "Merlin" was. I call him that because he had told me that the merlin falcon was his totem. It fit him. The merlin is an agile predator that lives on the edge of wooded areas in open spaces. It's solitary and highly territorial. To outwit its prey, it mimics the flight pattern of nonpredatory birds and then swoops in.

While I waited for word back, I looked into this idea of possession.

I had an encyclopedia of ghosts written by Hans Holzer, and one of the sections was about haunted people. He stated that true cases of ghosts attaching themselves to a person are not common. "The at-tachment represents an emotional problem that has not been fully resolved." These types of ghosts, it seems, have more opportunities to "get through" because they can manifest themselves in numerous places. When the spirit becomes demanding, it requires consultation with an expert.

I also read Richard Noll's account of possession in *Bizarre Diseases of the Mind*. He was a psychologist with some expertise in apparent "supernatural disorders." In his book, he discussed the case of a woman named "Trudy," a thirty-eight-year-old married teacher. In a psychiatric paper about her written in 1984, she described feeling a "force" come inside of her. This force began to suggest things to her and then to sexually assault her. It turns out that she had experienced several delusions before this malady struck. Still, the psychiatrists who examined her saw no evidence of a thought disorder or psychosis. They were utterly puzzled by her situation. Noll goes on to note that some psychiatrists refuse to rule out the influence of discarnate entities in mental illness—particularly dissociative identity disorder. Sometimes an exorcist is in order.

Well, I didn't know any depossession experts who were close at hand. Anyway, I wasn't possessed yet. Nevertheless, I did contemplate a case similar to "Trudy" described in a book called *The Entity*. It was about a woman in California who was attacked by a brutal, vile spirit every night. He raped her, swore at her, threatened her, and essentially trapped her. He didn't possess her, but he certainly attached himself to her. Even the parapsychologists who came in were unable to help. They went so far as to rebuild her house in a gymnasium so they could make a scientific study and find a way to deflect the phenomenon. They failed. She ended up institutionalized—which also did not end the attacks. As far as I understood, no one ever quite knew what that was all about.

I had heard several stories of people to whom ghosts had attached themselves—some of them quite possessively. A woman on Long Island had a ghost lover who interfered in any attempt she made to become involved with a living, breathing man. (Well, at least she got *something* out of it.) And certainly Wraith had attested to the fact that when Christian possessed him, it was usually for some erotic purpose. He had claimed that Christian wanted to use his body to reexperience the sensual pleasures of the flesh.

The idea of an incubus or spirit that has sexual manifestations has been part of Western mythology for centuries. Attempts to explain it as some wish fulfillment fail adequately to address the reported cases of those who claim to have been molested by a ghost. From a man staying at an English inn who had a most pleasant night, to women in their homes in New York, Florida, and California, erotic experiences with ghosts seem to occur almost anywhere. Not that all cases of possession are erotic, and not all erotic paranormal encounters become possessions, but given who we were speaking about, I had no doubt that whatever he might want with me was an issue both of control and of his own pleasure.

Possession is an alteration in a person's consciousness and behavior in some highly uncharacteristic way. Usually that person is thought to be mentally ill if dysfunctional, eccentric if not. Some psychologists who have a more spiritual bent claim that they have had cases where these changes in personality are accompanied by such obvious paranormal events that the best explanation is possession by a spirit. I've read that in many cases of possession, it was just some confused spirit getting entangled in the aura of the living. An unfortunate happenstance. Dr. Malachi Martin, a Jesuit who wrote *Hostage to the Devil,* claims that possession cannot occur without the consent of the victim. However, that consent can be subliminal.

According to Dr. Edith Fiore, who wrote *The Unquiet Dead,* the ten most common signs of possession are low energy, character shifts or mood swings, inner voices, substance abuse, impulsivity, blackouts, impaired concentration, anxiety or depression, onset of physical problems, and emotional reactions to reading her book.

I had an emotional reaction to it, but that was because she was too quick to diagnose a mental illness as a spirit infestation. She claimed she had seen over five hundred possessions in seven years and that over 70 percent of her patients suffered from possessions that would otherwise be diagnosed as mental disorders. Some of these people were hosts to numerous entities—as many as fifty or more. They were usually relieved of their symptoms with depossession techniques.

All of the things on her list are easily attributable to physical or mental causes, and all can generally be treated with drugs or therapy. I didn't quite buy into her beliefs, but I went on to read what else she had to say.

She pointed out that possession is a cross-cultural phenomenon. In China, ancestor worship translates into spirits who interfere with the lives of those who are not on good terms with their relatives. One Japanese cult believed that 80 percent of physical ailments were caused by possessions. The dishonored dead also showed up in ancient Egypt to bedevil the living, while Indians have a religion that identifies seven different bodies for each person. The lowest body is the physical, and each subsequent body corresponds to a different plane of reality, progressively vibrating at increasingly higher frequencies. The closest invisible body to the physical is the etheric, which psychics can see. Etheric bodies are on the lowest level of the astral plane, which divides the physical and spiritual worlds. Those on the highest are mentors or guides. The etheric entities, still trapped by their desires, might attempt to attach themselves to physical bodies. They can enter the body of those whose astral body has some defect.

This view has gained some popularity among spiritualists in our country. I'd heard that notion often and wondered how one could find and repair the defect. Was it like a slow leak in a tire? Or was it some personality disorder that caused an aberration in the way the aura formed around you?

One thing in this book made me sit up and take notice. Dr. Fiore mentioned that the existence of some spirits revolved around revenge. If they had been murdered, they stayed around to attack their killer in some way. If they already had a negative frame of mind when alive, their "vibrations" were lower than most, so it becomes easier for them to remain earthbound. They might try to possess the person who had done them in or even to kill him. Whatever that person was like in life he would continue to be as a spirit. When they attempt possession, that doesn't satisfy them, either, and they don't even realize that they are hindering their own evolution. If their death involved physical pain, they continue to feel it.

There was also a section devoted to people who are possessed by a spirit of the opposite sex. Generally, their hormonal systems are negatively affected and they go through a period of sexual confusion. Sex drive may increase or diminish, and relationships can be seriously damaged.

I guessed that if that were the case, it would be easy to know if Christian had possessed me. Or maybe not. I mean, we both found Wraith attractive. Maybe we had similar taste in men. I'd probably have to look for other mental or emotional signals.

Fiore and others have indicated that protection comes from one's own inner strength and evolved spirituality. You vibrate at a frequency too high for the lower beings to penetrate your aura, and spirits at the higher frequencies don't want to possess anyone. The aura is like an immune system. It weakens and you weaken. Any condition that causes you to lose consciousness, such as a trance or passing out, opens you up to potential possession. The same for substance abuse, serious illness, fatigue, loss and grief, or obsessive negative emotions. I noted that sitting in an unprotected séance or using automatic writing were replete with risk. As I understood it, Christian would have to vibrate higher to get to me, or he'd have to create conditions to bring me lower—illness, depression, bad dreams, and the like. I wondered if I could entice him higher. Induce him to desire to be healed.

This was interesting, but it seemed to me that if Christian *could* possess me, he would already have done so by now. I'd had the ring for two years. I'd been actively aware of the possibility of his existence for several months, and I'd certainly been fatigued during that time. I'd even experienced a terrible loss. At no point had he found an entry point in my aura sufficiently weak to let him through. In fact, it now occurred to me that his revelation of the "gift" he wanted only further strengthened me against him. Perhaps he'd hoped only to scare me.

While I was reading about possession, I came across a description of a type of ghost known in Buddhist and Hindu lore as a *preta,* or a Hungry Ghost. It resides on the lower segment of the Wheel of Life and has accumulated a lot of bad karma to work off. It exists in a state of perpetual hunger and thirst (like a vampire), and this torture continues until it balances its karmic debts. A *preta* can only escape its condition when certain rites are performed to release it. Sounded like Christian.

In fact, Wraith told me that Christian believed he himself had been possessed since birth by an entity, an Egyptian. It seemed, then, that possession was already a firm idea in his psyche. Whoever, or whatever, he was, I had to be more careful. It could very well be that he was gathering energy for an attack.

—4—

I decided to approach a folklorist from Delaware named Ed Okonowicz. He had written a book called *Possessed Possessions,* and I thought he would have some insight about my ring. He invited me to come take his ghost tour some Friday night, so I decided to kill two birds with one stone.

Of medium height, trim, and wearing glasses, Ed is always in motion. If he's not looking for more haunted places to write about in books like *Presence in the Parlor* and *Up the Back Stairway,* he's coming up with new ideas for a series of novels about a fictional place called Delmarva. He has enough energy to feed a legion of ghosts, if in fact they get their energy from us. Having grown up in Wilmington, he specialized in local legends and traveled into other states to present programs at schools, private gatherings, libraries, and special Halloween events. He gave me copies of his many ghost books, and when I read them, I knew I had to talk with him. Thus, was I on my way to Delaware for a Friday-night ghost tour.

On Pea Patch Island, east of Delaware City, a fort was completed in 1861. It was meant as protection for cities along the Delaware River, like Wilmington and Philadelphia, but ended up serving as a POW camp during the Civil War for Confederate soldiers. Thirty-three thousand men eventually were imprisoned there on an island that could bear only one fourth that number. Due to its deplorable conditions, it became known as the "Andersonville of the North." Approximately 2,700 prisoners died there, mostly from disease.

Ed led regular ghost tours to the island, accompanied by historical interpreter Dale Fetzer. Ed explained that there is no electricity on the island, which adds to the eeriness. It remains as it was during the Civil War era. Although they used dressed-up park personnel to create a ghostly impression, there has been at least one sighting during a tour that was not of one of them.

Ed and I met for dinner beforehand to discuss objects that seemingly were possessed by a spiritual power. He'd had a few mild encounters with apparently paranormal events, but he was not what I would call a believer. Nevertheless, he paid close attention to the stories he collected and listened with a sympathetic ear. One story that interested me was about a carved wooden chair owned by a Maryland antiques dealer, John Klisavage. This man had experienced several episodes of bad luck as he moved the chair around his shop. He finally learned that the chair had been built specifically for people who could send their spirits out from their bodies to travel to distant places. The chair "protected" them. That meant that it supposedly had its own energy source. I wanted to check that out.

I asked Ed if a spirit could truly haunt objects, and his response was that if spirits can haunt a place because of its significance to them, then he supposed they could also haunt an object—or at least use it for an after-death message. He mentioned a tale in *Possessed Possessions* about a jade ring. A young man named Kevin had given it to his childhood sweetheart, Holly, as a wedding ring, but the marriage did not last. Nevertheless, they retained a strong emotional bond. Holly placed the ring in a safe-deposit box. Then one day, Kevin was in a serious accident. While he was in the hospital, Holly opened the box and held the ring for a moment, then put it back. At that time, it was in good condition. When Kevin died shortly thereafter, she went to get the ring to place it with him. To her surprise, the jade had cracked all the way through.

She believed it was a special signal from him to her through a possession that had meant something to both of them.

There were sinister possessions as well. Ed also mentioned a wood-carver, Axel Gustafson from New York, whose carvings were associated with frightening events in the lives of several art collectors. According to neighbors who knew him, Gustafson seemed to be cursed. His attempts to support his family generally failed. He kept to himself and obsessively carved his animals while forcing his children to work. Both his wife and daughter died mysteriously, possibly by poisoning. After Gustafson died, his work became valuable to collectors, and a young couple, Suzanne and James Hofmeister, decided to find as many pieces as they could. They contacted Gustafson's surviving relatives, who treated them with suspicion and then moved away without a forwarding address. The Hofmeisters were mystified by this behavior until they started to collect stories from people who owned one of Gustafson's carved animals.

The first respondents told them that bringing a wooden deer head into their home had triggered intense poltergeist activity. They believed it was his spirit and it frightened them, so they left it outside. Another couple that bought some carvings started having terrible nightmares. Believing the pieces to be evil, the couple sold them, and things returned to normal. A third collector was afflicted with a number of injuries and illnesses after purchasing her piece. Yet the most disturbing story came from a man named John, a Vietnam vet.

He had bought a six-foot giraffe and stored it in a friend's barn. Subsequently, he discovered that the friend had inexplicably chopped it into pieces and burned it. John would not reveal the reason. Shortly thereafter, both of them died of cancer. Then John's house burned down with two more Gustafson pieces in it. The Hofmeisters have no explanations, but those who know the ghost world might say that Gustafson's obsession with the carvings, coupled with his apparent cruelty, might have created an emotional zone around certain items that radiated negatively into the lives of people who took possession of them.

Some objects seemed to have a lot of power—and it isn't always good. I asked Ed what he made of these stories.

"I recently read a book written by the exorcist of Rome, Father Gabriel Amorth," he said. "The chapters on haunted objects, houses, and pets makes a strong association with diabolical infestation, which is one of the six levels of 'extraordinary activity' associated with possession." Objects that seemed to have mysterious powers, then, were associated with something demonic.

He didn't have to convince me. My ring already seemed more sinister. However, Amorth's book had struck me as rather extreme, and I was more inclined to believe that Christian's personality, like Gustafan's, had left a negative aura than that I had a demon.

After dinner we went with the tour group on a boat called the *Delafort*. Once in the fort, Ed and I edged away and placed my recorder on one of the bunks in a room that had housed officers, to be retrieved later. I also took photos in the sally port, the kitchen, and out on the parade ground. I was rather shocked to get numerous orbs, particularly outside. Dave had mentioned that getting numerous orbs indicated the possibility of dust particles, but I got this effect in only about one out of ten shots; it made little sense that dust would show only a small percentage of the time—especially since the photos were taken in quick succession. Oddly, I got only a few in the dungeons, where conditions had been the worst—and where dust was more evident.

Ed said that ghostly figures had been seen in various places, usually in uniform or a dark cape, but the story that seemed most poignant to me was of an artist who had been painting the landscape. A young boy had approached her, soaking wet, and then seemed not to be there. She mentioned it to the park official, and he told her that a young boy had fallen from a boat two days earlier and drowned. He was wearing the same clothes that she had described.

On the way back, we listened to the contents of the recorder. It was rough, with a few loud sounds, but nothing intelligible. I wouldn't venture to say they were voices. However, I was pleased with the photos. Ed wasn't too interested in orbs, but I think he was happy to know that these pictures had shown manifestations. It surprised him that I had gotten so few in the kitchen, since that was one of the areas where many strange things had been reported. I guess orbs go where they want to go.

In any event, I had learned to take the possibility of a haunted ring a bit more seriously, so it was time to contact someone who actually had owned a haunted object himself. I didn't expect the added bonus of a good ghost story.

—5—

I drove further south to the upper Chesapeake Bay region in Maryland to visit Havre de Grace on the Susquehanna River. This little town is the home of decoy art, but I was there to learn more about the astral projection chair. The idea that an object could have some kind of energy that gave it the power to "know" and "do" things was just too intriguing to pass up. Before going to the antique store, I decided to check into a B&B that Ed had told me about: the Spencer-Silver Mansion. Built in 1896, it was a beautifully restored Victorian furnished with an impressive collection of quality antiques. The rooms were large and the atmosphere homey. As I walked in, I noticed parlors to the right and left, one formal and the other more comfortable. As it turned out, choosing this place added something more to my knowledge about ghosts that threaten.

Carol, a nurturing woman with pretty eyes whose casual manner made me feel right at home, ran the inn. She told me about a place in town where she once lived and had experienced three apparitions. One was a small girl with long brown hair just sitting on the steps. Carol nearly ran into her going down and literally jumped over the banister to avoid her. Then she turned and saw that no one was there.

The other two ghosts were more frightening, and it was her feeling that they intended harm. "I don't even like to talk about them," she said, "because I'm afraid it will attract them here." Nevertheless, she told me how one night she had heard two men in her home walking up the stairs. It sounded as though they were wearing heavy work boots. She was sure they were burglars. She decided not to wake her husband because she did not want trouble. If they thought the homeowners were asleep, maybe they would just take what they wanted and leave. However, she kept her eyes opened just a slit to keep watch. One man came into the room and stood by the bed. He dropped to his knees right by Carol and watched her. She was sure he could hear her heart thumping, and she believed he might attack her. Then the other man walked into the room and said that they ought to leave. The kneeling man rose and followed him out. When Carol heard no further noise, she woke her husband and insisted they had been robbed. She described the men. Her husband went down and searched the house, only to report that there had been no break-in. She was astonished.

Over the next few months, several people who stayed with them reported noise during the night of men in work boots walking around in the house, and Carol's young daughter claimed to see a man who frightened her in her room. It wasn't long before Carol learned something astonishing about the location of her home. A neighbor behind her pointed out the headstones that she had retrieved in the yard—the house had been built on top of an old cemetery. Carol noticed that one of the headstones was for a young girl, age four—about the age of the child she had seen on her steps. She wondered if the two men had been buried there as well.

For me, this story confirmed my childhood fear that ghosts go right to the one who's aware of them, and afraid. The image of that hovering man next to her bed stayed with me for a long time after the telling.

From the B&B I went over to meet John Klisavage, the tall and wiry owner of Washington Street Books. John loves to talk, and his shop had become a hub for strange and interesting people. Nearly every object has a story attached to it, and some things that come in are never going to leave because he loves them too much. John himself seems to be the embodiment of chaos theory. When he tells a story, he adds so many complicated sidelines that it's hard to follow the chronology, and yet it's all clear in his own mind. It's chaos only on the surface.

He was willing to discuss the chair, so we went to the local diner where we could talk all night without being thrown out. First he gave me a light blue stone that was "calling" to belong to me. It was angelite, mined in Peru and used to connect with higher powers. It was also used for telepathy, creativity, and astral travel.

"I'm a healer," John told me. I asked what he meant and got a tale that started with how he was born, included the chair and other haunted items, and wound through numerous connections with other healers and psychics. Pulling up the sleeves of his plaid flannel shirt, he told me to watch for goosebumps, because his story gave him chills.

He repeatedly warned me that I ought not to keep this ring because it could ruin my life. It could seduce me further into the darkness or be a portal for negative spirits, the way a Ouija board is. He believed I didn't know what I was getting myself into. "The more you focus, the more you bring him to you," he insisted. Well, that's what I was *trying* to do.

There are energy patterns, John explained, that will draw to them the energy that is like them. "He could lead you into his lifestyle. One day you could find yourself with a knife in your hand and wonder why." I just shrugged. I didn't foresee anything like that. And I wasn't parting with this ring, not without real evidence that it could do me some harm. Besides, Ouija boards hadn't worked, either. So far, not one prediction to me from any of these seers had come true.

I turned his attention to the story of the astral-traveling chair. John pulled out a set of photographs so that I could see it for myself, because he no longer owned it. I was impressed. It was an astonishing piece. Built in the 1860s, it had a wide seat—big enough for a very large man—and a back and seat ornately carved in dark wood. There were no arms. In back, two wings off the shoulders gave the appearance that it could just fly away, and down the center were carvings that looked exceedingly uncomfortable to lean against. The centerpiece was a Jack-in-the-Green face, and below that was an odd arrangement of human parts: a face, breasts, a man's muscled rib cage over a woman's smooth and plump belly. This arrangement also sported wings. On the seat were several carved symbols that represented the four winds.

"To work," John said, "the chair needs to be placed in the proper alignment with the earth." It had surprised him that so many people had entered the store and not seen the chair, although it was a conspicuous piece. He took that to mean that the chair had protected itself by making itself invisible. He also learned that the chair seemed to take energy from people who stood near it. Many people, including himself, felt completely drained by it.

A psychic friend warned him that it would draw both good and bad energies into the store and that it was better to be rid of it. He also said that someone would come to buy it who would know what it was for, and that a sign would indicate that John was to let it go: Every noise in the store would suddenly stop.

Before any buyers came, various people entered and told John ghost stories or added to his knowledge about magical objects like crystals and sacred objects. He believed that the chair was drawing them in. At one point he put it in the window, and suddenly business came to a halt. People came in but no one bought anything. The chair, he decided, had "protected" his store by keeping things he wanted to sell right there. He moved it. After that, twelve people came into the store and every one of them bought something. John did not think that was a coincidence.

Then one day, two men and a woman came in. They were dressed in black and sported strange hairstyles, as if they were members of a cult. One of the men did all the talking while the others remained silent. At some point while he chatted with John about the chair, John realized that the store had grown silent. All the motors that usually ran were off. That was the "sign," so John sold them the chair. He knew they were the rightful owners. His experience with it had opened his eyes to spiritual possibilities, so he set out to learn about his own inner energies so he could use them to help others. That's how he became a healer.

It was interesting to hear all of that, but I wanted most to learn about how a person could be protected in the spirit realm by something like a chair. Where did the energy come from, and how did it get attached to a chair? I had the impression from this tale that it had to be an object that had been designed and made in some sort of sacred ritual—although that did not really answer my questions. John did not have any answers, either, except that he was convinced that energy did attach to objects and I had to be careful. He worried that my ring had powers that I did not understand, and he felt certain that Christian was not in the light. John urged me to find a guide who could help.

—6—

When I returned from Delaware, I found two messages on my machine. The first was from Merlin. He had a voice that came from his gut, deep and grounded. It gave the impression of comfort and wisdom, and I was disappointed that the message was so brief. He would be happy to talk to me about his understanding of the spirit world, he said, but he wanted to do that in person. Could I come to Arizona? He gave a number to call.

By contrast, the second message was disturbing.

"I want the ring," Wraith said in that polished Southern accent. "Take it back to where you got it and leave it on the rock. I'll be watching."

I'd been waiting for that one. Wraith was far too attached to his ghost to give up an object like this so easily. For all I knew, he might ambush me, and I wasn't about to step into a trap. Besides, I still didn't know what Christian wanted. I'd give the ring back when I was ready, and on my own terms. Maybe.

I called Merlin. It was great to hear his voice again. It brought to mind his Native American features, his long dark hair, opaque brown eyes, and stocky build. I recalled how he walked in a solid, confident manner as if completely attuned to the earth. After so many years, we still had a connection and it felt as if I could just walk next door to visit him. I gave him a brief idea of what I wanted to know. He listened patiently and then said, "It's dangerous to contact these dark spirits. They're unpredictable. You'll be walking through fire."

His imagery was on target. "I feel like I already am," I said. "It's like this spirit is enticing me but putting up every barrier."

"Maybe the barrier is you."

He always turned things around on me, but I actually liked that trait. It made me keep my eyes open to possibilities I hadn't considered. "Maybe," I acknowledged.

I heard him draw a breath, as if he was not sure whether to say what was on his mind. Then he went ahead. "You should be an experienced shaman to do such a thing. And most of them wouldn't even attempt it."

"I know, but what if this man was murdered and won't be at rest until he's able to make it known what happened to him? What if I can help?"

He laughed. "I think you're not telling me your real motives."

He still knew me. He had a way of seeing beyond my words, and he knew that I had a thing for the devilish. Even so, it actually had occurred to me that I might be able to do something for this spirit. I made arrangements to come out there at his convenience so we could discuss this at length. In the meantime, he urged me to continue to learn all I could about communication with spirits, particularly about protecting myself. He also urged me again to think about my motives.

To that point, I hadn't really considered my motives. I wasn't even sure if I was the one who had initiated all of this. Wraith had told me that Christian had picked me, and it wasn't exactly over Wraith's dead body that I'd ended up with the ring. I'd been told that Christian came with the ring, and I'd been curious to see if that were true. Simply put, I wanted to see a ghost. Then, as I had learned more about how one contacts the spirit world, I'd had the sense that Christian wanted something from me. Now I was beginning to feel that while he might have some purpose, I had a purpose as well: I wanted him to find peace.

I did some research on the various forms of spirit communication and leaned about a place in Florida called Cassadaga. Earlier in the century it had been a spiritualist camp because the area was considered to be a "vortex"—an area where the earth's spiritual energy is more intense. Mediums and psychics of all sorts still lived there. I thought it might be a good place to see if I could get a consistent opinion on my situation. My only reservation was heading south again. That call from Wraith worried me. I decided not to tell anyone where I was going, not even Christian.

Seeking the Spirits

"GHOSTS ARE EVERYWHERE."
—DAVE OESTER

—1—

On the plane to Florida, I continued to read about EVP. I had *Talks with the Dead* by William Welch, a Hollywood scriptwriter with an interest in survival after death, Sarah Estep's *Voices of Eternity,* and *The Ghost of 29 Megacylces* by John G. Fuller.

The first book gave me a sense of what had happened with the EVP movement after Raudive's *Breakthrough.* I had left off in the early seventies with Bander's account and I'd wondered who had picked it up from there. I learned that others were carrying on experiments independent of Raudive and getting similar results. Welch was one of them. He was interested in finding some mechanical means for communicating with those who had passed on, so when he heard about von Szalay's work, he started up his own investigations. He referred to those on the other side as "technicians" and imagined them working hard on ways to break through. At one point, he mentioned that they might be able to help "receivers" (us) improve our abilities. That interested me. If ghosts could help me see or hear them, I was ready to find out how.

It was intriguing to learn that after his death, Raudive actually communicated with other EVP investigators, including Estep and Welch, although in the literature I'd read to that point, he mostly just said his name. Even Thomas Edison made an appearance, albeit to a psychic, but with instructions for how to modify some of the equipment and use the plans that he had devised for spirit communication just before his death. (Someone did build this machine, which consisted of an aluminum trumpet attached to an aerial that used potassium permanganate to amplify "ether waves," but got no results.) There was also a book, *Phone Calls from the Dead,* that documented numerous accounts in various places of people who had received calls from, and conversed with, dead people whom they knew. Sometimes they realized the person was dead, other times they only found out later. It was in this book that I learned a more specific definition of a thoughtform—what the blind psychic, Steve, had said Christian was. It's a psychic entity mentally created by someone and endowed with psychokinetic powers and it can take on a life of its own. In other words, people could be producing the EVP effects. That was another form of wishful thinking that did not fit all—even most—of the cases.

Then George Meek, a research engineer, arrived on the scene and in 1977 found a way to accelerate the development of paranormal connections. John Fuller wrote his remarkable story, and Meek followed that with a book of his own.

In the seventies, Fuller had written the account of his investigation of reports he had received about ghost sightings on Eastern Airlines L-1011 jets. Both crew and passengers had talked of seeing and hearing the voices of the deceased captain and flight engineer of the ill-fated flight 401 that crashed in the Florida Everglades in 1972. Eastern's management suppressed the reports for fear of losing customers, but the subsequent investigation uncovered the fact that parts of the fallen aircraft had been salvaged and used on other planes of its type. The ghost sightings continued, especially among those who had known the deceased, and complaints were so numerous that Eastern finally removed the parts from those planes.

Fuller applied all manner of investigative journalism to discover the truth, but the source of the alleged hauntings remained a mystery. He interviewed witnesses willing to tell their stories and discovered pages missing from logbooks for flights on which some of the sightings occurred. He was skeptical but open, concluding that something was genuine about this haunting, and his book remains one of the classic descriptions of paranormal phenomena.

I was curious to see how he would treat EVP, the subject of this 1981 publication. Typical of his style, he approached it with cautious curiosity. According to his account, Meek had contacted him with an incredible story. It seems that the ghost of a NASA scientist, Dr. George Mueller, had visited an uneducated man in Pennsylvania named Bill O'Neil, who possessed mediumistic abilities. Mueller had died fourteen years earlier, but he wanted to help O'Neil design some equipment that operated at 29 megahertz that would facilitate two-way communication between them. O'Neil contacted the editor of a paranormal magazine, who put him in touch with Meek. When Meek met O'Neil and checked out what Mueller had offered thus far (his social security number, his career history, and unlisted phone numbers of colleagues), he believed that what Mueller said was possible. Meek then funded O'Neil's efforts to continue to get information, and he helped put together a complicated device that would achieve their dreams. It was called Spiricom. After months of futile experimentation, on October 27, 1977, the first voice came through. Instead of the typical brief and mundane comments often recorded for EVP, this was a real conversation. The content concerned getting the controls right. They got nothing more for quite some time, but by 1980 they had held over twenty hours of extended dialogue.

People around the world who were experimenting with EVP were ecstatic. Many groups set about learning this technology and improving it. In 1982 Sarah Estep started the AA-EVP, joining together hundreds of experimenters in many different countries. Her own initial reaction to voices on tape was disbelief. She had seen plenty of fraud and delusion as a psychical investigator. She'd come across a book about "psi" discoveries that described EVP, and since it did not require mediumistic talents or special equipment, she decided to give it a try. Using an old recorder, she made the decision to try it every day for a week. Each morning and each evening, she recorded for two hours. She asked basic questions such as "Is anyone here?" But she received no responses. Growing bored, she decided to change her question to "What is your world like?" To her surprise, she got a voice on her tape recorder that said, "Beauty." That began a major effort on her part, recording daily, to continue to try to get contact from wherever these voices originated.

For the most part, messages were brief, such as "Come down, we must do good," and "We're going to help you." She reported that receivers frequently get requests for help, prayers, and guidance from souls who seemed unaware they were dead. She asked questions on specific topics, such as what their existence was like and whether rein-carnation is true. In *Voices of Eternity,* she reported her many results. One thing she said confirmed my own initial results: When asking how the entities are able to speak to us, one of them said, "I shout." While that seemed to be the case only with some, it did explain why the early responses I had received were loud and aggressive.

According to what Estep learned, the spirits are drawn to the researchers or brought to them by entities whose job it is to rescue lost souls. The messages sometimes appeared to be warnings of what it means to be unprepared for death. Some people think these commu-nications are from extraterrestrials. (I had already received e-mail from someone who feels certain that ghosts and ETs have some association, and I read some ideas on the Internet about how Spirit relates it all—human spirits and other planetary races—together.) More often, people recognized the voice of someone they had known. Estep feels fairly certain from her many communications that these entities are trying to help us to improve our lives and connect with them for some higher purpose. Eventually she moved from a tape recorder to using a com-puter with a microphone.

Spiricom ushered in the new field known as ITC, or Instrumen-tal Transcommunication—the use of multiple electronic systems for the purpose of communication. In 1983, Hans-Otto Koenig in West Ger-many develop equipment that used low-frequency oscillators. An acous-tics expert, he was invited onto an international radio show to demonstrate ITC. Koenig carefully set up his equipment under the scru-tiny of the station's engineers. When someone asked if they could get a direct response, a voice came through with, "Otto Koenig makes wire-less with the dead." It was a stunning moment, and it wasn't long before audio-video contact was also established and spirit images were seen on televisions.

With all of that, it still seemed that electromagnetic energy was a crucial factor in successful communication. Some people felt that we all have a certain amount of ectoplasm and that groups of people get better results because they make more ecto and energy available as a contact medium. I noted that there also seems to be an "experimenter effect." Those with a negative attitude hinder the process. (One wonders if their attitude somehow alters their available energy.) Having fun and maintaining a playful attitude appeared to help researchers get the best results—again, high energy.

In the nineties, an international organization was formed for cooperation among researchers of ITC, which flourished for two years.

"Enhanced ITC" included telephone conversations with spirits, pictures of the dead on television, extended messages through the radio, images through the fax, and text on computers. To my surprise, it seemed that some of those first generation EVP researchers, such as Jurgenson and Raudive, had died and returned as spirits to the next generation to assist them with refining the methods. They gave specific instructions about equipment and offered brief descriptions of the Other Side. Scientists in places like Luxemburg and Germany were collecting some very impressive technological data from a team of ghosts that called itself TimeStream. They wanted to help, although they communicated that being a spirit was not like anything that any living person could imagine. It was wondrous, even busy. None of our theories even came close to describing it.

Then trouble developed among the members of ITC, and the accounts of that research dried up. I soon realized that whether certain results were to be believed was a rather hotly debated political issue. In other words, some were apparently fabricated or faked. An American member, Mark Macy, intends to move ITC beyond this impasse.

From these books, and from sources online, I compiled a basic consensus about recording voices:

- *We can hear spirits talking among themselves as they wait to communicate.*
- *We need to use white noise or low-level music as a medium (humming?).*
- *One often must listen closely and repetitively to interpret what is said.*
- *The messages may sound like speaking in tongues or reverse speech.*
- *Researchers often hear their own names called.*
- *There is an acoustic window that only opens randomly and for a brief time.*
- *Sometimes messages change languages in midsentence.*
- *It is generally better to use an external microphone and earphones.*
- *Amplifiers can pick up weaker voices.*

I had already heard from practically everyone that one had to be in the right frame of mind to try to contact the Other Side. Thoughts about positive things drew "higher" spirits, because we "vibrated" at a higher frequency. Could Christian be helped to vibrate higher, or was he simply lost?

Some people shunned digital recorders because of the static, recommending only regular tape recorders, while other thought that digitals were the best thing that ever happened to EVP. Despite static, voices could be heard and amplified.

Some said you had to have a psychic connection with whomever you were trying to contact, and that the person needed to have a reason to make the connection, while others believed that this was all random.

Some claimed you needed to invoke protection with prayer or meditation; others had no such ritual.

Some play the recorder for a certain period of time and then play it back; others just go by instinct, using a Q&A format.

Everyone said—and they were right—that one needed patience and commitment.

What was becoming obvious to me was that, despite all this excitement about electronics and acoustics, there had been some communications that were clearly instructive. It seemed that existence after death was still occupied with learning and evolving. If we were self-limiting in life, we would have similar problems in the afterlife. If we were mean, unhappy, hateful, or intolerant in life, that would follow us. Better to think about developing the type of personality with which we wanted to exist for a very long time, because a more evolved state of mind at death meant a better chance of getting to higher places afterward.

I felt some degree of compassion for Christian. If he'd had such bad parenting that he'd become hardened and cold, then he was going to stay that way unless some mechanism was in place in the spirit world to assist such souls. In fact, Wraith had indicated the worst: *If you think he was mean in life, you should see him as a ghost.*

—2—

I arrived in Orlando and picked up my niece, Ming Lea Hower. She's a striking young woman, half Filipina, half Caucasian, with dark, almond-shaped eyes and smooth skin. She works at SeaWorld and has an interest in marine biology. Eager to learn how to ghost-hunt, she had jumped at the chance to come with me. Her husband, Jimmi, does not believe in ghosts, but he nevertheless warned her not to bring any home! She had not yet experienced EVP or ghost photography, and I figured that was something one must be there to really appreciate.

We were heading north to meet a pair of ghost hunters, Jeff Reynolds and Krista Mattson, in St. Augustine, a city that dates back to the sixteenth century. They had been to Cassadaga several times, and I hoped they could tell me more about it. We also planned to do a little ghosting together so Ming could learn how. And while there, I was to have yet one more near-contact experience.

As we set out, Ming told me that her friends at work thought she was crazy.

"Why?" I asked.

"They just think this is scary."

"It is. But that's why it's fun."

I didn't think she quite believed that.

The St. Francis Inn at 279 George Street in St. Augustine's re-stored district has several ghost stories. The Spanish residence was built of native coquina limestone (crushed shells in 1791), making it the oldest inn in the city. A weathered statue of Saint Francis among the banana trees greets all visitors. An interesting part of the inn's history includes a rumor that during the Civil War Confederate spies occupied the house.

We got a first-floor room on the enclosed garden courtyard. Furnished with an antique bed and armoire, it also had an electric fireplace. The haunted room on the third floor, 3A is usually booked long in advance. Things turn on and off by themselves, TV channels get switched, bags are knocked over, and people feel watched. It's called "Anna's Room," after a previous owner, although the ghost is said to be Lilly, a slave girl whose heart broke when her white lover killed himself. At the time of their illicit romance, room 3A was an attic. In 1845, Anna Dummett had inherited the place with her sister, Sarah, and they decided to run it as a boardinghouse.

One of the stories is a sighting of a black person's hand going down the back stairway banister, and another is of a black girl dressed in white seen in the hallway and in room 3A. People hear whispers and moans, and one guest said she heard a whisper that was definitely a male voice. Several guests have seen the black girl come right through the closed door.

Ming and I went down the hallway to check for cold spots, but found nothing unusual. For dinner that evening, we walked through the old part of town and looked for what we thought might be a haunted building. We settled on Harry's Seafood Bar & Grill. Serving New Orleans–style food, it offers an inviting courtyard and a bar inside. We sat at the bar. It turned out that the building, once a residence, is the oldest house on Avenue Menedez. The bartender, Mike, told us that it dates back to the 1740s. When I asked if there were any ghosts, he described the time he went up to the third floor and all of the windows slammed shut at the same time.

"You should go to the bar upstairs," he said. "Ask them about the ghost in the women's bathroom that goes right through you."

We followed his advice and met Jessica, a bartender on the second floor. She told us that she once had left a cameo necklace on the sink and the chain went straight up, like a magnet had pulled it. She had also seen a figure at the top of the stairs, and many others had seen a woman in a long white dress in the bathroom or smelled a very strong odor of perfume. The ghost apparently liked to mess up the tissues in the bathroom as well, and several people have reported the feeling of being closely watched in there.

I took pictures down the long hallway and in the bathroom, but nothing showed up. I didn't feel watched.

Soon a tall, lean young man with longish dark blond hair came in and sat at the bar. He heard us talking about ghosts and introduced himself. Apparently he was a regular there because the bar staff seemed to know him. His name was Todd and he said he was a psychic. The first thing he said was that I should not accept an invitation to go to Paris on New Year's Eve. "You will be asked, but don't go."

"I have no intention of being on a plane at all on New Year's Eve," I said. (Note: I never did get asked.)

Todd shrugged as if he knew better and told me that he was quite gifted. "I have healed the sick, found lost children, and foreseen major world events. I teach the work that I was sent to do. Time is running out for us and I teach people how to get over the bridge. Where there once was sun it will become cold and dark." He then said that I had only to ask and I would receive whatever it was I was after. "You block what you ask for. It's your intellect that gets in the way. You have a strong mark and you lead yourself into trouble now and then. But I see the mark of God on you. The power is there for you."

Before I could respond, he added that a man was standing behind my left shoulder, with his hand on me, talking to me. "He talks a lot," Todd observed. "He's talking to you all the time."

He was the second person to tell me that. Chanda had said the same thing. I told Todd about EVP and let him hear some of the responses I had gotten on my recorder. He heard the word *love*. "He loves you."

He was now the fourth person to observe that, but I couldn't hear that message at all. I handed him Christian's ring for a little psychometry, and he told me it was very old. "Thirteen people have owned it. Someone named Perry or Henry. And there was a woman, too."

To that point, his "readings" had been so general that they could have been said to anyone and sounded accurate (except maybe the man with his hand on my shoulder), but then he said something that surprised me.

"There's a book that's locked away somewhere," he said. "It's very important. The box will be opened a year from October and you'll be part of that."

Another seer who knows about the book in the box. I was beginning to think that was part of their repertoire—perhaps a line they learn at psychic school. How could two of them pick up on such a specific item? And was he predicting that I might see Wraith again? Still, he was probably right that my intellect blocked me from being more receptive. I didn't want it to, but I could not find a way around it.

We got back to the hotel and called Jeff and Kris. They had a suite on the second floor, so Ming and I went up to get acquainted. Jeff was a lean man in tight jeans with curly brown hair and a mustache. He exuded nervous energy that burned strong in his eyes. Kris had a softer manner. Blond and pretty, with large eyes and perfectly applied makeup, she could have been a model. These two had met online and had developed such a strong relationship that when Jeff asked her to leave everything in Maryland and join him in Florida, she did—in a day's time. "Our meeting online was somewhat mystical," Jeff said. "We seemed to be very in tune."

While Kris was soft-spoken and brief in her comments, Jeff was a wiry guy who liked to talk. He told us he was a firefighter, paramedic, and musician. He was hoping to now develop his talent as a writer. "I have a thousand stories," he said. Admitting that ghosts scared him, he nevertheless relished the hunt. Only when he felt them right there watching him would he pack up and leave. "If you can't control it, you avoid it."

Kris worked on a magazine staff doing advertising sales. They had only recently gotten involved together with ghost hunting and had become members of the IGHS, which is how I met them. Following the usual protocol between ghost hunters, they got out a scrapbook and showed me the photos they had taken of orbs. Some were filmed in Cassadaga, and Jeff was eager to tell me what a deeply serene and spiritual place it was. He had first gone there to gather information about witchcraft and herbs, and he realized that the place was a transformational vortex. "The older spirits there teach the younger spirits to advance." He was sure I would find people there who could provide help with my quest.

Ming interrupted our discussion to observe that someone was vacuuming outside the room. That seemed peculiar, since it was ten o'clock at night. "If we open that door," she said, "there won't be anyone there."

We laughed, although she did not mean it as a joke, but no one checked. To this day I don't know why none of us but Ming sensed what was happening, nor why *she* didn't open the door.

Eventually we went outside into the street that ran alongside the inn. I used my EMF meter to get readings while Jeff took photographs. At one point I saw the meter leap into the paranormal range and shouted to him to get a photo. He did, and between us was a filmy ectoplasmic cloud. The street was clear and every other shot showed no mist. I guess the meter worked. I had felt nothing myself, however, which disturbed me. If it was that close, I should have picked up something. A chill, a sensation. Was I ever going to develop any sensitivity?

We all went over to the Huguenot burial ground and I gave Ming my digital camera to try her luck. She got a number of good shots over the cemetery walls, which excited her. She reminded me of my own initial experience with a digital camera. Although the idea of seeing a ghost scared her, she thought this kind of ghosting was fun. I took a few pictures myself, but let her use the camera again while I operated the EMF meter. On one street corner where a still-unsolved murder had occurred, we got high EMF readings but no orbs.

We counted the evening a mild success and agreed to meet Kris and Jeff in the morning before we went on our way. Cassadaga was our ultimate destination. That night, after Ming got into bed, I said I wanted to try some EVP. She pulled up the covers, not altogether happy that she had to hear a ghost talking in the same room where she was going to sleep. I laughed and then turned on the recorder. I asked if anyone was there and got a very loud response.

Feeling suddenly vulnerable out there in the dark in the middle of the room, I decided to get into bed. I didn't need to know whether we had a ghost in the room.

That night an odd noise woke both of us several times. It was a tapping sound that neither of us could identify—not like someone knocking on the walls, but the tinny tap of an object against wood. It was clearly in our room, not next door or overhead. Neither of us wanted to check it out in the dark, so we suffered through it and woke up irritable in the morning. I looked around for the source of the sound, but couldn't place it. Then I noticed a glass globe, about an inch in diameter, on the end of the chain for the overhead light. It hung about a foot from the ceiling in the middle of the room. Just to see what it sounded like, I knocked it against the ceiling several times.

We looked at each other. "That's the sound I heard," said Ming.

I nodded. "That sounds like it, but look at it. It can't just hit the ceiling on its own." I tried bouncing it on the chain, in case it was just from people walking in the room overhead. It was too far from the ceiling, so I smacked it again with force and concluded, "It has to be hit to get up that high."

Ming just shrugged and finished packing. She didn't want to know.

Outside, Jeff and Kris had a surprise. "We asked the maid if she ever saw the ghosts, and you know what she told us?"

"What?" I asked.

"Just the little black girl who *vacuums.*"

My mouth dropped open. Someone had been vacuuming last night.

"See, I told you," said Ming. "You just ignored me."

"Wait, wait," I said. "I'll be right back."

I went into the lobby and asked the manager if anyone could have been vacuuming the night before on the second floor.

"That's impossible," he said. "The second-floor vacuum is broken."

Agghhh! That close once again!

—3—

We pulled into Cassadaga around noon. The idea that this place was a spiritualist center had put me into a high state of excitement. There would be mediums and psychics everywhere. Located on fifty-seven acres not far from Daytona, it was built in 1875 when a spirit guide advised George Colby to establish a community there. The church leased the land to its members, and that practice is still in place.

As we drove through the dusty little town, I thought we must be in the wrong place. The buildings here looked cheap and rundown, with mostly homemade signs on the roadside or in the window of a house for palm and tarot readers. I had the impression they expected potential customers to just go door to door looking for a psychic, but I wasn't going into one of these scrubby little houses. We drove from one end of town to the other, which took about three minutes, and then turned around. Although there was a park with a gazebo and a fountain, I did not find the serenity that Jeff had spoken about. I just wanted to leave. The place seemed like a trailer court, but with match-stick houses instead of trailers. With great difficulty, because there were no parking areas, we found a place to stop next to a general store.

"This is it?" Ming asked.

"I guess so." I looked at her. "I'll just have a look around. If the whole place seems like this, we'll just go. I don't have the impression that this place is any better than my local psychic."

We got out and walked across the curbless street to the Cassadaga Hotel. That place was supposed to be haunted by an Irish tenor who died there in 1930. Apparently he still likes his cigars, because people claim to smell cigar smoke in the area where he stayed. The hotel itself looked like the headquarters of a summer camp.

Jeff had already told us that the town's certified mediums, who spend several years getting official recognition from the spiritualist church, scorned those who rely on tarot, palm, or other devices. The latter group can just stake out some territory and set up a plaque advertising their availability, whether or not they've had any training. I wondered if the tension between these two points of view affected the town's spiritual aura. We went inside the hotel lobby, and I asked the woman at the desk if a room was available. I knew there was little chance, but thought I'd inquire. She acted as if I had insulted her. "People make reservations three weeks in advance," she said in a haughty voice.

"Well, yes, but it's a Sunday. I just thought—"

"I'm sorry. There's nothing."

Okay. So much for serenity. No room at the inn.

I had read in a tourist book that the energy in this place is strong, and Ming and I did feel quickly drained. In fact, the number of people there whose livelihood depended on tourists coming in for spiritual advice began to make the place feel to me like one big collective psychic vampire. If there was a vortex here, it was working in reverse.

However, I was willing to continue to look into it. I noticed a bulletin board on which a number of licensed practitioners were listed, along with their availability for different needs. I wasn't sure if I wanted a psychometrist, a tarot reader, a medium, or what. I noticed an overweight woman with short, brittle hair the color of a lemon working behind the bookstore counter. Her cheeks were red and she looked stressed, but I needed advice, so I approached her. She told me an appointment would cost $35 to $50.

"For how long?" I asked.

"For however long spirit is there."

"You mean I could pay that much for fifteen seconds?"

"Oh, no, of course not. It's usually at least half an hour."

I was stymied. If it was all about "spirit," and no one could tell how long "spirit" would choose to be there, or if it would even come, then how could anyone know that it would last longer than fifteen seconds? And what if it went for three days? This place was beginning to seem like a business, plain and simple. Ming wanted to leave.

"Let's have lunch and talk about it," I said. "I still want to find a medium or someone to give me a reading on the ring. Maybe I'll get a sign."

The lunch at the hotel was pretty cheap and mundane, ordered off of a menu that had been dittoed. (Did people still do that?) However, when we got the bill, we had been overcharged on three out of four items. I pointed this out to the waitress.

She flew into a rage. "I've worked here for six years and I know what the prices are! They're wrong on the menu."

I was shocked. Since when did a waitress yell at the customer for her own mistake? "Well, then," I said evenly, "maybe you should change the menu. It's just a cheap piece of paper."

She grabbed the bill and stomped away, making sure we knew how annoyed she was, and then came back and slapped it back on our table. She had removed the items altogether. Then she stomped away.

"Wow," I said, "this place is so warm and loving."

Ming laughed. "Let's go," she said.

"Yeah. I think I've just been given a sign."

We drove back to Orlando. When I later told Jeff about our visit there, he was surprised. "I have to ask," he said, "were you wearing that ring? It has been my experience that most of the people in Cassadaga are flawlessly perceptive. Could it be that they picked up on something that surrounds the ring? The darker side of *him* is bound to be detectable by those who are sensitive. It's just a thought."

Possible, perhaps, but I'm fairly perceptive, too, and it seemed to me that they were simply rude.

Ming felt that she had gotten a lot out of her first experience as a ghost hunter. That night was the opening weekend of a movie called *The Sixth Sense* and we decided to go. Ming's brother and my nephew, Marc, was visiting, so we sat around and talked about EVP and ghost photos before going to the show.

I think we were all astonished by how close the film came to portraying what we had just been discussing. EVP was used as one of the plot devices, and the idea of a little boy who can see ghosts reminded me of a few people I'd already met along the way. Jacqueline, for instance, whose mother had tried to exorcise this gift right out of her.

What struck me about the movie were the ideas that (1) ghosts see only what they want to see; (2) ghosts gravitate toward people who are aware of them so that they can finish their purpose; (3) they don't know they're dead; (4) if they do, they don't want to be dead; and (5) they might have business or they might just be mad and want to hurt someone. Whether any of those ideas was true I didn't know, but it surely would explain Christian in my life. It was still possible that he wanted me to discover what really happened to him, and if he did exist, he certainly saw only what he wanted to see—not that he was evil or trapped or even dead, but that he wanted revenge and was justified in getting it any way he could.

I had a lot to think about. I was disappointed that Cassadaga had been a dead end, but fortunately I was to continue my apprenticeship with Rick Fisher, the explorer-scientist over in Lancaster. I felt better with someone who had some experience. And I was looking forward to it, because it would be my first experience with videotaping ghosts.

—4—

From Florida, I went right to another haunted B&B, the Railroad House in Marietta, Pennsylvania, built in the 1800s to cater to the canal workers. The weekend was to be an intensive series of investigations. Rick, who had first introduced me to orbs, wanted to see if he could get ghost videos in my room with the infrared videocam. I had no objection, as long as it didn't "see" through my clothes.

I met Rick and Donna Chambers, who have owned the Railroad House for over a decade. Donna, a slim woman with dark hair and a lively manner, showed me around. There were colorful stencils everywhere along the ceilings and white plaster walls, with doorframes painted in colonial greens and reds. On the first level were two separate dining rooms and a kitchen, while the guest rooms were up a tall, narrow flight of stairs. My room at the far end of a long hallway was warmly furnished with Early American antiques that reminded me that I was in Amish country. A braided rug, quilted bedspread, and a dark wood mantel over the fireplace made it quite cozy. There were also two chairs and an antique dresser. Just outside my room was a door that led out to the back garden, a fenced area full of vegetables and flowers, where Anna Marie's ghost would appear.

I knew this tale from Dot Fiedel's book, *True Ghost Stories of Lancaster, Pennsylvania.* The young woman, Anna Marie, who wears a Victorian dress and wide-brim hat, had lived next door well over a hundred years ago. After the Railroad House opened, a chef in the restaurant was the first to see her, an experience that left him shaken. Later a waitress felt a sudden cold chill and then spotted in the garden a glowing figure that disappeared.

Rick and I had the restaurant's famous clambake dinner and I asked him more about his investigations. He said that he tried to get out whenever he could and used to do so every Saturday night. "All I think about is ghosts," he admitted. He was excited about our destinations that night because they produced results on a regular basis. An electrical storm was also building, and he felt sure we'd have a good evening.

After dinner, we traveled into the country to his favorite spot, the Haldeman family cemetery. It was dusk when we arrived, but darkness soon fell. The plot was small, containing only about twenty-five deteriorating gravestones surrounded by a low stone wall. Rick used his videocam while I took still shots and tried to get EVP. I noticed that I was getting nothing inside the cemetery, so I aimed my camera out into the surrounding woods. In nearly every photo, I had an orb—sometimes a very bright one. But why were they out there, I wondered? We stayed about an hour, and as we left, I turned around and took several shots. There they were, back in the cemetery.

Lightning in the distance alerted us to the approach of a much-needed storm. We wanted to get one more investigation in before calling it quits.

The next cemetery, Hans Graf, was another family plot, but this one was much larger, with the stones more regularly spaced. It resembled a military cemetery. On the videocam, Rick got two orbs gliding on the breeze, one after the other, out into the trees. I took a few pictures but concentrated this time on EVP. At one point, I asked, "Does anyone want to communicate?" I let it run and then listened. At first, all I could hear was the sound of a passing car and the noise of crickets. Then I heard my question and almost immediately had two separate responses, both of them very clear—Class A. The first response was the voice of a boy, perhaps eleven or twelve, who simply said, "Yes." Clear. Poignant. But he offered nothing further.

The second was weaker, more gruff, and somewhat alarming.

"Why are you doing this to us?" I pushed the ten-second reverse button and listened again. "Why are you doing this to us?" I was quite amazed by the clarity and anger evident in this voice. It was my best EVP so far, but this person was clearly annoyed. I wondered what we were doing that could make this spirit so agitated. Maybe he was not even talking to me, but it had felt rather personal.

Then it occurred to me: They did not like the flash from the camera. I wasn't sure why, except that it probably disturbed the peaceful aura of the place. Maybe it hurt their "eyes." I didn't know, but I surmised that this was why the orbs in the other cemetery had avoided us until we left. Maybe they didn't want to be near "the light." I'd read that in some near-death experiences, people felt the light actually sucking them toward it. Maybe these spirits were afraid.

We finished there and I returned to the B&B. I set up Rick's camcorder and "talked" to Christian, inviting him to move around the room and go in front of the camera. I asked questions such as "Am I getting any closer to knowing what you want?" and "Is anyone with you?" I got mostly aggressive responses. I asked whether I should contact a medium to help and heard "No." I told him to stop yelling, and finally I gave up. I felt a little silly speaking to the air, but if there was something for the camera to pick up, I wanted to do my part.

Rick came the next day and packed up the camera. He'd look at the tape later, he said. Then he presented me with a notebook in which to record the times, dates, and weather conditions for all my EVP experiences. I guess he'd figured out that I wasn't being very scientific. I had to remember who I was with.

He did his ghost-hunting workshop that night at the Railroad House and we went on Donna's ghost tour. One of the women who came showed me photographs of orbs, and I was astonished to see how large they were. Some of them were as large as people. I'd never seen any like that. Kathleen Benyo, part of the group, also got photos of what looked like long illuminated strings—"supercharged" orbs, I found out later—and some of them were around me. I wondered if there was a "photographer effect"—something in the person that made the difference. Some of them thought that these results were due to my ghost. I thought it might be a problem with the camera.

My ring drew some attention. I had spoken at Rick's workshop about my ghosting experiences, and a woman came up to me who said she was psychic. She told me that when she'd seen the ring around my neck, she had gotten the impression of some woods. She wanted to know what that was about, but she declined to touch the ring. "I think it's got negative vibes, frankly," she said. "Its power is male. There was something that got out of hand, some deal." She put her hand close to my necklace and said, "I feel like crying. It disturbs me. You have a secret connection to it that you don't reveal."

I didn't say anything, but she was right on all counts.

—5—

The next morning, I picked up Rick for an adventure. He told me he had watched the tape from the night in my room.

"And?"

He looked at me with a smile. "And you were not alone."

He went on to describe how orbs had come out of walls and gone into the fireplace, often in response to my invitation to move around the room. He was pleased with the results, which indicated responsiveness on their part.

We decided, since we were close, to go to Burkittsville, Maryland, where the legend of the Blair Witch had allegedly been the source of the film *The Blair Witch Project*. The psychic Chanda told me that she'd been there and that real energy was evident. "The locals tell me there was a witch," she confided, "but the rest is made up. I've been to the cemetery and the air is so tense you can cut it with a knife. It's one of the only places I have ever been where I actually felt afraid."

Our first view of the town as we drove in off highway 17 in the Catoctin Valley was the post office, which sat just down the hill from a rather large cemetery for a town that had nothing more than a few churches and some houses. Founded in 1824 as "Harley's Post Office," it changed to its current name four years later when Harley died. I took a lot of film photographs, unaware at the time of what was happening to my camera.

We tried some EVP in the cemetery but had no real results. We then walked down the narrow sidewalks, feeling resentful stares from residents inside their clapboard houses. We wondered why no one had capitalized on the elevated interest in this little hamlet. No T-shirt stands, no haunted fudge, no bundles of witch sticks for sale.

"I want to go into the woods," I said. "You game?"

Rick was along for the ride, and unless he longed to become a permanent resident of Burkittsville, he didn't really have a choice.

"I'm a researcher," he said. "I need to find out what this is all about."

Good enough.

We drove up a back road, which took us past a long, open field, and I thought about the plot of the movie. Three college kids team up to make a documentary about a witch that supposedly lives in the woods outside Burkittsville. They get lost, something follows them, one of them ends up missing, and the other two find a deserted building where the whole thing ends badly. They never come back and no one ever finds them. The story has roots in a folktale from Red River (now Adams), Tennessee, known as the Bell Witch. There are several versions to this tale, but like the Blair Witch, it's about a marauding spirit out to do harm. For three years during the early part of the nineteenth century, many people observed what the Bell Witch could do, including Andrew Jackson, who came specifically to see it. How much of it was true was anyone's guess, but it is sometimes cited as evidence that ghosts can do some real harm.

In 1817, John Bell, sixty-eight, had a large tract of farmland overlooking the Red River. In December, something began pounding on the back door late at night after everyone was in bed. Bell would open the door, but no one was ever there. He and his seven children tried to keep watch, but they never caught the perpetrator. The pounding continued for another five months, and then the entity came inside.

The children heard sounds in their rooms like furniture being moved, chains dragging, and rocks hitting the roof. Sometimes the covers were pulled off someone who was asleep. They tried an exorcism, but the spirit retaliated by dragging one daughter, young Betsy Bell, around by her hair.

Eventually, the spirit began to speak and the voice was deemed female. She said she was a former resident of the town, Kate Batts, and she hated John Bell. He began to fall ill, a swelling appearing on the inside of his mouth. In 1819, he died.

The spirit also went after daughter Betsy, breaking up her engagement and physically harming her in a poltergeist-like manner. Some modern theorists speculate that Betsy had been abused by her father and had reacted with telekinetic powers, enhanced by rage and hysteria. She never spoke about what had happened to the family, but the "witch" seemed never to have harmed John Bell with a physical blow.

That was not the case—at least from the movie's suggestion—with the Blair Witch. She seemed truly malevolent and capable of murder.

To my surprise, Burkittsville was actually a setting for Civil War action. There was even a battlefield. It seems that in 1862, thirty thousand troops converged on the town. At the Resurrection German

Reformed Church, the Union wounded were treated inside, while Confederate wounded were laid outside. Those who died were temporarily buried in the Union cemetery on the hill before being removed later.

We looked around and then found an abandoned building in the woods with a small cemetery nearby. This was the one that had scared Chanda so badly—the one that had negative energy. We parked by the road and got out. Rick went into the building, while I stayed out in the cemetery to take some photos. Then I saw a thin, dark-haired man not far away pounding a stake into the ground. I gotta admit, that spooked me, so I tried to stay out of sight while I made my way to the building. Pulling myself up through a broken door, I hid and watched the man retreat. I looked at my car and realized it would be quite a long dash to get back to it.

Since I was inside, I took some digital photos, noting as I did that the building had been a church. There were lines of pews and an altar. My first photo, taken before I even stepped all the way through the door, showed a mass of orbs of all sizes, but in every other shot I failed to get a single orb. It reinforced my feeling that they simply did not like the camera. It also confirmed that these orbs were not spots on my lenses.

Rick came up the steps from down below. "You should see what's down here."

I looked into the darkness of the stairwell, thinking only of rats. I didn't like rats. But I was here. I wasn't going to miss this opportunity. So, tentatively, hoping I would not step on something squishy that might leap out of the dark at me, I went into the cellar.

Rick followed me with his videocam, telling me when an orb had shot across the room at me. I tried not to think about one getting caught in my hair or sliding down the back of my shirt, but looked instead at the evidence of kids coming in and desecrating the place. No doubt this was a movie-inspired prank, but it certainly was creepy to see the Helter Skelter–like words painted large across both walls, "Stay the Fuck Away," and "He Is Always With Us." At our feet, drawn in white paint or chalk, was a pentagram.

I wondered at the wisdom of staying there much longer. It was deep into the afternoon and could get dark fast. I wasn't afraid of a witch, but I *was* nervous about that man I had seen. We decided to go back.

I returned home, and when I took the pictures in for developing, I received a call from the photography place. They told me there was something wrong and I ought to come and take a look. Okay. I'd been waiting for this. Other photographers had problems around spirits. I was interested to see what I had gotten.

When I arrived, the technician raised an eyebrow at me and rolled out the string of negatives onto the lightbox. She explained that their engineers and even the president of the company had examined this, but no one had an explanation. The entire first half of the roll that had been used in Florida was black. No pictures of St. Augustine or St. Petersburg. Second, things were transposed in some odd way such that the numbers showed the pictures to have been taken upside down. I had the camera with me and showed her that there was no way to load the film upside down. I looked through the negatives and recognized the Railroad House, the Burkittsville post office, and the cemetery, but all of these photos had extra sprocket markings in the middle, as if the top or bottom of the film had burned across them.

I sent the negatives to Dave Oester, who believed they'd been processed badly, but admitted that the odd sprocket pattern indicated the possibility of a burst of energy near the camera. "The width of the image decreases as it goes from left to right. This is not natural, so if your camera has not been acting strangely, then this roll may have been affected by spirit energy. It is almost as if you were in a very strong electromagnetic field, like a vortex or portal, that distorted the image as it was placed on the film."

I decided to take only the digital camera to Arizona.

gHost

10 *Things Are Not as They Seem*

—1—

Before I left, I moved to a new apartment. I was afraid that, given how modern it was, my ghost would not come with me. As soon as I was moved in, I tried to get some photos. Nothing. Then I tried EVP and got some strange, inconclusive responses. Unfortunately, I didn't have the chance to experiment any further because I had an appointment with Merlin.

Arizona is a land of harsh, dramatic beauty. Nowhere are the sunsets so consistently spectacular. Because of the diverse terrain, from mountains to pine woods to deserts to canyons, it became home to many different tribes of Native Americans. They had to be tenacious and resilient to force a living out of this dusty land, and they came to depend on the spirits of their ancestors to assist them. Their will to survive was tested every day.

Going to Arizona is like going home for me. I'd gone to college in Flagstaff and I already knew about some of the hauntings there. Old Town had the Blue Lady looking for her baby, and the Monte Vista Hotel housed several entities. This famous hotel, around since 1927, was home to many actors who were shooting films nearby and was even the site for a scene in *Casablanca*. A phantom bellboy, a wounded bank robber, and some murdered prostitutes are among the legendary spirits. Spooky as they may be, I heard a story from Flagstaff that tops any from the hotel.

Friends of mine, Crissi and Don, told me of their experience in a small rented bungalow on North Agassiz, built in the twenties.

"It was a snug little home," Crisis said, "with a sunroom, hardwood floors, a claw-foot tub, and a backyard for our dog, Bagheera, a 110-pound German shepard/Akita mix. Upon arriving, we took the dog into the house. He walked ahead of us, sniffing the sunroom floors, and then approached the living room. About halfway through, he stopped, whined, sat down, and would not move. It took us five or ten minutes to drag him out to the backyard. We attributed it to the new surroundings.

"However, four months later, I was sitting on the couch watching TV. Bagheera was dozing on the floor in front of me. Suddenly, he jumped to his feet and looked at the ceiling. Within seconds he was whimpering and cowering on the floor while crawling backwards out of the living room. He kept his eyes on the ceiling until he got to the hallway. I froze and stared at the ceiling, trying to see what it was that frightened this normally bold dog. I tried coaxing him back with me. He crouched down and looked at me, still whining and refusing to come back. This made me doubly nervous.

"I called Don and he said there was probably a squirrel in the attic, but I didn't think a squirrel would cause that much fear in a big brave dog. By the time I was off the phone Bagheera had rejoined me. I shut off the TV and looked at the ceiling, poking at it with a broom handle, trying to see if anything furry was indeed making its home in the attic. I heard nothing.

"Not long after that, my husband and I woke up to the sound of the plastic divider doors between the main rooms rattling violently. Our first reaction was that someone was trying to get in. But Bagheera hadn't warned us. Don got up and as he got out of bed the rattling stopped. We both wondered if our snug little home might be haunted. It always felt crowded."

I can't say I'd ever heard of a dog actually crawling backwards out of a room. That was impressive, but Don's side of the story was even more dramatic.

"In the middle of the day," he told me, "I was walking through the kitchen to the backyard. Off of the kitchen was a doorway to the spare bedroom. As I passed through I glimpsed out of the corner of my eye a young boy of four or five with brown hair. He was standing next to the bed in the spare room with his hand on the bedpost. I stopped and did a double take, but he was gone. Soon after that I started seeing lights flashing in the night, similar to flashbulbs on cameras.

"Then one evening I got up to go to the rest room, which was located off of the spare bedroom with a door that also went into the living room. As I opened the door to return I encountered a wall of white light that filled the doorway. Instantly all the hair on my body stood on end. The cold in the air was not normal.

"Soon after these experiences I asked our landlady if the house was haunted and she said 'yes.' She told me that while waiting for some prospective renters she used the rest room and an elderly gentleman and a young boy walked through two closed doors. Upon further questioning she told me that a family had moved here from California and the father couldn't find work. Soon after he killed his wife, son, and father, and then turned the gun on himself."

After that, Crissi consulted an herbalist who told her to smudge the house with sage and cedar during the full moon and for ten more days. "The smudging seemed to help," she said, "and the house felt less crowded, but the incidents kept cropping up."

Much as I'd like to see a ghost, I'm not sure I could live with them under those circumstances.

Not far from Flagstaff is Sedona. Before it was dubbed a spiritual power center during the early New Age movement, it was where we hiked on weekends. I did not find much in the way of hauntings here, although online I saw some pretty impressive photos of orbs. My plan was to meet Merlin and then get set up at the Inn at Jerome.

—2—

I met Merlin in Sedona, amidst the red rock beauty of Oak Creek Canyon. It seems that iron oxide and silica in the sandstone deposits creates a magnetic energy, and Sedona was deemed one of the power centers of the world, a virtual temple of dynamism. It had some fifteen to twenty vortexes (sources of magnetic energy), most of them near breathtaking rock formations. We had lunch at the vegetarian restaurant and then hiked out to the Boynton Canyon vortex, near Hoodoo Rock (also known as the Kachina woman—Kachinas embodying the life force from spirits of the departed). I didn't know if this was a male or female vortex, but it was near a "female" formation. I thought Merlin would better appreciate nurturing energy. I also wondered if a vortex might improve my ability to "hear." When I had lived closer to nature out here in the West, I recalled hearing the idea that our energy levels determine the truths of our experience. Getting an influx of energy from this area might reinstate my sensitivity.

A full-blooded Apache, Merlin looked the same as always, although I had not seen him in many years. His longish black hair had some gray, but his sun-darkened skin was still smooth and his brown eyes full of mystery. Lean and strong from working outside in the forestry service, he had a wife now and three children, one of whom was in college. Merlin was not actually a shaman, but he had gone through numerous rituals to get closer to the spirit world. He had a shaman's perspective, and he lived his religion fully. What I sought was a person who knew that the world was infinitely complex and that we as humans tend to select only a portion of the reality available to us. I knew from psychology that we tend to limit our intake. I knew that Merlin understood that.

In fact, we had met in a psychology course and sometimes talked for hours at the local Dunkin' Donuts about what makes people tick. It was his opinion that one must learn to create balance within oneself and with the environment. He did not understand my interest in dark subjects, and he thought that my "dance" was rather dangerous. He preferred a life of serenity. However, he had agreed with me that one does not just call something "bad," one tries to find out how it got that way so one could find the point of forgiveness.

When I explained to him about the ring, how I acquired it, and what I had experienced as a result, Merlin said, "Each thing in our lives is a test. This has come to you so you can find out something about yourself. Perhaps you need to know that you're getting in too deep."

"Maybe so, but I'm in it and I'd like to get some perspective. Do you think there's anything to this? I mean, people who claim to be sensitive react to this ring and they warn me that the spirit is bad."

"Show it to me."

I unlatched the chain and held the ring out in the palm of my hand. Merlin looked but did not reach to touch it.

"What is it you want to do?" he asked.

"I want to see if he's really here and find out what he wants from me. If he was murdered, I want the real story."

"You want more, but you aren't saying. I see it in your eyes."

I shrugged. "If I have a ghost around me, I want to see him."

"And then what? What if he doesn't leave? What if he's harmful?"

"I don't know. But I think that's making things more clear than they really are. I don't think he's a demon. I just think he's a ghost with issues that trap him. In all the theories I've read, no one seems to think very specifically about how to help these entities, besides just to exorcise them and send them away."

Merlin smiled, and the lines around his eyes deepened. "I think you're about to eat the sweet berries."

"What?"

"In some of our cultures, these are stories about beings that are not human but that masquerade as someone we knew. They try to trick us with things we want. Some call them skin-walkers. It's when someone leaves his body to travel spiritually and another spirit enters and takes over. You think it's the person you know, but it's not. He can't get back in. The same can happen with an identity. The person has left an energy mark in terms of who he was and a spirit can wear it and make you think you're contacting the person. The false spirit can be whoever that person was because the traits guide how it thinks and acts."

I'd heard about this. Someone had called them "extradimensional beings." I hadn't eliminated this possibility, or that of ETs.

"I'll tell you one story," he continued, "and you decide what you think. The young men and women of one tribe were taught never to eat a certain type of berry unless they had first been through a ritual of protection and purification. The young people accepted this, but one day they were out in the woods. They saw the berries. One of the boys wanted to taste them, but the others warned him not to. He said if the berries could be eaten, they could be eaten equally with or without the rituals. He didn't understand that the rituals woke up the good spirits. So he ate a berry and found it to be sweet. He urged the others to try it and some of them did. What they did not know is that the berries belonged to the evil one and now their souls belonged to him as well. They hadn't protected themselves. When they returned to their tribe, they weren't allowed to come in because they couldn't be saved. They lost everything they had known. Their existence now was to serve their new master, which meant that they were to tempt other innocent souls into consuming the sweet berries."

"So they became demons," I said. "Or these skin-walker things."

"Not demons. They were human, but not quite human. They could make you think they're just like you or me. But their only purpose is to ensnare you."

"And you think that's what my ghost is. One of these?"

Merlin smiled. "I don't pretend to fully know the ways of the other world. There may be more than I understand—including more kinds of spirits than I know." He reached into his shirt pocket and pulled out a small tuft of feathers, tied together like a fly-fishing lure. "What I do believe is that some things are good and some things are bad. When those forces are greater than we are, you have to ask the good to give you help. You can't do it on your own." He handed me the feathers. "These are from the falcon. Keep them with you. They may seem like nothing but feathers, just like those berries seemed like nothing but berries, but I think there's more than meets the eye."

I accepted the soft brown and white feathers and thanked him. Then I said, "It's possible to be in the darkness without being corrupted by it. Christian may try to seduce me or test me, but he may also be curious about what can be done for him."

"Your tolerance for these things makes your walk precarious."

"I guess. But the shadows have always been my home. Maybe I'm like those vampire hunters who were half vampire. They have a special attunement because they have one foot in that world, but they don't practice the vampire's ways."

Merlin smiled. "Maybe you are. But I think you should remain aware of the possibility at all times that this Christian is not who he seems. The voices mean nothing. That could be anyone imitating him. Has he told you anything that makes you sure it's him?"

I shook my head. "I definitely think I'm getting voices, but it's hard to make out what he's saying. He's told others some things they couldn't have known that make me think he's the real thing, but he's said nothing obvious to me. And it's easy to just answer yes and no. I agree with you that whatever seems to be attached to that ring—or to me—it may have nothing whatsoever to do with Christian. But even so, if you were to venture contact, what would you do?"

Merlin shook his head. "I wouldn't. Nor would I advise you to, but if you insist, then you should first make a study of the ways of the spirits. There are many different types and you should try to understand where the dangers lie. If you remain naive, you could get yourself into real trouble."

"But it's difficult to learn. Most of the stuff out there is either from fundamentalists who have no appreciation for nuances or from New Agers who sound like alchemists. I came to you because I figured you'd have a more experiential perspective. I mean, you live close to nature. You have strong spiritual resources. It's not just doctrines to you." I stroked the soft feathers in my palm as I said this.

"And that's why I warn you not to do this," Merlin repeated. "But if you must, then you should gather good people around you to assist you. You'll have to leave your body to meet him, I think, and you'll need people who can chant to keep you anchored and safe. You can only truly see these entities when you escape your physical limitations. And you don't want him to come to you first, because he may get too close. His anger, as you see it, may not be a reaction. He could be gathering his energy to make an attack."

"Can these spirits push you out of your skin and just take over?"

"They might if you're weak or ill and they really need your body to go do something. You must have a very strong identity to even approach them. You must be the warrior and go to him. But I still think you need to know him and you're not yet using your own resources. Didn't you just get a degree in forensic psychology?"

"Yes."

"And didn't you study this type of person in depth?"

"I guess."

"Then perhaps that's what you need to do. Look at what they did and see the demon at work. If this Christian is anything like them, you'll know what you're trying to confront. If there was a skin-walker in someone, for example, you'll see how he made that man behave. And if these people can be helped or healed, then you just have to transform the psychology into spiritual principles. You're capable of that. You're also capable of knowing when you shouldn't eat the berries."

I accepted that. I realized that I'd separated this world from my other fields of expertise and it was time to understand that, demons and extradimensional beings aside, the soul of a human could be approached psychologically, whether dead or alive. In a way, I was doing a psychological autopsy.

In cases where the manner of death is unclear—as with Christian—a psychological autopsy assists the medical examiner to resolve the mystery. The idea is to discover the state of mind of the victim preceding death. In a suspected suicide, for example, it's important to rule out accident or autoerotic asphyxiation. The investigator gathers a database that consists of an examination of the death scene, documentation pertaining to the death, interviews with family members and associates, and all relevant documents pertaining to the individual's life history.

In a suspected suicide, questions would be asked about the victim's stress level and any major changes in his or her life, such as marital separation or losing a job.

Although I did not have access to a complete database about Christian, everything Wraith told me about him leading up to his death contraindicated suicide. He was young, attractive, energetic, and about to leave Wraith for someone new. It made no sense. The only scenario that supported suicide was that he had gotten in over his head with some drug lord and chosen his own way out. Even so, his manner of death was more clearly indicative of murder.

So as a ghost, he might want revenge, and also as a ghost, he'd have traits similar to those he had in life: angry, self-loathing, violent, sadistic, self-centered, sociopathic, and decidedly dangerous. Would he even want to be healed?

Sitting here with Merlin, in this magnificent land of red rock formations, I sensed what I could lose should I get too close to someone who wanted only to hurt others and possibly to claim my soul. It was the first time I had second thoughts. Perhaps the vortexes here had power after all.

I thanked Merlin for his help and his gift and promised to let him know what happened. Then I went to Jerome.

—3—

I drove up the steep slope of Cleopatra Hill, just below Mingus Mountain, noting how precarious the layers of houses looked. They were built on stilts along switchbacking roads that hairpinned from right to left, and reigning over it all of these wooden structures was the enormous Jerome Grand Hotel. I noted several buildings that exploited the town's ghostly atmosphere, such as Spook Hall, the community center. I pulled in late in the afternoon and quickly found the Inn at Jerome on 309 Main Street, where I was staying. On the first floor was the Jerome Grill, and the guest rooms were overhead. The place was built in 1899 and was said to be haunted. That's why I was staying there.

I spoke to Dennis Schulyer, the general manager, and his wife, Juanita. Both had stories about this restored glass-front Victorian building. Of the eight guest rooms, several had shown strange activity. Juanita had heard laughing in the hallway, and in the "Victorian Rose" room, a vase of flowers had flown through the air and crashed onto the floor. She also felt watched in a room they called "Kiss and Tell," to the point that it made her skin crawl. Dennis reported unexplained voices, names being called, and strange events like glasses and pans inexplicably falling off kitchen counters.

A guest claimed that in the Victorian Rose, a shadow of a man crossed in front of her and went behind the door. That same figure had also been seen in the Jerome Grill downstairs, and one cook felt it brush against him (although this might have been an experience with the phantom cat, which has also been seen on the premises).

In the room I was to occupy, "Lariat and Lace," the person cleaning it reported that she saw shadows of people, which disappeared. Once the armoire door had forcefully slammed shut. I was told that this room once belonged to the bossy madam, Betsy, who had run a brothel there, and another maid named Joanne said that she constantly heard voices saying things like, "When are you going to clean this?"

When I arrived, there was a woman waiting for me; she gave me the keys to my room, told me to go on up the steps, wished me well, and left. No one else was there and no staff lived on the premises. I had the place all to myself. As I dragged my bags up the unusually tall carpeted stairway, the place felt haunted . . . and deserted. I liked it. I came up into an open space that had been made into a Victorian sitting room, which seemed the perfect place to set up a recorder during the night. I introduced myself to whatever spirits might reside there. Then I walked into a long, dark hallway to find my room. It was only steps away, with a bathroom further down the hall.

In this room was a monstrous handcrafted, four-poster step-up bed with down pillows and a barnwood armoire. With all the horse paraphernalia in the room, it was distinctly Old West. I had the feeling that Christian liked it here and was communing with other spirits. I'm not sure I'd have been pleased with that had I known then what I would soon find out.

Founded in 1876, Jerome had once been a booming mining town populated by 1929 with over fifteen thousand people. Over one billion dollars' worth of copper, gold, silver, zinc, and lead had been taken from the mines. Although fire burned down the town on three separate occasions, it was always rebuilt. It became such a center of opportunity that in 1927 they built a large state-of-the-art hospital, which served the entire valley. Then copper prices fell, and by 1932 two thirds of the people had left. The mine was reopened, but then closed again in 1953, at which time the place became a veritable ghost town, with less than one hundred tenacious inhabitants. It is now a national historic landmark, a thriving tourist town of over four hundred residents and a haven for artists, writers, and antiques dealers.

The town closed up early, so I went to the Haunted Hamburger restaurant for dinner, where from the patio I could see the sunset over the valley. Off in the distance stood the San Francisco Peaks. I sipped an iced margarita as Margie, my waitress, told me that she was looking in the closet by the dumbwaiter one night when something tapped her on the shoulder. She turned and no one was there. Another time, two girls argued over who was going to go upstairs to the storage area and get a trash bag. Just then the dumbwaiter came down on its own. Inside was a trash bag.

In fact, many of these buildings had a story, and as I walked along the streets that evening, I got orbs in a high percentage of shots. At one point I asked Christian to show himself on camera, and my next shot was of a single glowing orb right in the center of the photo. I remembered my manners this time and thanked him. Then I sat out on the ledge that overlooked the Verde Valley and the tiny lights of Cottonwood. I wanted to think about what Merlin had said.

I had with me a note that Wraith sent about his attempts to get Christian out of his life. I got out a small flashlight and read it over.

I was disturbed all the time, unable to retreat from his presence. He haunted every thought. I grew afraid of simple things, like brushing my teeth or anything that came with a mirror. He often appeared there and it scared me. My life became a series of macabre adventures that kept me off balance. He came every night, taking me into the darkness. Whenever the sun came, I wrapped myself in a blanket to hide, although I knew there was no hiding from him.

I called someone I knew who was involved in spiritualism to see if I could be rid of him. He told me it would be difficult, especially since I had let him in. He told me to renounce my love for him and for things that had belonged to him. I didn't like that option. Those things were part of me. I wasn't sure I could forsake all of that but I was willing to try.

I went to a church and made a vow to abstain from yearning for Christian. I spent almost an hour on my knees. Then I hurried out of the church to get ready for the evening. I intended to show no interest in him or what he wanted to do. I fell asleep under my bed, but was awakened by a whisper. I thought I had dreamed it but then I felt the bed rising and cold air all around me. I closed my eyes and repeated my vow.

Suddenly everything was still. I opened my eyes and turned

*my head and there he was, lying next to me. He just lay there
staring at me, with the bed hovering over us. Then he spoke.
"How cute," he said, "that you thought you could hide." Then
he laughed and said, "You'll never be rid of me."*

As vivid as this was, I still wondered how much of it was
Wraith's imagination. I just couldn't tell. Others had attributed similar
feats to demons or ghosts, so it wasn't that he was necessarily halluci-
nating. If I'd had him as a client in therapy, I might have spotted certain
patterns, but a few brief messages and the confessions from a single
night fail to yield sufficient information, particularly not about what it
might take to help this spirit move on.

The things Wraith told me about Christian reminded me—
rather disconcertingly—of Gary Gilmore, who'd been executed in 1977
in Utah for two pointless, cold-blooded murders. I'd read his brother's
book about their family, and what caught my eye was the experience
his mother, Bessie, claimed to have had. She believed that as a girl
playing with a Ouija board, she conjured up a ghost that had attached
itself to her family. When one of her sisters was killed and another
paralyzed in an accident, she felt certain it was the ghost. Then she
married Frank Gilmore and found out that his mother, Fay, was a
medium who could get spirits to materialize. One night while at Fay's
house with three of her sons, including Gary, she learned from Fay that
there was to be a "special" séance to contact a spirit who had died under
the shameful suspicion of murder. Bessie stayed away.

After the ceremony, Bessie found Fay in a state of exhaustion
with an expression on her face of fear and helplessness. Bessie woke
up later that night to the feel of being touched, and when she turned
over, she was looking into the face of a leering inhuman creature. She
jumped out of bed and saw Fay, an invalid, staggering toward her,
insisting that she get out *now*. "It knows who you are!" Bessie looked
in Gary's room and saw the same figure leaning over her son, staring
into his eyes. She grabbed the kids and ran. Fay died shortly thereafter
and Gary began to have terrible, shuddering nightmares that he was
being beheaded.

Bessie saw the entity again in a house they moved into near
Salt Lake City, and that's when Gary began to get into trouble. He also
continued having dreams, swearing that something was in the room
with him. Bessie concluded that the thing had taken over her son's
soul. His life thereafter was filled with angry, malevolent energy that
seemed bent on self-destruction. He developed a rebellious streak, acting

out in school, running in front of trains, exploiting friends, hanging out with a bad crowd, and engaging in petty crimes. By the age of sixteen, Gary was in jail. Even in prison, he acted out with violence, and one psychiatrist indicated that Gary wanted to die, specifically to bleed to death. Then just three months after winning parole by insisting that he needed another chance, he went out and killed two men in cold blood.

If Wraith was telling the truth, this sounded a lot like Christian. He had believed himself possessed by a spirit and he'd seemed bent on violence. The comparison got me to thinking that some people can't be reached, no matter how hard we try. They have such a strong legacy of negation that there's no penetration of light. If God is the spirit of expansion, then Gilmore's demon and possibly Christian were spirits in a state of contraction. They want life around them to shrink or be destroyed.

Merlin was right. If I used what I knew from criminal psychology, Christian was probably a lost cause. If he was stuck in some ghost limbo, he was there because of who he had been—and probably who he wanted to be. My belief that I could help him could get me into a lot of trouble.

As I sat there on the ledge, I took a few photos, and to my surprise they showed a progressively increasing number of orbs, like they were coming in at me from the valley. I felt a little vulnerable out there and decided it was time to find out what was at the inn. As I climbed up the steep and shallow concrete steps to get from one level of the town to another, I could see how it had become a ghost town: from people falling down these steps and breaking their necks!

—4—

As usual for me, the night was uneventful. I tried getting EVP in the room, to no avail. At least there was comfort in the fact that these recorders didn't always get voices on them. That would have meant it was caused by some defect in the machine. I walked up and down the halls trying to get photos. Negative (as the ghost hunters say), except for one faint orb outside on the porch. Nothing in my room, either. I left the door open, but that didn't help. Even the sitting room produced no results.

Several times during the night I woke up. At one point it seemed I was in the midst of a dream, although I thought I was awake. I felt someone gently touch my face, which seemed wet, as if I'd been crying. I put my hand to my face and it was definitely wet, but I didn't know why or what the moisture was from. I was sure that someone was actually there in the room—someone who was tense and agitated. I heard no voices, but it seemed as if someone was trying hard to get my attention. I listened for a while and kept my eyes open in the dark, but saw and heard nothing. However, the sensation of something wound up and angry or frustrated remained. In the morning, I assumed it had been a dream.

When I told the story to Dennis, without hesitation he said, "That was Betsy!" He said that other experiences with her were like that: She was agitated, angry, and demanding.

Hmm. There's something about me and female spirits in haunted inns.

Although the Jerome Grand Hotel was closed for renovation, I was invited in to have a quick tour. Once the United Verde Hospital, it had sat vacant for forty-four years before it became the hotel in 1994. I had taken photographs the night before, getting amazing shots of numerous orbs, so I was curious to know more about the place. A young woman in town breathlessly told me that a caretaker had killed himself there. While vacant, lights were seen going on and off, and I was told that one could hear ghostly coughing, labored breathing, and sometimes even screams. In 1935, a man was caught under the elevator, although it was in perfect working order, and afterward lights could be seen in the elevator shaft. There was some suspicion that he had been murdered.

There's also a female specter called the Lady in White, seen by several people. Apparently she can melt jewelry because one guest claimed to have found her gold necklace and earrings fused together. The third floor has a little boy who wanders about. Voices are heard in empty rooms, and the switchboard even receives phone calls from unoccupied rooms. When the operator picks up, the only thing on the other end is static. A psychic who visited from Sedona claimed that the spirits had not been patients at the hospital but people who had worked there. The Lady in White was apparently a nurse.

LaWanda, a lively older woman with a gracious manner and polished appearance, generously agreed to a limited tour. After telling me some of the stories told by guests and staff, she took me up to the second floor. We entered the oldest self-service elevator in the state, and on the way she told me that in the rest room on that floor, a woman who was looking into the mirror felt a presence trying to take her over. She got her husband to come in, and he felt something odd, too. Also, some female guests on the third floor had insisted that a man was in the corner of their room. They both had seen him before he disappeared.

We got to the second floor and stepped into a long hallway full of doors. LaWanda told me to just walk down the hall and stop if I felt something. She did not want to say anything more. Knowing I'm not sensitive, I wasn't optimistic, but I started down the hall. About ten feet away, I stopped. I felt something grip the back of my head, and chills shot down my back all the way to my feet.

"My God!" I said.

LaWanda smiled. "That's the place," she said. "There's something there. A lot of people feel it."

I thought I was never going to get warm after that chilling sensation passed over me, but I was pleased that I'd actually *sensed* something for once. Maybe those "technicians" were working on me after all.

I then spoke to one of the partners, Larry Altherr, and he mentioned an interesting tale. It seems that a band of Native Americans told Phelps Dodge, the mining company that owned the building, that they wanted to get inside with their shaman. Some of the workers were nervous about spirits and they thought this huge empty building was key. The overseer, Andy Peterson, let them in and left them to do whatever they planned. After spending the night trying to oust them, the shaman said, "We can't help this place. They're not leaving and we're not coming back."

Wow. No wonder Christian liked it here.

Larry also told me about the caretaker who in the early eighties had hanged himself in the engineer's apartment. He was an alcoholic barred from seeing his wife, who was dying of cancer. When he failed to show up at his regular hangout one day, the police chief went looking for him and found him in the empty building. That same police officer reported seeing lights come on when the building had no electricity. He even went inside to check it out, found no one there and no lights on, but when he came out, the lights were still on. He just went on home.

Just before leaving town, I stopped at the Gift Shop of Jerome, where Carly, the shopkeeper, assured me that most of the buildings in town were haunted. She herself had had problems with the alarm and she'd heard footsteps in the empty space overhead. Stormy days were especially active.

It appeared that the shaman was right—they weren't going away. I hoped Christian wouldn't stay behind. Or maybe I hoped he would. In any event, I came away with the knowledge that I *could* feel things. And that, at least, was a start.

When I returned home, I started to read more about EVP. Merlin's suggestion that I travel astrally to meet Christian face-to-face seemed beyond my skills. I preferred the more mundane attempts to record a clear communication.

I wrote to Dr. William Roll, a paranormal researcher who had actually spent some time in the sixties with Frederich Jurgenson in Sweden. Among other techniques, they had used a radio receiver, tuned to an empty band. Jurgenson apparently had a guide, "Lena," who instructed him on how to get better recordings. Roll was skeptical that the sounds he heard were the voices of discarnate entities, so he was unable to give me any guidance.

I turned to Sarah Estep, and she laid out a clear technique. The tape recorder to use for home taping, she said, is either a reel-to-reel (difficult to find) or a cassette tape deck with an amplifier or speaker and an external microphone. "You make a short recording," she said, "and always use a sound source. I like air band, but not all radios have them because it is limited in content—just about airplanes landing, taking flight paths, that sort of thing. If your radio doesn't have an air band, you can tune to FM or short wave. Have the volume of the radio just loud enough for you to hear, and for 'them' to use its energies and vibrations (along with yours). Then, at the end of your recording, you must wear headphones."

Time to get more equipment.

Apparently white noise in some acoustical range was needed to make the communication work well, and the spirits have to get close to the earth to link with us. However, they don't want to get contaminated with lower level densities that come from our negative cognitive and emotional patterns. Electromagnetism appeared to be our common link, since all of life involves electrical charges and ghosts seem to register on equipment that detected that.

I soon learned that Bill O'Neil of Spiricom had died. I wondered what that had meant for the experiments. Then I read how, after death, he had communicated to other experimenters that "they" (the ghosts) were now experimenting with systems tuned to 68 megahertz. He had become one of the "technicians." To my mind, this was amazing. Who better to advise those researchers at the frontiers than once-living people who knew the equipment? Given the fact that much of the earliest work was done in the sixties and seventies, there could be an increase in those first-generation researchers who might now be able to offer better insight from the other side.

While I appreciated all the physics and technology, I was mostly interested in what they might say about what lay beyond—especially for spirits like Christian. Most of the brief descriptions indicated that for the enlightened ones of good heart, the realm was amazing and rewarding. However, there were those who spoke of misery, entrapment, depression, and great difficulties. I guess it wasn't all heaven.

I was back in my new apartment and I now wanted to experiment. Specifically, I wanted to know if Christian had accompanied me home. I had a small light on, but the rest of the place was dark. I tried some EVP, and it sounded like there were several voices at once. I picked up my camera, lifted it into the air, and took some photographs. To my surprise, I got seven orbs in the picture. For the next couple of nights I continued to get results. That puzzled me. No one had died here. I did some research on West Windsor Township, where my apartment was located, but found nothing out of the ordinary. The peaceful Leni-Lenape Indians had lived nearby, but no battles were recorded. Washington fought too far away to have affected this area.

By the fifth night, the orbs were increasing in number and I was getting very confused. Ghost hunters encourage people to go to cemeteries or some haunted site for photos, yet I was getting better shots right here in my apartment. It reminded me of a movie, *Truly, Madly, Deeply,* where the ghost of a woman's lover returned and then invited all his friends to come watch movies. Her apartment became a hangout for ghosts. I sent the following note out to several fellow ghosters:

> Six nights ago, I was getting what seemed like more than one voice on EVP, so I took a picture. There were seven orbs hovering in my apartment (with no history of deaths on this property). Each evening thereafter (and a few times in the afternoon), I got EVP and a number of photos that contained at least one orb. I noted that an orb seemed to show up consistently (but not always) in the same spot near a painting I have, and I used the meter to check for EM levels. It went to 4. The next day, there was no elevation. Then last night I was reading a book, completely engrossed for an hour. (Interestingly, the author advised people to read while doing EVP to keep their mind from being so intensely focused on the results.) At that point, I took a picture. There were some 30 orbs in my room! Does anyone have any ideas why they would be here? I don't think they inhabit this place. I think they've come from elsewhere.

Rick Fisher from Lancaster responded with a brief note: "Usually when there is a spirit around, there are several. They gather together much as humans do. They will also seek out those who are trying to contact them and that is what you are doing."

Like in *The Sixth Sense*. But how many would come?

Kat's reply, characteristic of a New Orleans bent, came next: "When you look for ghosts, they look for you. They are probably intrigued with you and your work. These could be your ghosts that we pulled up in that séance. My guess is that they know you want to see a ghost and they know you want to know the truth about them. I think they've been with you all along. Without the EVP and photographs, you would not have noticed them. I really feel that they are reaching out to you."

Ed Okonowitz from Delaware suggested focusing on the painting. He thought I should take it out of the room and check the levels of energy after it had been removed. He also suggested I try it in a new location. "Perhaps your interest in the paranormal has awakened some energy or 'visitor' who is trying to get your attention," he observed.

One more thoughtful response came from Dot Fiedel. "I have read that a death on a property is not always necessary or consistent with a haunting. Possibly the land itself was the site of some traumatic event or of a village, meeting place, or observation point—a place where a repetitive occurrence involved a living entity, therefore leaving an 'imprint' of a prior occupation. There is a theory that the geographical electromagnet characteristics of certain regions show higher than average strange occurrences."

I didn't know what to think, but I hoped it meant a greater possibility of a paranormal encounter. Of course, it could just mean that the camera was picking up some other anomaly, but if Christian had invited in some friends, I had to get moving on my quest to figure him out. I had some insights, but still no clear direction. Then I got motivation from other sources.

—6—

I heard again from Wraith. It was a postcard with a Louisiana postmark and just one line, written in red script: "It belongs to me."

His communications were becoming decidedly less friendly. Now I really knew I had to get this quest resolved. If I kept ignoring him, he might come looking for the ring.

Then shortly after I'd taken the photos, I picked up my recorder and discovered forty minutes of a recording that I had not made. I don't usually run it longer than a few minutes. Somehow the record button had been pushed, possibly from the bag in which I carried it. I turned it on to listen.

There were the usual grunts and growls, and a few sounds that seemed like someone talking. Then I heard myself in the background. I recognized the conversation. I'd been on the phone talking with a friend. Superimposed over what I was saying were aggressive male voices that seemed to be arguing.

I played it back to listen again. I was astonished to hear someone yell, "Get out of here!" A little later, I could hear someone say, "This is *my* house!"

Geez, was he talking to me? Hey, this was *my* house and I wasn't going anywhere. Who were these two, anyway? I heard more of the same, but it was difficult to make out the words. In several spots, there was definitely an argument. I wondered if Michael and Christian were fighting over me.

But I had no time to figure it out. I had several expeditions planned on which I wanted to test another piece of equipment: the Sony videocam with infrared Nightshot.

Trick or Treat?

"DEATH IS ONLY A HORIZON; AND A HORIZON IS
NOTHING SAVE THE LIMIT OF OUR SIGHT."
—ROSSITER W. RAYMOND

—1—

I went first to Ann Arbor, Michigan, where I'd grown up, and it seemed a prime opportunity to try an experiment. When I was an adolescent, there had been a serial killer in the Ann Arbor/Ypsilanti area, and I became completely caught up with his boldness and stealth. At the time, the killer had seemed so elusive that some people believed he had paranormal powers. They called him the Devil. Once, while cops were inside investigating a site, he actually left lilac blossoms outside, one for each victim—in broad daylight! There were seven victims in my area, and the person finally convicted for the last murder but implicitly attached to the others was twenty-year-old John Norman Collins. Every bit the handsome and charming all-American boy that Ted Bundy was, he had plans to become an elementary school teacher.

It was a time when few people really understood the concept of a serial killer. We'd had the Boston Strangler a few years before, but the idea of a man randomly killing young women in a prominent college town was unnerving. However, it was the end of the sixties and race riots had rocked nearby Detroit. We felt unsafe. Then a young woman—the first victim—turned up missing.

On Tuesday, August 8, 1967, the *Ann Arbor News* described the first of the "coed murders": "A body found yesterday afternoon on a Superior Township farm was tentatively identified as that of a nineteen-year-old Eastern Michigan University coed who disappeared without a trace July 9."

The body turned out to be that of Mary Fleszar, who was last seen by a roommate when she left their apartment near campus to go for a walk. She was five foot two, weighed about 110 pounds, wore glasses, and had brown hair.

Two guys I knew found her. They were preparing to plow a field when they heard a car door slam. Thinking they might witness a pair of lovers, they sneaked closer to the foundation of the former farm-house, a sort of dumping site and lovers' lane combined. The car door slammed again and an engine turned over, but by the time they reached the area, the car was gone. They noticed fresh tire tracks in the weeds and followed them to a spot where they caught a putrid odor. Then they spotted a blackish-brown form with leathery skin, which they thought was a dead deer. Flies crawled all over it in the summer heat. The carcass appeared to have a head, but it was rotten and shape-less. Then one of them realized that the ear looked human, so they ran to get the police.

The responding officers immediately recognized the body as hu-man. It was nude, lying on its side, facedown. One forearm and hand and the fingers of the other hand were missing. Both feet had been severed at the ankles, and animal bites were evident on the skin and bones. The medical examiner estimated that the victim had been dead approximately one month, and she was quickly identified as the missing coed. The autopsy found evidence that she had been stabbed in the chest about thirty times. The lower leg bones had been smashed just above the ankles.

Detectives who examined the crime scene said the body had been moved at least three times, possibly by the killer, who apparently had returned at least once. It was first placed on top of a pile of bottles and cans, then moved five feet south. Later, it was moved three more feet. Clearly, whoever was out there that day was there to see her.

The next body would not be discovered for a year, but over the thirteen months after that, five would be found in roughly the same area. A teenager at the time, I was drawn to the sites, but I did not know why. Over the years, I found myself visiting those areas again and again.

Now that I have studied violent crimes up close, I believe I know what I was seeking. I was trying to sense the residual aura of a person so untroubled by moral laws that he not only could kill someone but stay close to his victim even after her death. I was experiencing my own defenselessness. These murders repulsed me, of course, but psychopathy is still one of the most compelling mysteries in the field of psychology. Even now with my background and expertise, these places still haunt me—just as Christian haunted me. There was some connection. Whether or not he was really a ghost, who he had been in life offered that same kind of disturbing mystique.

So I was going back to the sites, but this time I would take my camera. I brought the ring as well. He could "come" or not as he pleased—I figured the key was more about how it affected me. If I was ever to develop intuition with this skill, this had to be a good place to start.

My sister Ruth agreed to go with me. She did not understand my fascination with these murders, but after her experience with orbs in Gettysburg, she was more curious about them. We planned our expedition so that we would arrive at the site near dusk. As I looked at the map, I noticed how close we would be to the other murder sites. On the way, we passed by where the youngest victim, a thirteen-year-old, had been tossed on the roadside. Only a few more miles and we'd reach the cemetery where another one had been shot in the head. Even thirty years later, I felt gripped by the feeling that a killer had driven these roads, searching for places to dump a body. When we reached our destination we checked to make sure this was the place and then waited in the car for the sun to set.

I noted that the temperature had dropped considerably in the past hour and was now in the thirties. I really dislike ghosting in cold weather. I hate to be cold. And you have to watch that you don't breathe out while taking a photograph, because on digital cameras your breath can look just like ectoplasm.

I glanced out at the clearing where the body had once lain for a month. It had to be haunted, and I became more certain of that as darkness closed in. This place really disturbed me because someone I knew actually heard the killer there just before they found the body. It was like sitting one person away from him on a train.

"Okay," I said to Ruth. "It's time. Are you going with me?"

She considered this for only about three seconds before she said, "No, someone has to stay in the car in case we need a fast getaway."

"Okay, but that's how you'll be depicted—as the chicken."

"That's okay."

Knowing that no further argument would induce her to join me, I got out of the car. In order to get closer to the site, I climbed over a pipe, watching my footing in the snow, and then walked through prickly weeds that grabbed at my jeans. The foundation of the old farmhouse was about fifty yards away. I walked the property's perimeter and took photos along the way. The place was still as trashy as it had been back when the police had sifted through the garbage for clues and had found the victim's orange dress. I took several shots and checked a few, only to see that I wasn't yet getting any results. I decided to stop checking my photos and just concentrate on the aura of the place. My feeling was that I would get the best results at the old foundation, so I snapped several from different angles.

In a way, this was a test of how I'd developed in this ghostly business. I'd been at it for a while now and I wanted to see if I could trust my instincts. I knew I was supposed to be asking the ghosts for permission, but I always seemed to forget that part until after taking a photo.

Then I tried a bit of EVP, but it was windy and the sound of cars from the nearby road kept intruding. Also, my fingers were freezing. I figured that because I was so cold, I was probably not in a very good space for concentrating properly, so I gave it up and took a few more photos.

Eventually I tramped back to the car. After a final look at the site that had made me so aware of how close murder can come to ordinary lives, we drove away.

My experience here represented my first photography at a site where a body had actually lain, since I'd not had a digital camera at the Borden home. This was also a crime that had deep resonance for me. At the time, at the instigation of some friends who thought I resembled the victims, I actually tried to bait this killer. And I'd come close. I'd been hitchhiking from a spot where one of the girls was picked up the very next day and killed. It was stupid, but it was the experimental sixties, and we were young and invincible. I might have been the girl who lay by the side of the road or on the old farm. The victims spoke to me of my own fragility.

Ruth and I then went home. I wanted to hook the camera to

the television and search through the photos on a large screen that had brightness control. I had learned that sometimes orbs remain invisible on a photo until certain shadings or brightness brings them out. At first, there was nothing, but I doggedly went through each one. Several more showed only weeds. Two of the foundation shots showed nothing, and I wondered if I was developing any feeling for this after all. I'd been so *sure,* and everyone had urged me to develop confidence in my impressions. I was feeling disappointed, sure it had been a failed expedition, when in one photo I spotted a very clear orb up near some telephone wires. I went to the next photo. There they were: a dozen or more orbs hovering just inches over the abandoned foundation. Ruth and I both exclaimed at once over this result. Yes, something still haunted that place. It confirmed my feeling about scenes of violence. The auras lingered. And this one lingered within me.

I still had something more to investigate while I was there. One of my close friends during those crazy adolescent days eventually killed herself. She had gone out into the middle of the road one night and was hit by a truck. The place was not far away. Her tragic death was linked in my mind with the murder victims. Maybe it was the times— the social chaos, my own impressionable years. Or maybe it was that she had influenced my own near self-destructive impulses, which unlike her, I'd managed to turn around. Her name was Judy, and her sister Wendy invited me to come and explore the old building where they had lived with their parents. Now they ran a banquet business in the building, and all of the bartenders who worked there swore that they had seen the figures of a woman and a child walk through the basement area. Wendy told me that she thought the woman was associated with a theater that the building once had housed.

I went over to the place and set up the videocam. Thus far, I had only set up Rick's cameras, so I wasn't too experienced with this piece of equipment. I knew by touch where the buttons were and that you could only run the infrared light in darkness. So despite being unfamiliar with the building, I went alone into the dark cellar, which was all set up with tables and chairs. I ran into a post and felt terribly vulnerable as I fumbled with the camera. I have to admit, I was scared. It was a large space and felt incredibly open down there. This was where the ghosts lived (so to speak), and I felt I was trespassing on their domain. But I went ahead and hooked the camera onto a tripod and aimed it toward where the ghosts had been sighted. I opened up the LCD screen so I could watch for a few minutes, pressed the record button, and hit the infrared switch. Almost at once I saw an orb fly at me from the wall. I jerked away and had to restrain myself from running up the steps.

This was different from still shots. By the time you develop one of those and know you have an orb nearby, it's gone. With the video-cam, you're right there when it's happening. You see the orb go through a wall or come at you. It was spooky in every sense of the word, but I steeled myself to remain, and soon saw another one emerge. At that point, I decided to just let the camera pick up whatever was down there. I left it running and sprinted up the steps.

Wendy was fascinated with my adventures. She looked so much as she had years ago that I nearly felt that Judy was still around. Her oversized shirt, loose pants, and long curly hair reminded me of my hippie days. We talked about her impending trip to Europe and the art and poetry she had done in Judy's honor. At one point, after several glasses of wine, Wendy suggested we go to Judy's grave.

I wouldn't have suggested it myself, but I was quick to grab my Olympus and the voice recorder. First we went to where she had died, but both of us felt, contrary to folklore, that she would not have stayed in this place right next to a highway. Wendy then drove us to the local graveyard where her family plot was located. We had to park on the road and walk through the snow to get there. On several of the stones I passed, I noticed names of people I had known. Then we arrived at the large stone with Judy's name on it, among the names of other family members. We stopped and stood for a few moments in silence. This was poignant for both of us. We missed her, but we both knew how difficult her life had been, and how unhappy. Ordinarily I might have felt that I was trivializing Wendy's loss by doing this, but she insisted, so I took half a dozen shots of her standing there. I noted with surprise that in two successive shots, there was a single orb. At first it appeared to be at a distance, but then it was close by, hovering near her. I wondered.

We went back to her place to check the tape, but there were no more orbs, and not even a hint of an apparition.

Finally, it was time to leave. I had an appointment in Gettysburg. However, my brief time here did yield some insight. Having followed up my visit to a murder site with one to a suicide site, this whole business with Christian was taking on new meaning. Merlin had been right. Looking at Christian as the criminal that he was had dimmed his luster as a ghost. I didn't want him around me. But the possibility that he was so filled with self-loathing that he had killed himself softened that. In short, my sense of several aspects of who he might have been were sharpened here. Nevertheless, if he did not get better at communicating his needs or telling me his real story, I could not do much for him. In that case, I had to start thinking about what I should do with this ring.

—2—

I got more experience with the camera at Herr Tavern in Gettysburg. Mark Nesbitt, historian and author of the *Ghosts of Gettysburg* series, had invited me to participate in several days of investigation, which included the tavern and his own place of business, the Ghost House. Through trial and error, and with a few tips from Rick Fisher, we both learned some things that weekend about ghost video photography.

Mark's greatest strength may be his ability to explain history without being obnoxious. When he took me to Iverson's Pits, I felt I could almost see the events he was describing. "Iverson was flat-out dumb and it cost about four hundred men from the 12th Carolina their lives. He was hung over. He just told them to go give 'em hell. They had no idea where they were going. They wandered out and got within eighty yards of the Yankee guns. Within seconds, they all fell." His manner is relaxed, enlarged by a sense of humor and an air of confidence that comes from his endless hours of study. You want to know more, so you ask. He'll tell you, adding tidbits that make you want to study the subject yourself. "They buried them by scooping out a grave, rolling a body in, then scooping out another grave, and that went on for three hundred men. That's a helluva long trench." He'd be terrific in the classroom. Of course it helps that he tells some good ghost stories. "Laborers on the farm later claimed there were ghosts out here. They could hear bullets thumping and men screaming."

Mark's a solid guy with a twinkle in his eye and an eagerness to make life fun. Once a park ranger, he came from Ohio in 1970 and settled in Gettysburg. After five years, he quit the Park Service to research and write. In addition to several historical accounts of the Civil War, he wrote five volumes of the *Ghosts of Gettysburg* series based on stories sent to him. That enterprise spun off into a whole business revolving around ghosts, including tours and videotapes.

Mark himself had a passing interest in ghosts and thought the books would succeed as human-interest items. Then Rick Fisher came along and showed him how to do ghost photography. Mark was amazed when through night-vision binoculars he saw an orb coming at him through the roof of Sachs Bridge. It looked like it was going to pass right through him when it paused, turned, and went out the side. "I saw that. I can't deny it. It's getting harder to be objective about it all. I know it's an energy source that we don't understand yet." He also had experienced a drop in temperature at the same time that people got pictures of orbs around him. "It was at least twenty degrees colder."

His fourth ghost book reflected this shift. He began to think there was something to it, and he went out and got his own set of cameras and meters. He was convinced of the electromagnetic quality of the orbs. Further, he spoke to a "dowser"—someone attuned to the vibrations of the earth—who explained to him that quartz is a conductor and pointed out that some of the most haunted battlefields in the country stand atop ley lines. These are geomagnetic paths of energy that link ancient sites of spirituality, such as Stonehenge and Glastonbury in England. The strongest energy lies at the intersection of these ley lines. It's also been said that spirits prefer to travel along ley lines, using them as an energy source. Mark researched this and discovered that Gettysburg rests on a mass of rocks such as granite and feldspar, which are crystaline in form, and it is the crystal that supposedly conducts spiritual energy. He also believes orbs exhibit all the traits we associate with ghosts: electromagnetism, coldness, movement through solid objects, and invisibility. He's hoping that soon they'll be proven to be ghosts. "It's every historian's dream to have an interview with a Civil War soldier. Maybe this is the way we'll do it."

I was staying overnight at Herr Tavern out on Route 30 West. Built in 1815, it's on the National Register of Historic Places. In 1828, Fred and Sue Herr turned it into a public house and ran it for forty years. The battle of Gettysburg started close by, at a spot a little over a mile outside the town center. When the Yankees were driven back, Confederate artillery took up their positions on Herr's Ridge and among the tavern's buildings. A Union shell crashed into the second floor. Soon the wounded filled the place and many died. Six were buried there. Surgeons came in and turned the place into an instant hospital. Body parts from an explosion contaminated the well.

Today the inn has twelve guest rooms, a bar, restaurant, and banquet facilities. The sitting rooms overlook areas of the battlefield. The ghosts are thought to be Fred and Sue; apparently Fred liked room 2, where I was staying, because the guest book in there contained many references to "Fred" being around between 3:00 and 5:00 A.M. The most commonly reported manifestation was a rattling doorknob, but one guest said that someone grabbed her hand in the middle of the night.

There had also been tremendous racket in room 2, as if someone was demolishing the furniture, but a check always shows the room to be empty, with everything in its right place.

Workers that Steven Wolf and his wife Sharon hired to renovate the place claimed that they felt the presence of ghosts. One person said that she was nearly shoved down the stairs. Steve himself heard someone ask for a beer when the bar was empty. He also confessed to frequent outages of the electrical system.

Mark had set up a live radio interview with Jim Cooke at 5:00 the next morning, and we were about to go meet him for dinner. He was bringing a psychic, Karyol Kirkpatrick—the same psychic who had done the radio show at the Farnsworth.

Mark was impressed with her. He had taken her to one of the battlefields and she had named several states—Georgia, Texas, southern New York, and Philadelphia. Mark had pointed out that Philadelphia was not a state and she had shrugged and said, "That's what I got." Mark then found out that the soldiers that fought there had been recruited from Pittsburgh and Philadelphia. They also came from Orange County, New York, on the southern border. "I didn't know about that unit," Mark said. "So there was no psychic bleed from my mind to hers. She definitely picked up something." He did not think she had researched the place ahead of time. Since they had refrained from telling her where they were taking her, she'd have to have done a lot of memorization to be that specific.

On the way to Kracker Jacks to meet these two, I mentally urged Christian to make himself known to this woman in some overt manner, if only to prove himself to me. I wore the ring on its chain in plain sight, hoping she would pick up on it. Once in the restaurant, I immediately felt restlessness in the air around me, as if Christian did not want to be around this woman. It was the first time I actually thought I could "read" him, although it could have been my own projection. I wonder why she affected him—or me.

At any rate, it seems that he didn't stick around. When Karyol talked, she usually closed her eyes and adopted the same loud, full-voiced authority that Mariah, the theosopher in New Orleans, had exuded. She proved to be religious and "centered in the light." She even told me that, because she was nearly taken over once by a deceased psychic, she puts oil on the soles of her feet to prevent spirits from entering her.

When she said nothing throughout dinner about the ring, and even seemed to avoid eye contact with me, I finally asked if she would read it. She took it in her hand. "I was intrigued by this when I saw it," she said, then added, "I see a white-haired woman, and there's a sense of a loving relationship and a diamond. It was turned over to you in love. I think you inherited it."

That disappointed me. None of it matched what I knew. Perhaps Christian had declined to "pick up the phone." However Karyol did point out that energy of some kind was flowing through the ring. She didn't know what it was. (I later learned that her first impression of me gave her some concern: She thought I was dealing with something too close to the edge and would get into serious trouble. She had avoided me because she did not want me to ask her any questions about it.)

After dinner, Mark and I set up two videocameras in my room. We joked about the spirits hovering around my bed, and I told him the stories I'd heard about sexual entities. He knew someone who claimed she had one in her house.

"Hey," he said, "a little succubus never hurt anyone."

I laughed. "I'll take an incubus, if you please."

After he left, I turned out the lights and went from one camera to another, watching through the screens, until I finally had to get to bed. I didn't see anything, but that didn't mean there was nothing to see. I tried some EVP, but received only faint results. Karyol had mentioned that the voice is an energy imprint and it was possible that whoever I was trying to communicate with couldn't do any better.

Since I had to meet the others at five in the morning, I missed any manifestation that Fred might have offered. I arrived at our meeting place and found out that Jim and Karyol would be late because their alarm clocks had malfunctioned—two clocks, both brought from home. A spooky start to a spooky day. When everyone was together, we went off to Sachs Bridge. The idea was that Jim would broadcast our expedition live and report any interesting events. As he interviewed Mark, I walked off to the side and got my first good shot of ectoplasm. I had one on the side, got another one on the roof, and two more inside the bridge. All of the other shots were clear, with a few orbs, so this effect was not the result of morning mist. The ecto was also too far away from me to have been condensation from my breath. Jim stood at the head of the bridge, asking if anyone was getting anything. I laughed because I had a photo with five orbs around him and his wife, Maureen. Karyol talked about a woman who had been raped there. She said there was a lot of sadness.

Back at Herr Tavern, we went through the rooms while Karyol

read the spirit energy and told the radio listeners about who she thought was there. She mentioned that it had been a surgery and noted that the floors were sticky with blood. There was also something about a treasure and someone named Jack. In my room, she said a man was sitting in the chair. I sat down in it to see if I felt anything. Nothing. I didn't doubt that some psychics have genuine impressions, but I didn't enjoy just listening and accepting whatever she said—even if there were some evidential confirmations. It was like riding in a taxi when I wanted to drive myself. I went off to do some EVP.

At one point, I was telling the story of Christian's ring to Sharon Wolf and Karyol overheard me. "If I were you," she said, "I'd get rid of that ring. Get it far away."

That surprised me. It had been her initial feeling that it was given in love. "But you didn't sense anything evil when you held it," I said.

"Nevertheless, I think you need to be rid of it. It could invite something in."

I shrugged. I already knew I had to start thinking of a plan. I did not want to push Wraith any further than I had to.

—**3**—

The radio show ended and everyone went in different directions for the afternoon. I had made contact with a sociology professor at Gettysburg College named Charles Emmons, and I went to meet with him. His wife, Penelope, was a talented medium, and he considered himself a student of spiritualism. I told him only briefly about my haunted ring, and we found common ground in our desire to probe further into this world while also maintaining an open-minded objectivity. I wanted to meet him and see if he had any sense of Christian.

Charlie was developing his own mediumship by studying the lives of other mediums, attending a spiritualist camp in New York, and experimenting with devices like a psychomanteum. The psychomanteum dates back to ancient Greece, where gazing into a reflective pool would produce images or messages from the dead. People today use a dim light and mirror. You sit in a comfortable chair, lit from behind, and situate yourself in a way that gives you a view of the mirror without seeing your own reflection. Experiences can range from visions to apparent communication with deceased loved ones. Generally people who do this have some question they want answered. In his various books, researcher Raymond Moody discusses his results with these "facilitated apparitions." Although 85 percent of his clients make a successful contact, sometimes it happens after they return home. In other words, ghosts can follow you.

Although Charlie spoke tentatively about his experience with receiving spiritual messages, he'd had moderate success. He called himself a student medium, but some of his messages for other people, who confirmed their contents, were sufficiently detailed to make him the equal of people I have met who claim to have full mediumistic abilities. Charlie was not always sure about the details he was receiving, but he had learned to stop editing himself. He once had told a man attending a spiritualist meeting that there was something he had forgotten. Charlie sensed that it was a round object but felt too uncertain to add that detail. The man himself realized that what he had forgotten was a medallion—a round object—that he had wanted to use to contact his deceased father. Charlie learned from that experience to just go with his impressions.

His own first attempts in the paranormal involved him in psychokinesis, in which he managed to beat chance in a dice-rolling experiment. His interest eventually took him to China, where he studied Asian experiences with spirits. He was gratified to find no significant differences from those reported in our culture, which tended to confirm the universal nature of ghostly phenomena. He then wrote *Chinese Ghosts and ESP,* and it was this book that brought him to my attention.

Charlie was in his basement office on campus when I met with him. He had grayish hair but a young face. Glasses shielded his eyes somewhat, but his expression was deliberative. Lean and of average height, he invited me to have a seat amidst his pop-culture paraphernalia. He pointed out a few items like his Energizer bunny, Spiro Agnew wastebasket, and psychedelic pet rock. I noticed a lava lamp and several Santa Clauses. Further into the densely packed office was a 1940s Zenith floor-model radio. I sat on a couch while Charlie took a seat in his office chair. As we talked he told me about his research. In a recent psychomanteum experience, he believed he had actually seen images in the mirror of a time and place associated with his childhood.

We talked a bit about EVP, and he described a spirit recording he had done in the Farnsworth, where I had spent the night on a previous trip. He played the tape back and heard a male voice, but when he went to play it again, it was no longer there. Yet he had not imagined it, and another person who was with him had also heard it.

At some point in our conversation, Charlie said, "This may be really inappropriate, but I'm very curious about your ring. I'd like to hold it."

I took it from around my neck, slipped off the chain, and gave him the ring. He closed it in his hand and shut his eyes. During his silence, I attempted to feel something myself. That experience of restlessness with Karyol had been provocative.

It wasn't long before I thought I sensed a solid column of energy directly in front of Charlie. It seemed that someone—Christian?—was standing slightly to his left, but knee-to-knee, and looking down at him with a challenging smirk.

Then Charlie began to talk. "What I see is my mother. She's telling me that this is something I don't want to know."

Hmmm. Like Charles in New Orleans with Jacqueline.

"Now I see this sort of dense grass, almost like bushes, and it's growing and blocking her out. I can't see her anymore."

"Like you're not supposed to listen to her?" I asked.

"Yes, like that." He stuck his left hand out in front of him. "I sense something right here, like he's standing here. It's male energy. I see a lot of hair, dark hair. He's large."

That surprised me. It was exactly where I thought Christian might be, but once again it sounded more like a description of Wraith.

"There's agitation," Charlie continued, "and worry. He has some unfinished business that involves two things. Something from when he was alive and something that involves you. He has some intention toward you." He opened his eyes to look at me, as if asking for confirmation, then added, "It might be romantic. I sense that he has a sort of confused intimate intention toward you. It's as if he wants to get real close, but it's a mixture of emotions, negative and positive, not knowing what he would do if he could get there. It's rather overbearing."

I shrugged. I suspected that Christian had some intention, but I didn't think it was romantic. It could be an attraction to my spirit, as Wraith had said, but if it was, it was angry and confused.

"There's live energy in this ring," Charlie said, repeating others before him. "It wants to be worn. He wants to wear it."

He closed his fingers around it again and concentrated. I thought I felt the energy recede, as if it had moved away and given up—perhaps expended itself.

"He says that there's nothing I can do about it anyway," Charlie told me. "I see him changing and forming into an object." He struggled to describe it and came up with a piece of black, faceted obsidian floating in the air. I had no idea what that could mean, but it was clear to both of us that this was all he was going to get. He tried again and felt only the energy in the ring. He handed it back and I put it on the chain. Before I left, we agreed to keep in touch about any progress that either of us made into the spirit realm.

To my mind, we'd already made some progress. Charlie seemed to have received an accurate message that whatever was attached to this ring was not good, and we'd both felt energy of some kind in the same place. It had been male. For me, it was interesting to have experienced it twice. Although it was only subjective confirmation, I was happy to know that I'd had different impressions each time and that each was somewhat confirmed by the responses of the parties involved.

—4—

Later that day, Mark and I went together to Pennsylvania Hall on the Gettysburg College campus. Built in 1837, it now houses administrative offices, but during the battle it became a makeshift surgery. Hundreds came in for amputations or suturing, or even to die. Limbs were tossed out the window into a pile.

Ghost stories here include sightings of soldiers in the cupola, where sentries had watched the battle's progression. Even more frightening was the experience two women had one night while working late. They entered the elevator and pushed the button for the first floor, but it took them to the basement instead. When the doors opened, they saw a scene of horror that they would never forget. Impossibly, blood-spattered physicians were operating on moaning soldiers, sewing up wounds and amputating limbs. The women became frantic, punching the elevator button to go back up when a ghostly orderly caught their eye. He took a step toward them as if to get them to come and help, but the doors closed before he could reach them. The women reported this horrific experience to campus security, but an officer who checked found no one in the basement.

I wanted to go down into that building myself and get some pictures. It was locked, but we found a way in and got into the elevator. Mark then told me that someone else had had an experience similar to the two women's, which confirmed for him their apparent emergence into a time slippage. We wondered if it could happen to us. I felt the elevator descend and held my breath, hoping . . .

No such luck. The doors opened to show a basement full of some very unghostly storage. Even my pictures and EVP were negative, but it was eerie to walk around in a place where the ghostly imprints implied that many men had gone through some frightful emotional experiences. Bodies and limbs had piled up in here and blood had coated the floors. Much as I wanted to see a ghost, I wasn't so sure about a phantom amputation.

That evening I stayed in the back bedroom of the Ghost House on Baltimore Street—Mark's tour office—to continue with the weekend's investigation. I'd already seen photos of orbs in here, so I went right up to the attic to take more. I got two small orbs, but no responses on the recorder.

I decided to see if I could pick up some EVP in my room. I'd heard about a dog barking at an empty corner and several orbs that had shown up in photos of two kids. I turned on the recorder and asked, "Is there someone in this room?" On playback, I heard a low rumble.

"Did you die here?"

"Yes."

"Can you give me a name?" The two-syllable response was strong but not altogether clear. Randy or Henry or Charlie.

"Were you a soldier?" Could have been yes or no, but it was emphatic.

"How old were you?"

"Twenty-three in the war."

That last part, "in the war," was clear and even a bit startling. Again, I have to say that I would hardly have anticipated an answer like that. Granted I was at a Civil War battlefield, but I still would not expect it to be that specific. It couldn't be a subconscious projection. I let Mark hear it. He was surprised, too, at the clarity of that last phrase.

He showed me a history of the place and told me that when a carpenter was renovating the section that dated back to 1834, the door kept swinging closed when he walked over to it. The brick and wood house had been built in two sections. During the battle, the second story offered a place for Confederate sharpshooters to find their mark, while houses to the south and north served as field hospitals. Mark had brought Karyol in to do a psychic assessment, and she mentioned several areas of the building that appeared to be haunted. In the basement, she noted that there were images of injured people and blood. Upstairs she felt something about someone named Mary, and in Mark's office she was sure she could hear children playing with marbles on a wooden floor, despite the carpeting. She also felt someone named Henry present there, and subsequent research indicated that Henry Comfort had been an owner.

Later in the room again, I ventured to see if Christian was around.

"Say my name," I instructed. To my astonishment, he—or someone—did.

"Katherine Ramsland." My entire name. When I played it again just to be sure, it was clear. I asked others to listen, and they heard it, too.

I then asked if "Charlie" was in the room. I got no response, so I asked if he needed help. What came back sounded like "Go away." It was tricky talking to these entities; if they didn't know they were dead, it probably wasn't a good idea to assume it, since that could interfere with their illusions and possibly drive them away.

I then asked how many were in the room and thought I heard "sixteen." I asked about ten more questions, with little response, and then heard what sounded like, "Katherine, help me."

I stopped recording and sat perfectly still. Someone was asking for my help—*my* help specifically. But who? And what was the problem over on that side? I didn't like to think about what it must be like to be floating around, seeking a way out, pleading with living beings for assistance. That seemed truly a nightmare. And that soul was trying to contact me. I then asked, "What's the name of the one who needs help." I thought that someone said, "Christian." I asked him to repeat that but got nothing.

These little blips of phrases are the most baffling aspect of EVP. Some need to be followed up, but they leave one with no opportunity to do so. The feeling was like standing on a street corner as a car drives by and someone rolls down a window to cry for help. Then the car is gone. I used the recorder to ask again who had spoken to me, but got no further with this. I ended the session with a vague feeling of something not done that desperately needed closure. I went to bed and hoped that if I dreamed, I might get an answer.

During the night, I heard a wooden door slam somewhere on the second floor. I responded by pulling up the covers. Mark told me that others staying alone there at night had reported the same thing. When I got up in the morning, no doors were closed. We had also set up two videocameras, which recorded a few orbs going through Mark's office. So it seemed that I was not alone.

At dusk that evening, Mark and I made a trek to the Triangular Field, up by Devil's Den. Named before the Civil War, Devil's Den is a maze of huge boulders where intense battles took place. Nearby is a creek called Bloody Run, which was said to have turned red from all the blood. Across the road from the boulders is the Triangular Field, known to some as the most haunted area of the battlefield. Soldiers from Georgia and Texas fought through this field, and many fell and lay in agony from the shrapnel and minié balls that exploded in their flesh.

When Mark did the research for his book *Thirty-five Days to Gettysburg,* he focused on one soldier in particular who had been killed here. "He was with the 15th Georgia, so I know his name and I've talked to his relatives. I even found his grave in Savannah. I know this guy intimately. I come out here every July 2 about five in the afternoon because that's when he was killed. I actually put his diary in the book. His unit was attacked and he writes about it, but then the handwriting changes. It turns out that his brother had picked up his diary after he was killed and added a note about his death."

Mark had the names of the men who had served in the various regiments in the Triangular Field. He didn't know how many from his list had actually died there, but his plan was to call the roll as if he were an officer and to have me catch what I could on camera. We knew that many people had experienced disabled camera equipment in this place, so we were prepared for the worst.

Behind us, we both had a videocamera rolling with infrared lights.

Mark reeled off a few names, holding his digital recorder, and I snapped some shots. I got one orb not far from him. When we played the recorder back, we listened to him calling out names. After one, we heard a distinct, "Yessir!"

We were speechless for several seconds afterward. As he searched my face with an astonished expression I'm sure was matched by my own, Mark played the recording again, as if needing to confirm what had just happened. We hadn't imagined it: There it was, in the silence of the Pennsylvania dusk. "Yessir!"

Mark went back to use his videocamera while I remained deep in the field. I took some shots and got one photo with several orbs. Then I went around the perimeter of the field, where soldiers had run through the woods, and took more shots. One was a true prize: ectoplasm and an orb in a tree. To be sure, I took some photos while breathing out into the cold air. It looked nothing like what I'd just gotten in the tree. In fact, I had to breathe really hard to get a shot of the mist in my breath, so that effectively canceled out the suspicion that my ecto was just a photo of breath condensation. I was pleased.

Mark told me that he'd caught an orb following me on video,

"just like a puppy." I wondered "who" it was. I got a few more good shots, but when it finally grew too cold to stay outside, we packed up and went to set up a camera in the Ghost House.

As soon as I entered the attic and set up the equipment, I could see orbs highlighted by the infrared beam. I recalled that Rick Fisher had gotten a tape up here of two orbs in flight and had recorded a breathy voice saying, "Catch me." It felt weird knowing these things were there with me right at this moment. Mark thought that it would be interesting to leave the videocamera running by itself, so I left it in place and descended from the attic. I talked with Mark's girlfriend for a few minutes and then we left the building. Mark told me later that when he viewed the tape, the orbs were active while I was talking, but once we left, there was nothing more.

I wondered if they responded to the energy of people nearby. Or if perhaps they fed on it. We needed to do more experiments.

—**5**—

It was one thing to take my videocam to a reputedly haunted place like the Ghost House. It was quite another to set it up where I lived. I'd already gotten numerous still shots of orbs in my apartment at all hours of the night. Some of the photos showed dozens of orbs, of all sizes and densities. It made me wonder about what they actually were. I'd also gotten orbs in a horse barn back in Michigan, at the urging of my sister Donna, because many people there felt the place was haunted—by horses. I began to wonder if the orbs might even be some kind of transient electronic pollution.

I asked Rick Fisher, with his more painstaking approach, how he logically justified his belief that orbs are actually ghosts. While carefully pointing out that no one knows for sure, he said that when you take into account the meter readings, the temperature drops, and the fact that the orbs seem to react to external stimuli, you have to at least consider that an intelligence of some kind is present. "We get them in places where death or some strange event has occurred and they respond when we ask them to show themselves on film. You see them come out of the walls." He reminded me about the voice recorded in the Ghost House as two orbs flew by. Unfortunately, when I asked him why I would get so many in my apartment, he didn't have an answer.

I continued to think about this: Even if orbs were ghosts, were they only attracted to certain types of souls, such as those who are open to them? Taking these photos each night had given me the chance to study some of the finer nuances. I wondered if the videocamera would

An orb hovering over the military cemetery at Gettysburg.

Monument at the High Water Mark, Gettysburg Battlefield.

The bedroom where Abby Borden was murdered (and where I slept).

Witch Memorial, Salem, Massachusetts.

My first vortex, near the bridge Washington's army crossed to win the battle of Princeton.

Orb hovering over the former field hospital for Washington's army, Princeton, New Jersey.

Orbs hovering over the Princeton cemetery.

The haunted room of a three hundred-year-old farmhouse.

Haunted room with an orb, taken just after the previous picture.

Rick with a video camera and an orb over his head.

Orbs inside Fort Delaware.

Ghost hunter using an EMF meter to indicate when to take a picture.

Ghost hunter using a thermal scanner. He said, "Take a picture now!" And there was the orb.

Orbs hovering in an old church, Burkittsville, Maryland.

Jerome Grand Hotel, Jerome, Arizona.

In Jerome, Arizona, I asked "Christian" to show himself, and this is the picture I got.

Orb in motion in my apartment.

Odd orb activity in my apartment—possibly caught in motion.

Orb on the painting in my apartment.

Taken after raising a lot of dust—looks very different from the bright, opaque orbs.

Ectoplasm and orb on a haunted inn, New Jersey.

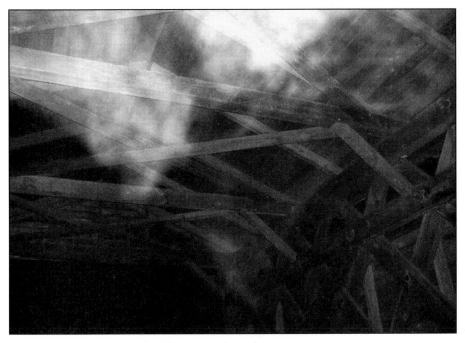

Ectoplasm on Sachs Bridge, Gettysburg.

The Ghost House, Gettysburg.

On the porch at the Ghost House 1.

On the porch at the Ghost House 2.
These pictures were taken simultaneously.

Mark Nesbitt doing a roll call at Triangular Field, Gettysburg Battlefield.

Ectoplasm and orb at the edge of Triangular Field, Gettysburg Battlefield.

Orb hovering in front of the Logan Inn—taken in the afternoon with black and white film.

Haunted painting at the Logan Inn.

Haunted painting with vortex, taken during the eclipse.

Witch's Ball at the Logan Inn.

Room 520, the Chelsea Hotel—it looks like dust, yet no other photo of the room came out like this.

Room 520, the Chelsea Hotel—this orb appeared while Rosemary and Kitty were engaged in energy rituals.

open up more of this world to me. It wasn't long before I realized I'd added an essential piece of equipment.

The first night, I waited until midnight and then turned out all the lights. I took a few still photos, which showed me nothing, and then set that camera aside to turn on the videocamera's infrared light. I watched through the LCD screen as the Nightshot brought a perfectly dark room into focus, as if it were daylight. So far, so good.

For a few minutes, I patiently watched the screen. I thought I saw some flashes of a white circle on the closet doors, almost as if they came though it from the other side, spotted me, and receded. Then I saw one bright flash in the area of the light switch. I stopped the camera and rewound the scene.

Yes, there it was. It was present for just a split second, but it was clearly an orb. Right there over the light switch.

I moved the camera to a new position and caught another one floating across the rug. Then two large bright orbs came down from high on the wall over the desk.

After that, there was nothing.

I got similar results for the next few nights, but I soon noticed that they seemed to be coming and going in the vicinity of the desk. It was an old desk that I had acquired when I bought a house owned by a woman who had fallen, lain for several days on the floor, and then died in the hospital. I couldn't imagine that she would haunt this desk, but then I had no idea what significance it might have had for her.

I pointed the camera at the desk and watched. A few small orbs came in and out of the space between the desk and the shelf unit where my television sat. When I got impatient, I decided to move around to catch their attention. I waved my arms in the air, silly as that looked, but to my surprise, it got results. A fairly sizable orb floated toward me, followed by several more coming up from the rug, as if startled.

Was it dust?

I did the same movement again, but this time got no response. Interesting.

Then it occurred to me that the reason they were so fascinated with the desk—particularly the one side—was that all of my electrical equipment was plugged into an electric outlet strip that lay on the floor. Maybe they preferred to be near electrical sources. I had gotten a lot of orbs in still-shots hovering over the television screen.

That brought to mind an article I had read in *Fate* magazine about using electrostatic generators as ghost bait. The authors had claimed (erroneously, I found) that most ghost activity occurs on cold, dry nights. They tried out some generators that they said got results. Among them were the Wimshurst and Van de Graaff generators, which produced static electricity, and the Tesla coil, which also created EMF fields. I looked these up. I was interested in the Tesla coil but was afraid it might mess up my computer, so I ordered the Van de Graaff instead. I wondered if, given the amount of activity in my place, I might be able to "feed" them a bit of energy so they could materialize into something.

Still, the idea scared me. I mean, what if I created an apparition right there in my living room? Would pulling the generator plug also pull the plug on it? Or would it be like Frankenstein's monster: Once created, there would be no controlling it.

The device consisted of a hollow steel bulb atop a stem that housed large rubber belts. The first night, I turned it on and watched it produce sparks in the dark through the bulb. It was loud and annoying, but I gave it some time to work up an electronic sweat. Then I got out the camera.

To my astonishment, the orbs came flying at me, away from the generator. I had the distinct impression that they did not like it, although clearly it had the effect of getting more floating white objects into the air.

Just to be sure, I cleaned out a dust mop in front of the camera to see what dust particles looked like in the infrared light. They certainly didn't look like orbs. I tried raising dust from the rugs by jumping on them. Nope.

I continued working with the generator over the next week. In that time, I caught one orb coming at me in a rather diffuse state before forming into what looked like a floating cigarette, dropping into the rug, and vanishing. I recalled that ectoplasm had been observed appearing in similar shapes, which were thought to be the raw material of apparitions. I saw another that seemed to form into a fist and another that looked like a handkerchief picked up off the desk and thrown through the wall. Two orbs danced upward together before disintegrating, and one night, as I turned on the camera, I saw what looked like a luminous wave. Unfortunately, it was gone before I could record it.

Despite all this activity, I decided that none of us in the room liked the generator, so I sent it back. I feared that I might lose all my orbs. In fact, for several nights after those generator experiments, there were none. I hoped I hadn't driven them away. Then one night, staying up late to finish writing a chapter, I took a photo and they were everywhere. I was relieved.

In the meantime, however, I decided to try to eliminate other, more mundane explanations for the orbs, so I started with queries to the technical staff of some of the camera companies. To Sony, I wrote:

When I use the infrared, I often get these perfectly round white balls sometimes floating and sometimes zipping through a room. They are not bugs or dust. I know people who use your Mavica digital cameras and they get still shots of these things that show balls of light of varying sizes which are invisible to the eye. So they are there, but they are only visible on infrared or digital. I've seen these photos and videos posted on websites as evidence of ghosts. They are not from sources of light, camera straps, insects, reflective surfaces, lens flare, or drops of water. Can you offer any explanations? I'm not convinced these are 'ghosts,' as many are, but they are certainly invisible, they certainly move around the room, they go through walls, and even as they are floating by the camera, they suddenly just disappear. Some people using thermal scanners or EMF meters get readings when these things are present that indicate drops in temperature or blips in electromagnetic energy. Any ideas?

Sony thanked me for contacting them and sent the following response: "Regretfully, we are unable to offer an explanation for this phenomenon." Olympus merely said that it must be dust or moisture in the air.

I asked some people I knew who worked with digital imaging and they had no explanation either, apart from suggesting that there was a source of light exposure that the eye could not see. Jana Marcus, the photographer who had experienced some kind of anomaly in New Orleans, thought they were round because the lens was round, but I had other shapes as well, and when I asked her about these, she was stymied.

I wasn't long after I began experimenting with the generator that I noticed something very odd on the television screen. I had some photos of orbs all around the screen, but had only recently noticed that something else was happening there. Drawn in the dust, all over the screen, were small marks, like fingerprints or the imprints of something bounced against the screen (little white balls?). I went over and looked more closely. It appeared that someone had drawn a finger through the dust in the form of several designs. One was a question mark. The others were more detailed: a bunny with what looked like a noose around its neck, a basketball that appeared to be punctured by a blunt object, and a very erotic male image that I won't describe here.

I was puzzled. I wasn't likely to draw on TV screens in my sleep. I had not had anyone over in months, and these designs appeared to be recent. The lines were free of dust. I'd heard of demography, where writing mysteriously appears on someone's body, but not this. Tentatively, I moved my finger along one line of a drawing and realized no dust was there. It was clear that this was quite recent.

I called Kat and described it to her to see if she'd heard of anything like this before. She was, after all, a ghost historian and had heard almost every ghost story that New Orleans had to offer.

"Someone's obviously trying to communicate," she said, "but why would they be so enigmatic? Why not write in words?"

"I don't know. I don't even know if I've described the drawings correctly. That's just what they look like to me."

"I've heard of something similar to this. The owner of Lafitte Guesthouse was planning a trip, and ashes came out of the fireplace. Then the words 'Don't go' were written in the ashes in French. The ghost there was a little French girl. He went on his trip anyway, and while he was gone, New Orleans got hit with the worst hurricane in its history and he lost a lot of property. He wished he'd been there to protect it."

"Well, maybe this is a warning. Like I'm the bunny or something."

She didn't know. She wasn't sure what it meant.

I then called Mark Nesbitt in Gettysburg, since he was familiar with the electronic angle. His first words were, "I'm going to quit dusting my TV!" Then he said that this incident did not surprise him.

"It doesn't?"

"No. Think about it. A television screen is sensitive to electrons. An electron gun is aimed at the screen, hitting it with negative electrons, so it will attract things that have a need for electromagnetic energy. The dust sticks to it because it's charged in some way." He reminded me that there were accounts of faces of deceased people appearing on the screens of televisions that are turned off. Why couldn't they also use it for messages?

"I guess they can, but I wish they'd be more clear."

I thought the ghosts were trying to teach me that they were never going to be anything but enigmatic with me because I wasn't receptive enough for a real communication. Or perhaps it was the Decline Effect—we just weren't meant to get that close.

Recently I had spoken again to Mariah, the theosophical minister who thought Christian was a demon, to remind her that I was coming to New Orleans soon. I hoped that she could still guarantee me an experience of seeing a ghost. However, Mariah was ill. She might not even make it to the Big Easy while I was there, let alone do all the prep work necessary to make this experience happen. Needless to say, I was disappointed.

"It took me a long time to recover from that last encounter," she told me. "I couldn't get rid of those girls who were murdered. When you deal with victims, they want you to experience their pain. I can't help them and it gets very frustrating. I've got my own pain to deal with. I don't want theirs, too."

"They didn't leave you?" I asked.

"Not for several months. The problem is that when they die like that, they go into the Veil of Illusions. They don't get over being dead. Their lives were cut short and they still have life energy that they pump into their new experience. But they're incapable of giving you blocks of communication. They just don't give you the information you need to help them to understand."

I thought about this. "Maybe that's why I'm always getting the same stuff from Christian. He never gives me something I can really use."

"He's a one-note soldier. He has to give up the crap to grow as a spirit, but he is a demon. He's achieved what he set out to do in life. I've meditated on this. He's all the way there, I can assure you. Those two women told me they were tortured. He tortured the young one in front of the older one."

"But that's not how his energy seemed to you at first."

"I know better now. I've spent time on it. He's putting his energy into your aura to make you attract bad things. That's what he wants from you. To move away from that, he needs to school himself to get more information. There are teachers on that side and he needs to find one. But that's not what he's doing."

We ended the conversation with Mariah saying that she would try to get to New Orleans, but I knew that she'd had it with Christian and would not try to help me. Jeff, the voodoo medium, had backed out as well, and Mimi, the witch, had other plans. Kat said that she would conduct a séance herself, so we made plans.

My niece, Ming, flew in from Florida to continue with her ghost-hunting lessons, and Kat picked us up to go to lunch. On the way to the French Quarter, Kat used her car phone to check in with her assistant for messages and sensed that something was wrong. The woman on the other end denied it. Kat hung up, but bothered by her gut feeling, she called back. Finally, her assistant admitted that she felt drained by a series of dreams she'd had over the past two nights. Kat listened, reassured her, and then hung up. She told me the contents of the conversation, and we looked at each other. Here we go again.

At lunch we discussed Christian and what we ought to do about him. Kat thought he was probably much weaker than we all realized and that's why he used tricks to scare people. She told me that one of her young granddaughters could see spirits, and after my last visit when we had conjured Christian with the psychic board, the little girl had told her that behind the door in Kat's office she could sense a ghost that frightened her. When Kat asked why, she lowered her gaze and said, "It's a vampire."

"She said that?" I asked. "A vampire ghost?"

"That's what she said," Kat responded. "I'm sure that was him behind the door. What other ghost could be a vampire, too? I think you should really push the envelope with Christian and see what you get."

"Easy for you to say," I laughed. "You don't live alone."

We talked about what we would need for a séance and then parted company so Kat could run errands. Ming and I went off to O'Flaherty's Irish pub on Toulouse Street to explore some of the French Quarter's haunted buildings. About fifteen minutes after we arrived, I was told I had a phone call. Puzzled, I went into the bar to find out who it was.

"I figured it out!" Kat shouted. "I tracked you down because I needed to tell you this while I was thinking it. I know what he does!"

"Who?"

"Christian! I know what he's up to. He goes after the naive and weak and unsuspecting. I came back to the office and found out that the series of dreams my assistant had were about being murdered. She dreamed about her grandmother approaching her and hanging her upside down like a gutted pig and cutting her throat."

That startled me. Another dream that was alarmingly close to how Wraith had described one of Christian's murders.

"It's him, I know it's him," Kat continued. "I think maybe he comes around here for some reason. I'm sure it was him that my granddaughter sensed. Maybe he's here because you're here."

"You know, there's one other possibility that we haven't thought of," I said. "What if the dreams are all from Wraith?" I hadn't told anyone that I thought I'd seen him the last time I was in this city. "Maybe he's astrally projecting or something."

"I don't know. Let's just do the séance and see what we get."

Kat came fully prepared. Miss Mary, my unpaid assistant who had seen the ghost before my friend Corey died, agreed to join us. With Ming and I, that made four. We set up a table in our hotel room.

Kat had her psychic board. She said a loud prayer of protection. Then we started. I did some EVP first and Miss Mary thought she heard the name Corey. I wasn't so sure, but the planchette on the psychic board went to "Listen." Kat said that was a message to just use the recorder, so she stopped and we concentrated on the recorder. Again, while we got results, it was a matter of interpretation. At no point did I think Christian was there. The voice was not the one I was used to. It was much more faint.

"I think you protected us too much," I told Kat.

She admitted that she was very grounded and that she'd blessed the séance instruments to keep them free of negative vibrations and evil influences. "I may have had an entourage of spirit guides keeping him out."

We went on for over an hour, but the séance came to an end without advancing my understanding of Christian. I was even a bit worried that he had not communicated with me in some time. However, he seemed to be up to his usual tricks with our dreams.

The next morning, Ming told me that she'd dreamed that her mother told her that *she* had dreamed she was going to cut Ming's throat. Another dream with a knife and a slashed throat. Was Kat right that he was trying to affect those people around me who weren't aware of him or guarded against him?

I, too, had a dream, a very vivid and graphic one, but it did not share the same bloody themes with these others. Without going into detail, it had to do with making myself vulnerable through my desire to do something for a man that was impossible. He allowed me to think it was possible because that was how he was going to trap and kill me. It felt like a warning dream for my protection, and I wondered if it might be from Corey. More symbolic than brutal, it had left me feeling wary.

I told the dream to Kat and she said, "I think he'll do anything to make you feel vulnerable. That's how he gets power. He stayed away from the séance because I'm not afraid of him. I give him no power. He's weak. That means you can be rid of him if you want."

I had to wonder if I really wanted to.

It was time for me to go, so we moved Ming to a better hotel in the Quarter, the Place d'Armes. Before I left, we played around with the recorder. I didn't want to scare her, since she'd be there alone, but she wanted me to go ahead and see. (Later she regretted that decision.)

I asked a few questions about who was here, etc., and didn't get much response. Then I said, "Tell us your name." When I played it back, I nearly dropped the recorder. As clear as could be, as if he were right there in the room, he told us.

"Christian."

What Is a Ghost?

"GHOSTS CONTROL THEIR OWN DEFINITIONS."
—ANTONIO GARCEZ

—1—

Given how clear that voice was, I decided to return to my EVP research. What I really wanted to know was how to set up a machine like Spiricom. I checked my original sources, but the actual description seemed elusive. It had something to do with the interplay of high-frequency signals that in turn created a lower frequency signal—making more energy available than the traditional white noise managed to do. I asked Mark Macy, who had been part of an international organization to promote the development of ITC, and he had said that for now things were on hold, although there had been more experimentation lately with video images and computers. Then I ran across a letter written to *Fate* magazine by Terrance Peterson. He claimed that Spiricom was a fake. He'd received tapes from the machine, just as George Meek had, and he gave them to a speech pathologist who reproduced the effects with an artificial larynx. It was Peterson's contention that a fame-seeking Bill O'Neil had duped Meek.

While this seemed contrary to the picture that John Fuller had painted of a publicity-shy O'Neil, Peterson went on to imply that Sarah Estep of the AA-EVP also thought the whole thing was suspicious. She received a Spiricom machine from Meek and had asked O'Neil to invite the dead scientist to talk to her. When the dead George Mueller asked for directions to her house, she began to have doubts. Nevertheless, if Spiricom is fake, then Peterson does not explain how O'Neil and Meek managed to get private details about Mueller, including the location of a book that seemed all but lost. It's also difficult to say how an uneducated man like O'Neil could have known all the sophisticated information that he relayed. In addition to that, Mueller appeared on a television screen in 1991 to a group of ITC researchers. That alone indicates something apart from fraud.

I had to find out, so I sought out Sarah Estep and asked her myself. She said, "I worked with Spiricom for a month and had results. Not like O'Neil's, but I still had a number of voices that came through. Most people think everyone should have identical results with a special system such as Spiricom. This is not the case. Everyone has his own unique energies and vibrations—as unique as our fingerprints. For that reason, what O'Neil did with Spiricom could not be expected to carry over to others. Unfortunately, the developers of the system (and George Meek had some very bright engineers working with him) expected many others to have the same results. Of course their thinking was incorrect. O'Neil was a gifted medium to start with. He had the 'right' kind of energies, compatible with many in spirit, to draw them to him while he was taping."

She confirmed some ideas I'd already read, namely that the EVP/ITC operator had to possess mediumistic capabilities. "I feel everyone is mediumistic to a certain extent," she said. "Some admit it; others shudder at the idea. But there are mediums and there are mediums. Everyone who tapes [records spirits] uses these abilities, whether they are aware of them or not. The maestros of the tape recorder have outstanding abilities. They are psychologically open, in tune, and want contact very much with other dimensions. I imagine you already are aware about the 'bonding' that can go on with people in our world and entities in other worlds. Those that have the best results not only have very special mediumistic abilities, but they are able to bond with the invisibles. In this world, we bond (or not) with certain people we meet or are in our lives to one degree or another. It is basically the same with other dimensions and other worlds. Good equipment helps, but the person using it is probably close to 90 percent responsible for the results."

Estep rekindled my interest in Spiricom. I especially liked the idea of the bonding. It reminded me of the ghost companion idea I had as a kid. I then learned that another researcher, Swiss electronics expert Klaus Schreiber, had studied Spiricom and invented Vidicom, a device specially adapted for television. He captured the faces of deceased relatives on a videocamera, but when Schreiber died, others were unable to make it work as he had, suggesting another operator effect. Then a team in Luxemburg became quite successful at getting messages and images from entities that identified themselves as "TimeStream." I'd already seen this group mentioned and now I was able to learn more. The essential message was that the consciousness of the universe was strictly spiritual; it creates all physical and psychical form. It's all Spirit. If we, the living, have any hope of getting our act together, it's going to involve some connection with that part of ourselves.

Then I listened to a CD called *The Ghost Orchid,* which included some of Raudive's voices along with those that others had recorded. There were clearly male and female voices, and sometimes I could make out the words, but often it seemed that they were so ambiguous that no one could know for sure what they were saying—especially when one factored in the multitude of possible languages involved. The CD had been made in April 1999, with an introduction that summarized the state of the art to that point. "Obtaining EVP is a difficult and arduous pursuit," read the booklet, "with many setbacks and fallow periods, and the conditions needed to make successful EVP recordings are largely unknown."

I was disappointed, but not altogether dissuaded. Someone had written in Estep's newsletter that they had taken an EVP recording of their deceased father to be analytically compared by a voiceprint expert to what they had of him on tape as a living person. The voices proved to be the same. That was hopeful, but it seemed that in my case—unless Christian himself improved the communications—they wouldn't get better even with better equipment.

I also learned about other things that researchers such as the Ghost Research Society in the Midwest were using: negative ion detectors, Geiger counters for radiation levels, and oscilloscopes. One investigator even measured the galvanic skin response (GSR) of people who claim to see apparitions. He found that the lower the GSR, the less resistant the skin is to magnetic energy. If you bring together a person like this with a haunted building on a heightened energy spot like a ley line, you get a combination that improves the possibility of such encounters. This seemed to indicate that some people are chemically more receptive to anomalous experiences. I had also read that people with certain brain-wave patterns make better conductors than others and the same was said for the ability to relax.

In other words, if I wanted to contact ghosts, I'd probably have to stop living a life of deadlines.

—2—

I was to meet another woman with sensitivity to the other world in New Hope, Pennsylvania, a ghost-filled town if ever there was one. On the banks of the Delaware River in Bucks County, it lies a few miles north of where George Washington crossed the river in 1776 to win the Battle of Trenton. He had rested his troops in and around New Hope that fall while he gradually collected boats. At the time it was a mill town called Coryell's Ferry, built along a trade route for the Leni-Lenape Indians. After 1790, it was renamed New Hope, and it has recently been transformed yet again into an artist's colony with plenty of offbeat boutiques.

In the early part of the century, this area was considered the Genius Belt. Writers and artists of great renown had bought the old houses and formed a community of kindred souls. S. J. Perelman, Dorothy Parker, George Kaufman, Pearl Buck, and James Michener all found the idyllic countryside a welcome retreat from Manhattan. Visual artists like Joseph Pickett, and potters, engravers, and sculptors also sought inspiration in the serene settings. Subcultures of all kinds flourish here, from witches to tattoo artists to musicians. Outsiders are insiders. Marginality rules.

Even ghosts love the place. Aaron Burr, for example, had sought refuge in a house in New Hope after his duel with Alexander Hamilton. It's said that when his spirit isn't walking Wall Street in Manhattan, it's here at the scene of his notorious seduction of the daughter of the man who had granted him sanctuary. ("She should feel lucky," was his legendary retort.) Then there was newswoman Jessica Savage, who'd drunk a fatal after-dinner cocktail of brackish canal water outside Odette's. People claimed to still see her. In fact, nearly every inn boasted of at least one spectral resident, from Hans at the Black Bass Hotel who was stabbed to death in a fight, to the primitive artist Joseph Pickett, seen painting along the banks of the creek behind the Wedgewood.

Whenever I drive there, I watch for the phantom hitchhiker. He pops up in various places on the road wearing a brown leather jacket and hauling a knapsack. Apparently he's particularly memorable even for a ghost, and stands out to those who spot him—even on dark nights—because of his piercing blue eyes. I thought sure I saw him one night along River Road, and I'd wanted to pick him up, but unfortunately I wasn't driving.

I was to meet Adele Gamble at the Logan Inn. This inn has an extensive history of haunting, particularly room 6, but sightings and other odd things have been reported almost everywhere in the building. The South Jersey Ghost Research Society says that room 18, just above room 6, is also haunted, and there have been reports that a double-locked door opened by itself in room 15.

Built in 1722 and furnished with colonial pieces, it is the oldest building in town and has gone through a number of owners. In 1828, it became the Logan House, reportedly to honor an Indian chief. Originally a tavern in pre-Revolutionary War days, George Washington's men frequented it (and no doubt he slept there, too). Part of the basement served as a morgue for bodies that had to wait for burial until the ground was soft, and I heard one story of a man who had been found down there still alive.

At the top of a very long set of stairs is the portrait of the grandparents of a previous owner, Carl Lutz. Many people have commented on the scent of lavender perfume, which was the grandmother's favorite fragrance, that seems to emanate from it. I was later told that people who have taken photos of it, often find the filmy image of a figure superimposed on it.

Also interesting is the witch's ball, a peach-colored glass sphere that now sits behind the bar. A witch's ball was a charm used to ward off evil spirits. This one, which has since been authenticated as quite old, was found one day in the cellar and placed carefully inside a glass case near the bar. At some point it vanished and was not seen for several months. Then it reappeared exactly where it had been originally found, in the cellar. It was put under glass once again, and once again, it ran away from its new home. New owners actually locked it up, but it continued to disappear and reappear.

Spiriting glass orbs away is not the only activity that goes on here. Several apparitions have been seen, such as the fully dressed colonial figure in the dining room. Other figures have appeared in the haunted room, an area where things turn up missing or rearranged, and some say it's the spirit of a little girl who drowned in the canal. She's also been seen outside by the tree in the parking lot.

Several members of the staff have heard their names called out when no one was around, and one person who heard a disembodied voice was shoved up against a freezer. Things get moved around in the restaurant, too, and once a basket of Melba toast was set out, but turned up empty. There are also noises. Some guests complained to the owners one morning about a loud party that had gone on until 3:00 A.M., though it was soon revealed that the last guest had departed the bar at 11:00.

Most interesting to me was the story of a guest who had checked out of room 6 at 4:00 A.M., claiming that someone had been choking him. He claimed that he had never been so scared in his life. When he'd felt the hand on his throat, he'd woken his fiancée, and she also had felt the intense threatening energy. The staff was doubtful, since they believe that "Emily," the ghost in that room, is only a trickster and would never hurt anyone. Emily was the daughter-in-law of the couple in the painting and had died in the building. Perhaps she was just trying to pull the pillow out from under him, as she has done with others.

—**3**—

For our interview, Adele and I were allowed to use the garden dining room where the colonial soldier had been seen. That added a spicy atmosphere—perhaps he would show himself. Adele is a soft-spoken, unassuming woman who has a keen sensitivity to paranormal events. "I really don't say I'm a psychic," she hastened to tell me. "I think we all have the ability to do this, but a lot of people bury it out of fear." To get started with psychic phenomena, she took a parapsychology course, studied the life of gifted psychic Edgar Casey, and used meditation.

Her own first experience had occurred when she was going on a picnic with some friends. They had all put money into a kitty to have a good time, but she told her husband that she didn't feel right. "Money is going to be missing," she said. She didn't know what this meant or how it had come to her, but it felt right. When someone went to get the kitty, it was gone. After that, Adele noticed how she had become attuned to things that were about to happen.

It wasn't long before she made the acquaintance of Adi-Kent Thomas Jeffrey, the local ghost researcher and author. Adele went on her New Hope ghost tour and then did a séance with her. It was then that she had an experience that seemed positively ghostly. "There was a window beside me and on my other side was a large antique hutch. My hair was long and I was just sitting there. Then something grabbed me and yanked me back. They told me that standing right beside me was a tall figure of a man."

Adi has since passed away and Adele has edited her last book on the area, *The Haunted Village*. Being so involved with ghost research, she has had plenty of time to come up with a theory. She believes that ghosts are energy that has been left behind, like radio waves in the air. "If you're sensitive, you'll pick up on that. I think they pass on to a higher plane, and a lot [of those] that are still here are still doing a job that has to be done. Those that go through the motions over and over, like a rerun, don't know where to go. They're comfortable there. But in all honesty, does anyone really know?"

She believes in helping those who ask to move on, but if they're not interested in going, they won't ask for help. "I pray for them and tell them to relax and follow the light. There will be someone there to transport them to a better place. I believe that. You can feel that you've helped them. They pull away. They're gone."

Adele has spirit guides who first came to her in a meditation to be her protectors. She describes one as tall and the other as a short figure. "They don't say much, but they always pull me back if I go off track."

I had already mentioned my "possessed" ring, and now I asked, "Do you sense anything around me?"

She was quiet for a minute, seeming about to say no, but then she asked, "Is there something with a man? That's really strong. There's a man around you and you don't seem to be too happy with this relationship. He looks tall with dark brown hair, combed over. He's not being honest with you."

"How can a ghost be dishonest?"

"I wasn't necessarily picking up on a ghost. Whoever he is, he's right there."

"What could that be?" I asked. I hoped it wasn't some kind of bilocation from Wraith.

"I don't know. He's on the left side of you." Exactly where Todd from St. Augustine had told me a man was standing, talking to me. "He has something to do with your ring. He's looking at you. He's smirking. That's terrible to say, but he is. He's attached to you. I think you need to protect yourself. Does he come to you in your dreams?"

"I think so."

"Are you powerful in the dream?"

"Sometimes." That was stretching it.

"That's good. But I can't understand why he's not being more specific with you. You should resolve this as quickly as possible and get rid of him. I think he's strong and has such deep anger. He's trying to use you to get rid of the anger, but it's not working because your subconscious mind is much stronger than his." Adele went quiet and seemed to be reading her sensing of the situation, slowly, haltingly. "Some of his anger might be from that, because he can't control you . . . and make you do what . . . he wants you to do. He's not going to let go until . . . all is answered and is done . . . the right way."

She came out of her near-trance and said, "His anger is like the atom bomb. It's just out like tentacles and he doesn't know where to concentrate it. He's got so much, he doesn't know where to place it."

"What can he actually do?"

"He's going to try to go through you to finish something or right a wrong that was done to him. But he's so angry that he's blocking it. He's not giving you the right messages. He can't tell you what happened. That's what you need. How can you help him if he's not clear?"

She actually seemed distressed on his behalf. She advised me to mediate more and to seek out a good psychic. I didn't tell her that nearly every psychic I'd spoken to thus far had reached this same impasse: They had an idea that the man was with me, that he was attached to the ring, that he was very angry, and that he wanted me to do something about it. Could it be that Christian, or whoever this was, was just too confused to convey what he needed?

I left the Logan that day without knowing I was soon to be back for a rather exciting night.

—**4**—

Now, three months later, I was spending the night in room 6 of the Logan during the lunar eclipse. Maggie Smith, the Logan's manager, had invited me to come and I couldn't resist. I was already aware from Dave Oester's IGHS site that solar flares seem to affect paranormal activity. I'd also gone out ghosting in December when the winter solstice full moon—the brightest of the millennium—was 14 percent larger than usual. I had gotten some very good results that night.

Now I had room 6 at an optimal time. This had to be good. I had already heard a story from Adele Gamble about her own experience in room 6. She had been meditating in the chair, and when she turned and looked, she saw several entities. "There was a man who looked as solid as any person, and a woman who was transparent, and the child was really transparent. I asked them why they were there and they said, 'We're just travelers. We were just passing through.'"

To maximize the possibilities, I looked up near-death researcher Raymond Moody's directions for contacting spirits. He found certain techniques to be effective for creating the mood. Two of them were easy: get in touch with nature and contemplate art or antiques. The Logan was filled with antiques and it sat on a pretty canal where I could go for a walk. Moody also felt that a happy, playful mood worked better than heavy concentration. In fact, sometimes being too determined to get contact can block anything from happening. I recalled that once when I was taking photos in my apartment in a sprightly frame of mind, I got the most activity that I'd ever had. It's also important to be enthusiastic and to have a sense of confidence that something will occur.

If there is someone you want to contact, Moody says, use a memento, like a photo. I wasn't sure I wanted to bother with Christian here, but I did bring the ring. I'd certainly take him if I couldn't get anyone else. Moody also recommended a light meal so as to avoid both lethargy and the distraction of an empty stomach. Interestingly, he noted that people who had a lot of potassium in their diets were better able to use imagery, while people who took extra calcium seemed to be blocked. He also recommended against caffeine. Exercise is good, because it aids in both alertness and relaxation. Above all, keep it playful.

For a week before going, I took extra potassium and left off the calcium supplements. I worked out in the fitness room every day. I ate very little (although I couldn't resist the fabulous dinner served at the Logan that night.)

I arrived during the first snowstorm of the year. The eclipse would begin around 11:00 P.M. It seemed a perfect time to be staying at what has been called one of the most authentically haunted buildings in the country, and I felt that I'd done everything possible to become more receptive.

I went right to the room and sat in the chair next to the antique bed. I noticed that the double full-length mirrors could serve as the perfect psychomanteum. For an hour, I stayed in the room, just meditating and allowing whatever forces were there to experience me. I also managed to grab a quick nap to prepare for the long night's vigil. Later I went for a walk in the snow, recalling some of the stories told about the various houses. The town was quiet as people remained indoors out of the weather. It seemed a ghost town.

When I came in, Rhonda, the night staff person, asked me if the room was cold.

"No, it was stifling," I told her.

"That's odd. I noticed that the other day, and when I turned it to cool, it stayed hot. That's very unusual in that room."

"I finally just turned the heat off. It's too hot in there for ghosts."

She smiled.

I asked how many people were in the place that night. "Just one other guest, you . . . and 'Emily.' "

Perfect.

When I had dinner that night, I was the only one in the dining room, so I decided to get my camera. I snapped a number of photographs, getting nothing at first, and then I got two white globes in the corner. Just then, Meghan brought out my pasta with sun-dried tomatoes. I showed her the picture.

"That corner," she confirmed. "That's where people have feelings." She then told me about how a place setting got rearranged on her. On another occasion, a waiter had laid out all the napkins into fan shapes. He had turned away and when he looked back, they were all undone.

"Well, this room is beneath room 6," I pointed out.

After dinner, I went outside. It was still snowing lightly, so the photos I took were too confusing to determine what I was getting. Snow looks amazingly like bright orbs, especially close to the camera. Stymied, I went in and asked Rhonda if she would take me into the cellar. She was eager to help. I gave her the still camera and I took the videocamera. By this time I had equipped it with an extra infrared light to extend its range. Rhonda took me to the stone fireplace where bodies supposedly lay in piles or were cremated, and we spent about fifteen minutes trying in vain to get something with one of the cameras. We relocated to another area and still got nothing.

"I was sure you'd get results down here," she said, "considering the history."

Just then, Randy the bartender came down. "Did you go in the wine room?" he asked. "That's where I get strange feelings. And that's the house's foundation. It's the oldest part and still has the original support beam."

Rhonda led me to the locked room. It was a very small space, about six by eight feet, but I set up the camera while they waited outside and almost at once got a quick, bright flash of an orb. Then one came out of the wall to my right, and two more flew at me across the bottom of the screen.

"They're in here!" I said. "This is it!"

Randy and Rhonda came in, but the disruption stopped the action. I asked if I could be alone in there for about ten minutes. During that time, I spotted about half a dozen more orbs, mostly small and quick.

While the basement proved to be a fantastic experience, I didn't want to miss the lunar eclipse. I set up the videocamera in my room and then went outside to catch the celestial display. It was getting extremely windy out now, which I have found is not great for ghosting. I walked around in the frigid temperatures, hoping to get some photos of other buildings, but it was still snowing just lightly enough to show up in the photos as small sparkles. I gave it up, but I was reminded of Peter Straub's *Ghost Story,* one of my all-time favorite fictional ghost tales. Set in a small town during a snowstorm, it soon becomes apparent that some paranormal force is manipulating the weather to build a trap.

I returned to the inn to watch the black shadow cross the moon. However, I could stay out only so long, so I went back in to check the videocamera. It was nearly midnight. On the way up the steps, I impulsively took three or four photos of the large painting of the Lutzes. Although I had not seen it for myself, Adele had told me that she had a photograph of this same painting that showed several ghostly faces around the picture. If there was any opportunity to get an interesting image, I wasn't going to miss it.

Then I went into the room and checked the recording in there. I had placed the camera so that the closet would be included in the frame, since Adele had the feeling that that area might contain some sort of portal. I saw nothing throughout the half hour of recording but the bed and closet door.

Then I checked through my still photos. Some outside showed snow—couldn't use. One clear orb on the front of the building—good. The staircase—nothing. The Lutzes—nothing, nothing. . . .

"Oh, my God. . . . oh, what is this?"

I stared at the LCD screen, not quite believing what I was seeing. I almost hyperventilated as I realized that I could make out a distinct series of large white orbs issuing out of the photograph and forming into a thick column of some kind of vaporous substance. I went back to the previous photo to see what the effect of the flash looked like. It was barely discernible and certainly nothing like this! I had a fabulous photo of a vortex that was a near-apparition. Incredible. And it was right in the middle of the eclipse.

Clearly the moon was good for more than just romance and werewolves.

I had to sit down. I was stunned. I had not imagined that I would really get something like that. Then I rushed out to the painting with the EMF meter and ran it along the surface. There were no abnormal readings until I stepped away to the right. A blip showed me an area of unusual energy, but that was quickly gone. I went back to the painting and still got nothing. Whatever had been there was gone.

When the bar closed at 1:30, Randy called me down to get some photos of the room. I spotted the witch's ball and asked if I could place it on a table where I could get a better shot. He helped me with that. I shot two pictures, and in one of them, on the wall behind the ball, was an orb. Cool.

Randy then locked up and left and I was there, with only one other guest. He had already gone to bed, so I had the place essentially to myself, while the wind raged outside. I looked out at the moon, bright now and without its blood hue, and then went to my room. While in there, I thought I heard something so I opened my door. There was a strong odor of pipe tobacco. That was strange, since I hadn't smelled it when I was in the bar. I walked down the steps and continued to smell it, but it was not as strong on the first floor. I definitely smelled it near the painting, but then as I walked back to my room, there was nothing.

For a while I sat in the room and attempted to contact mirror apparitions, but nothing came. This exercise is no easy thing. I then checked the camera and with dawn only two hours away, I gave up.

Still, I felt that I'd advanced somewhat in my ghosting skills. Now that I'd gotten something that seemed most definitely paranormal to me, I felt more confident. I wanted to rethink some of those theories about ghosts that initially had propelled me into this project, especially as applied to Christian. I'd learned a lot thus far and I wanted to try to understand it all. To me it made sense to view ghosts in terms of the way the mind and body work.

—5—

First, I want to put aside explanations like psychological projection and the extradimensional entity theories. If we allow that ghosts are souls or memories of some kind that survive the physical body, and that they have an emotional component, then it's possible that what I call body memories are a factor. Bear with me here. It seems complicated, but it's really fairly simple. Basically, it goes like this:

> *Consciousness, reason, and emotion are components of the mind.*
> *When physically alive, mind and body*

*form an interrelated unit, each part operating on
information-based energy.*

*When consciousness leaves the body, it retains a residual
body awareness.*

*Body awareness fades unless certain patterns of emotional
encoding anchor it to the body.*

*Consciousness then becomes like a phantom limb, aka,
ghostly phenomena.*

*The only release for a ghost is to shift the emotional patterns
to diminish body awareness.*

Only recently has it become clear that mind and body are essentially a unit. We can thank the French philosopher René Descartes for this. Back in the 1600s, he proposed that our minds were distinct from our bodies. Essentially, the body takes up space and the mind does not. His logic wasn't that great but was supported by religion, which seeks to establish an immortal soul that can exist separate from the body. Since that time, the divided nature of our identities has been firmly entrenched in our culture.

Recent work in a field called psycho-neuroimmunology (PNI) indicates that mind and body in fact work together as a unit: the mind, or soul, is a form of energy that is present in every cell of the body. Much of what we experience is the result of thoughts converted into physical information and then stored as chemicals that affect the emotions. The more intense the information, the stronger its impact. Each organ in the body processes specific emotional energies, and even if the energy known as consciousness leaves the body at death and continues to exist, that does not negate how intricately linked it is to the body while in the physical realm. Dr. Candace Pert, research professor at the Department of Physiology and Biophysics at Georgetown University Medical Center, is one of the pioneers in this field. Her work is documented in her book, *Molecules of Emotion: Why You Feel the Way You Feel.*

According to Pert, the chemicals in our bodies form a dynamic information network that links emotional experience with physiological systems. Thus, certain long-term or intensely felt emotional states become physically encoded into our cells, forming what she calls our bodymind. Our thoughts enter our bodies as energy and each becomes part of the other.

In this way we develop body memories. Our body gets used to a certain emotional state in certain repeated situations, such as daily routines. For example, whenever I walk, I use that time as inspiration for writing. However, if I change my exercise routine, nothing comes, because my body has come to associate mental creativity with walking. Another example would be growing up in a home where there is a lot of energy; if your body absorbs that, you will gravitate toward people who may recreate that for you in relationships.

In other words, the emotional energy flows into the body's energy. Briefly, the brain sends signals to other parts of the body via neurotransmitters—information carriers—which influence how we process our emotional experiences. Our cells take in information, organize a network of actions and reactions, link one physical system with another, and even show evidence of learning. How does this happen?

There are molecules on the surface of our cells called receptors, a class of protein, which is where neurotransmitters attach themselves. Each receptor acts as a keyhole, scanning all the information available to find the right "key"—the chemical information that will unlock and activate that cell's function. Receptor molecules float on the cell's surface but have roots into the cell. They respond to energy and chemical substances by vibrating. A typical nerve cell would have multitudes of receptors on its surface, all functioning as scanners: They are receptive, and alert, to only a certain type of substance. The right kinds of chemicals bind with the receptors through an information match, and the body becomes one large network of information processing, much like a telephone network. The binder and the receptor strike the same note, so to speak, and resonate, opening the door to the message.

The message then reaches the cell's interior and gives any one of many commands, such as to divide, to build proteins, to produce more (or less) of the chemical it produces. These minute activities can translate into larger behavioral and mood changes. For example, if a cell is activated to produce more of the neurotransmitter serotonin, the person may feel much calmer.

The whole process is directed according to receptor selectivity—that certain receptors respond only to those binding molecules with which they are programmed to bind. Opiate receptors bind only with opiate substances like morphine or endorphins. In other words, your moods can become part of the cellular structure via chemical transformation and the cell can produce chemicals that affect your moods. So that's how the body can affect your emotional state.

Applied to Christian, assuming we are correct about what we know: When alive, he spent a lot of time being angry and violent. That got stored in his body and evolved into a body memory. The physical tension that resulted anchored and fed his emotional state, so that anger became part of who he was and how he would feel much of the time.

Take this all a step further with ghost theories that link phantom activity with a strong emotional event like murder, suicide, or sudden death.

We like to believe that our emotions are guided, and can be controlled, by our conscious, rational brain. We believe that environmental information is processed through our intellect, which directs an appropriate emotional response. We see a bear, our mind tells us to run. However, our brain circuits are actually primed toward our more volatile emotions, responding more strongly to fear than to reason.

Joseph LeDoux, a neuroscientist at the Center for Neural Science at New York University, discovered a parallel pathway for information that goes straight to the emotional centers. It seems to be activated during distress. The information is routed from the thalamus to the amygdala, which is part of the brain's emotional headquarters. The amygdala's job is to scan information for danger, particularly with regard to what it "remembers" from previous dangerous situations.

In the framework of the mind/body, the brain and emotions work together in response to a body memory. If a certain situation once seemed dangerous, that same (or a similar) situation will trigger an alarm. The body will react without the person giving thought to how rational or appropriate the reaction is. The amygdala sends out a distress signal to the entire brain, signaling physiological responses such as a more rapid heartbeat, sweat, heightened blood pressure, and the release of hormones that prepare us for defense. We respond before we even consciously grasp what may be happening. The message reaches the emotional brain faster, blocking out the thinking brain. By the time the fear or anger—or even rage—floods the thoughts, the reaction already feels correct. The thinking brain is hijacked.

The amygdala is mature at birth. It gets busy right away processing emotion-laden situations before we have a chance to think about them. It then makes judgments based on past events that we may not even remember. It stores the raw material of our most primitive and basic emotional memories. Even crude similarities can spur eruptions. If your mother neglected you, you may act out against a spouse who walks away during a discussion. The memories, not the situation itself, trigger the emotion.

With ghosts, it makes sense that some hormonal surge may have been triggered at death that was linked to fear, even terror. My own theory about Christian was that he did not die willingly, and that his sociopathic acts were developed as a defense against his true vulnerability. I think that much of his life was lived in fear and his death was a repetition, but more enhanced, of a pattern with which he was all too familiar. From what little Wraith told me about him, he probably experienced a sense of abandonment as a child. His mother, a religious fanatic who despised homosexuality, no doubt distanced herself from him. I'm convinced that he did not feel loved and his violence was an acting out of his fear and anger—emotions that he retains as a spirit and that may even give him his entire substance. That is, his early fears were initially processed through his primitive brain—the amygdala—and then sufficiently reinforced throughout his life to be preserved as a body memory, which became foundational to his entire physical/emotional identity. Anyone who telegraphed to him that he was not loved was going to be a potential target, including and especially Wraith. There were times when Wraith feared for his life, he said, but he also indicated that he set Christian up to feel distanced. If Christian was leaving him, then perhaps it was because their relationship had become one of such great conflict that it seemed to Christian a repetition of his prior home life.

During feelings of abandonment, the amygdala kicks in, getting hormones pumped out to help cope. It is a physiological sensor to an emotional situation strewn with danger. The person develops a bioemotional hypersensitivity to any situation that triggers body memories of vulnerability. If he dies in this emotional state, and it's also a chronic part of his physical/emotional being, then it transfers to his departing consciousness and continues to remain anchored in a physical body that no longer exists.

So if this is Christian's state, how could I make a difference? Was I stuck with this angry spook? I didn't think so.

From research in neurology, I learned that hyperemotionality can be induced to relax, allowing reason to mediate. Our brains are created not just for defense but also for connection. If he could be made to understand that his fear and anger keep him in a perpetual state of hovering, nonevolving existence, and that he could in fact find something better, then it could be that the electromagnetic spirit neurology that ghost researchers believe spirits are composed of might be shifted. It means reworking his emotionality. In essence, he's like a phantom limb.

Now ordinarily we think of phantom limbs as something amiss with the brain circuitry: that the brain still thinks there's an arm when there isn't. Thus, it gets sensations from nonexistent fingers, although there's no sensory input. This can go on for decades. Even those born without limbs can feel them. The sensations are not constant, but fade and return unpredictably. Phantoms can feel more real than other limbs that are actually there. Occultists think that this proves the existence of an astral body. Others say the brain creates the sensations, within the neuromatrix that creates a body image. The brain itself generates perceptual experience even when there is no external input. "We do not need a body to feel a body," wrote a neurologist named Melzack. Nevertheless, in his scenario, we would still need a brain. But if we think of a spirit or consciousness along the lines of astral projection, where it can leave the body and still have all its body memories, then a ghost may be considered this kind of phantom limb. It once had a body so it can still feel a body, in part because its emotional life was once intricately connected to the body. It can "remember" the body.

To add yet another layer to this idea, some scientists believe that we exist inside memory fields, rather than memories being located inside us. Karl Lashley's experiments with mice in the sixties indicated that they could "remember" a path in a maze even with 90 percent of their brain removed. In another experiment, successive generations of rats ran the same maze with increasingly fewer mistakes. Each was raised in isolation from the others, and yet somehow the thirteenth generation acted as if they had experience with the maze that they didn't have. Then years later, a group of rats with no biological connection to the earlier groups performed just as well as those that had learned the maze through trial and error. The possible conclusion is that memory may be stored outside in nature, not in the individual.

Here's another fact. It's possible to evoke a memory by stimulating a certain part of the brain, but when the same area is stimulated again, a different memory is evoked. This also lends support to the idea that memory gets processed from energy rather than stored in a specific place in the brain.

Dr. Melvin Morse proposes that there may be a universal memory bank through which memories from all kinds of people and from all different eras can be accessed. As we get closer to death or trauma, the ability to process memory seems to intensify. He attributes this to activation of the right temporal lobe, which to his mind is our means of connection to the metaphysical. He feels that memories can and actually do exist independent of brain functions. If that's so, then the emotional identity that is wrapped up in a body memory can exist without a body. But let's take this a little further.

Princeton physicist John A. Wheeler thinks that the mind is woven into the fabric of the universe, and that means that memories are stored all around us in the patterns of life itself. The memory that seems to be in our brain may be coming in from the universal memory field via the right temporal lobe. That means that people may be able to process memories that are not their own, experience false memories as real, and be wrapped up in memory energies when they leave the physical body. I've watched John Edward, the medium who does a show called *Crossing Over,* deliver uncannily accurate information to people about deceased relatives. Yet each time he speaks, and they acknowledge the truth of what he says, he could be doing nothing more than tapping into a memory field informed by the people he's addressing. Perhaps those who have "crossed over" *are* speaking to him, but when he says that he gets his impressions through feelings and symbols, that sounds like sensitivity to a memory field. To be convincing to me, the spirit should offer true information that the receivers do not know, but can confirm.

At any rate, the right temporal lobe appears to act as a receiver and transmitter of memory-formed energies. The body gives off energy currents, and it could be that body memories form in the physical body but then can move out through the temporal lobe to become part of a larger energy field that supports them. Thus, an emotional identity that started in a situated body can eventually exist independent of it. Given that possibility, we can understand Christian as electrical energy formed through body memories, which means we can accept him as a ghost, but we still have to understand him via what he was when embodied.

The body is the voice of the emotions—when angry, we lift an arm to strike out, for example—and when the relevant body part (or entire body) is gone, the emotion can still linger. With some work, Christian's anger could be diminished and recreated as a form of energy that would connect him to other spirits or help him to cross over. If the defense mechanisms cannot relax until it becomes clear that all is safe, then the crux of the matter is to make Christian feel safe giving up his anger. It may be that he needs to be heard first; his anger needs to be taken seriously. Thus far, his response to existence has been violent—which is no way to attract love except from those who love violence (like Wraith), and then one cannot very well feel safe. Christian probably felt admired but not safe. Not feeling safe, he retained a hot emotional state, preserved as an alarm deep within the amygdala.

My own fear of him could seem like a pattern similar to that of people in his life: his mother, former lovers, friends who spurned him. If I were to embrace him, it would be different from what he is used to. Initially, it might make him uncomfortable, but eventually he might be persuaded to drop his emotional defenses. He certainly has ceased to yell the way he did initially. I don't know if that was in response to my request or just a matter of his growing used to communicating that way. As I write this, I think he may still be angry and afraid, but perhaps I can create a way for him to experience a different emotional pattern. The emotional system that is defensive cannot shift into a more adaptive state unless it calms down.

One path toward encouraging a shift in Christian's emotional state is to ponder Wraith's typical pattern of relating to him: adoration, manipulation, lying, dependence, eagerness to surrender to him, tendency to lay blame on him, and viewing him as an intellectual inferior. He demanded information while Christian withdrew; he wanted attention and pampering; he wanted Christian to do what *he* wanted to do. Wraith set Christian up to be the parent from whom he wanted everything but from whom he got very little in the way of emotional support. Christian was then stuck in yet another distant relationship. Theirs was the dynamic of mutual need and mutual resistance—a common pattern that only promotes fear and anger.

So that's my theory.

But it may all be irrelevant, anyway. In communication about the spiritual state to ITC experimenters, the deceased Friederich Jurgenson— one of the first to get EVP—once indicated that "All your scientific, medical or biological speculations miss the mark." I guess I won't really know till I'm on that side.

In the meantime, I still have to decide what to do with the ring.

Lord of the Ring

—1—

There were still many sites to visit and people to learn from. I knew there were still those who wanted to advise me about the right way to stalk ghosts, but I wanted to get closure on the ring. I called Mariah in Louisiana for her latest theosophical analysis, and she said that she'd gotten past her negative feelings and now believed that we should be praying for a soul like Christian's to find rest. To her, the ring didn't matter. To me, it did. Wraith wanted it back, and many people had warned me of imminent possession if I kept it. Thus far, I'd had it three years and nothing had happened to me, except a few bad dreams and some weird drawings. Even so, it seemed appropriate that I'd finish it where I started, and that was with Rosemary, the close friend of the reporter whose disappearance had launched me on my vampire escapade. She had also gotten me my first reading of the ring with Steve, the blind psychic, and she'd had some ghost experience of her own.

One day she was riding on the passenger side of a car just as dusk was setting in, and she spotted a man off to the side of the road. She couldn't see his face, but he appeared to be wearing a uniform. Because of the unusual buttons on the coat and his broad-brimmed hat, it struck her that he might be an apparition from the Civil War. As she stared at him, she experienced a bad feeling. "It was the sense of lost hope or total despair," she said. "I didn't know who he was, but he was clearly just without any hope." Although they passed him quickly, Rosemary was unable to shake her despondency.

The next day, she stopped at her mother's house. While she was there, the phone rang. The news was that Rosemary's uncle had just committed suicide in California. While she was upset, she made no connection between the two events . . . that is, not until several years later.

In a discussion with her widowed aunt, she mentioned the odd entity she'd seen that had made her feel so badly. As Rosemary described what he'd been wearing, her aunt looked at her in shock. "Those were the clothes that my husband was buried in," she said. She went on to explain that her deceased husband had designed himself a uniform with special buttons and a broad-brimmed hat, and told her some time before he shot himself that this was the clothing in which he wanted to be buried.

The coincidence was too uncanny. It occurred to Rosemary that she had seen his spirit in the final stages of despair, projected out to her just before he'd taken his life.

Throughout the course of my investigations, I had spoken with Rosemary to get her perspective. There were times when she thought I was safe, but also times when she cautioned me. She even told me that once when I popped into her mind for no apparent reason, a black onyx ring she was wearing broke into several pieces.

"It did?" I asked.

"That's good," she assured me. "It means that you were in a bad situation and whatever was going to happen to you happened to the ring instead. It protected you."

Another time when we'd met for dinner, she reached for Christian's ring but pulled back. "He doesn't want me to touch it," she'd said. "It will break his communication with you. He's very jealous. He wants you all to himself."

Since Rosemary had her own tarot deck, I invited her to meet me one night at the Chelsea Hotel in New York City. I had picked this place for a special reason.

There are numerous haunted sites in Manhattan. In Charles Adams's book, *New York City Ghost Stories,* I read about supernatural experiences in restaurants, theaters, hotels, and private residences. One that had interested me was the Morris-Jumel mansion on 175 Jumel Terrace. Built before the Revolution, it once had served as George — Washington's headquarters. Although it's apparently haunted by five ghosts, the one most people claim to have seen is the specter of Eliza Jumel, who was made rich upon the death of her first husband, Roger Morris, when he fell onto a pitchfork in 1832. She went on to marry former vice president Aaron Burr. According to Hans Holzer, there was some suspicion that she had killed her first husband, so Holzer took a psychic into the place to try to discover the truth. The psychic channeled the man's spirit and heard him say that he had indeed been murdered—and been buried alive. When her marriage to Burr failed after three years, Eliza became reclusive and then demented. It was said that following her death, each night after midnight there came a loud rapping and sometimes she would appear in a white dress. In 1964 she appeared to half a dozen schoolchildren who were touring the house, and they identified her from her portrait.

However, since the mansion isn't open to the public during ideal ghosting hours, I decided to look for another place.

I went to the Chelsea Hotel. Located on 222 West 23rd Street in the area of art galleries and flea markets known as Chelsea, this eleven-story building went up in 1884 as a residential co-op. Designed by French-born architect Philip Hubert, the front sports the intricate ironwork lace of French Quarter balconies. So does the interior staircase that winds around and upward from floor to floor. Some 75 percent of the 250 units are occupied today with long-term residents, while the rest are available for lodging. The hotel's reputation as a "cauldron for creativity" came from the numerous artists, writers, actors, and other creative types who have stayed or lived there. Among them were William S. Burroughs, Dylan Thomas, Mark Twain, Eugene O'Neill, Tennessee Williams, Bob Dylan, Thomas Wolfe, Arthur Miller, and O. Henry. Andy Warhol filmed *The Chelsea Girls* there, and several prize-winning works were penned there, including Wolfe's *You Can't Go Home Again* and Miller's *After the Fall*. One musician, Schizo, said that he'd never written before, but at the hotel, he wrote forty songs.

In fact, that was the reason I picked it.

Wraith had said that Christian wanted to be a writer. To my mind, a place where writers had produced some masterpieces and where some had gone into various dark states was the perfect ground on which to try to call him forth. A few had lived there till they died, such as poet James Schuyler and composer Virgil Thomas. Rosemary, who also had resided there and who had been attuned to the vampire culture for many years, seemed the best person to help. She said it housed many ghosts. Perhaps some of them were writers.

One of the sad stories from this place tells of the slow suicide of Welsh poet Dylan Thomas. In 1953, he went from his rooms to the White Horse Tavern. He claimed that night to have seen the gates of hell and then proceeded to drink seventeen shots of whiskey. He made his way back to his room, where he collapsed. He was taken to a hospital, but too late: He died there at the age of thirty-nine.

One of the reservation clerks told me that every Halloween the elevator constantly stops at the first floor. That's where the infamous room 100 was located. On October 12, 1978, Sid Vicious, former bass player for the nihilistic London punk group, the Sex Pistols, called the police to report that someone had stabbed his girlfriend, Nancy Spungen. They arrived and found her in her underwear, covered in blood, lying beneath the bathroom sink. She had been killed with a hunting knife. This couple had a record of arrests for substance abuse, so Vicious was arrested again. He was bailed out but ended up dead shortly thereafter from a heroin overdose, unwittingly supplied by his own mother.

To my mind, I was gathering a variety of spiritual energies— creativity, suicidal despair, murderous rage, vampiric attunement, and ghost. I had the ring and Rosemary read the tarot. A storm was coming in. The conditions seemed right. Whether or not I saw a ghost, I felt sure I'd discover something important.

I got to the hotel around dusk. One of the men there told me the room I was getting had been the residence of Pete Hamill, a fiction writer and editor of the *New York Post.* I was happy about getting that close to the creative spirit. If Christian didn't drink it all up, maybe I'd get some. Victor, the bellman, took me upstairs and on the way he explained that room 100 had been reconstructed and made part of another apartment so that people would stop calling. "They still send flowers and want to stay there," he said. "We don't want a reenactment, so we eliminated the room."

I was lodged in 520, a spacious suite with double doors, a kitchenette, two double beds, a round wooden table, an empty bookcase, and a red and black sofa. Over the ornate fireplace was a huge gold-framed mirror, and next to it was an antique dresser with another ornate mirror. When Victor left, I took some photos. Negative. I went over and sat on the couch, waited for any traces of dust to settle, and took three from that angle. Again there was nothing, so I remembered my manners and asked for permission. To my surprise the next shot showed the room absolutely filled with orbs. Against one purple wall was a rainbow of white bubbles. The next photo showed less and the third just a few lingering dots on the wall. Could that be dust after three previous shots showed nothing? I didn't know, but whatever they were, I thought this room would work fine.

—2—

I waited in the lobby for Rosemary. Looking around, I found myself admiring the enormous paintings and the sculptures. It really did feel like a museum in there.

Rosemary came in, wearing a clingy purple knit dress over a light green T-shirt. She wore her black hair loose down her back and had on several sparkling necklaces and rings. I started to take her up to my room, but she refused to use the one open elevator because it had always "tricked" her. "They'll remember me," she insisted, meaning the spirits. Since the other one was stuck on eight, she finally had no choice.

I had Merlin's feathers with me and wanted to ask Rosemary about using astral projection to find Christian. She had told me that there was a time when she actually had to resist her astral body's urge to travel. When I suggested that I try it, however, she said, "I wouldn't advise it. I think that's dangerous."

Merlin says yes, Rosemary says no. What to do?

I asked if she wanted to go get dinner and she said, "No. We're here in the room now and we can't be coming and going. They need to see us and get used to us so they'll come around." We ordered out, in accordance with her former routine. Rosemary lit two tall candles in glass containers, placing one on the floor in a corner and the other on the bookcase. She also lit a small candle that she placed between us on the table. We were not to blow them out. I aimed the videocamera at the table, shut off the lights, and turned on the infrared.

Rosemary took out a long silver string on which was placed a series of beads about three inches apart. I asked what it was. "You can call it a pendulum," she said, "but it once was a necklace. I broke it and then found out it could do this."

She held it high with the fingertips of her right hand and indicated that she would ask questions. When it swung from left to right, that was a yes. Back and forth was no.

"Do you remember me?" was her first question. "Have you seen me before?"

I didn't know whom she addressed, but as she went on with more questions like these, I realized it was one or more of the spirits who resided there.

Then she asked about Christian's ring, watched the pendulum, and indicated to me that I no longer needed it. Apparently Christian can be with me without it and is with me all the time. Great.

After more questions, with the pendulum swinging wildly in response, she handed it to me to hold and she asked a few more. I tried hard to keep my hand still, to keep from influencing the pendulum, yet it moved quite dramatically nonetheless. When I asked if I should get rid of the ring, it went in a circle.

"It doesn't know," said Rosemary.

Another impasse.

We finished with that and she told me that this was the best that the pendulum had ever performed. She thought it was something in the room. She said that when she'd first walked in, she'd sensed five people sitting on the couch. One had been Asian. I looked at the far end of the darkened room. I was going to sleep in there.

We checked the camera and I spotted an orb gliding across the floor. I was about to mention this when Rosemary jumped toward the door and shouted, "No! No! Not that one!"

"What?"

"Not that one, not that one!" She seemed to mean the orb.

"Are you afraid? There's nothing—"

"No. It's bad, it's nasty. I don't want that energy. When those things come around, everything escalates."

I thought she'd fly out the door, so I turned the camera off. After some time she seemed to settle down. "It's gone now," she said. "The room is clearing. It's different."

As usual, I hadn't felt anything. And she had reacted without knowing that I had seen an orb through the viewfinder.

Then Rosemary took out her tarot deck, laid out a colorful scarf, and shuffled the deck. This was different. Before I'd always been asked to do the shuffling.

"What are you seeking to know?" she asked.

I was ready for that. "I want to know what I should do with the ring."

Rosemary looked at me and then drew some cards. She laid them out in several piles. The first card up was the two of Pentacles. "The decision you must make is up in the air. You've been waiting and watching. You're disappointed because there have been no fireworks, nothing dramatic." True. She drew more cards and went on. "You're fascinated with the ring for its male phallic power. I don't mean sexual, but the exciting male energy." True again. She looked at several cards together and said, "The original owner, not Christian, but the one who had the ring turned his back. There were broken dreams. That person is the one defending the story. He makes Christian into an emperor."

That sounded like Wraith, but as far as I knew he was not the original owner. I still didn't know that much about Michael.

Then Rosemary addressed me. "This card says you think you can bring justice to this situation. You hold the ring like a treasure, and there's a young man involved whose opinion you value. He's not the one who gave you the ring."

Then she addressed the ring itself. "The ring gave you focus and a sense of satisfaction. It turned you toward the spirit world and took you away from what you were doing. It served a function for you, although you still think you can bring justice."

She picked up the scattered cards and shuffled again. The room felt very warm to me so I picked up the thermal scanner. It didn't show me any orb locations, but I read the temperature at seventy-five degrees. I wondered if that was too hot for ghosts.

The first card up told Rosemary something interesting. "The original owner of the ring was a blond man." Another card revealed that it was a blond gay man. At first I shook my head, thinking of Michael, but then I remembered something about him being Swedish—and blond. "The ring," Rosemary continued, "has been like bondage to them, but it was self-inflicted. They were controlled by it because they wanted to be."

That certainly had seemed the case with Wraith. Perhaps with me, too.

"You hold it by your own choice and you can walk away from it if you want. It's been valuable to you. You use it to gain strength from the idea that you're not alone. You use it to keep you company. You've made it a centerpiece and that makes it a crutch. It gives you strength because it's not real. And you have an attraction to strong, dominant powerful male energy that's not always nice."

Then she shuffled once again. This time I felt chills. She was getting too close to truths I didn't talk about. "We'll give it three choices," she said, "and see how the cards align with each. One, you keep the ring and continue as you have. Two, you put it in a box and hide it away. Three, you give it to someone else."

"What about just getting rid of it?"

"Let's stay with just the three for now."

Rosemary laid out the cards in three rows. Then she stared at the candle flame as she spoke each option again, as if seeking an answer there. I saw no change. Apparently she didn't either, because she returned to the cards.

"For the choice of keeping it as you are now, the previous owner is with you. It's the same card as before. You're looking to him. You've been getting messages. He enjoys traveling with you."

I wondered about the television drawings. Apart from that, I had received no clear messages, unless she meant the EVP.

"For the idea of keeping it in a box, the cards say there's indecision and fear of ruin and disappointment. But there would be freedom and relief. If you gave it away, it could be inspiration for someone else. It could travel more with another person, but it also could be disastrous. If you give it away, the whole story could be gone." She looked at me. "Did you ever consider giving it to a psychic museum?"

I shook my head. "No." I never considered giving it to anyone.

She then shuffled again and three cards fell to the floor. She picked them up and looked at them and then said, "Those make no sense." She placed them in the deck.

"Wait," I said. "I'd like to know what they were. They may make sense to me."

Reluctantly, Rosemary drew them back out and laid them on the scarf. I didn't see what they were, but she read them as, "There's a pissed-off man and a woman who has the power, and someone who's trying to get away. See, that makes no sense."

"In fact, it does. I understand it. But what about the idea of taking the ring back to where I got it?"

"It would be better if someone stole it. You could just drop it in the street and leave it behind." She picked up the pendulum. "Should Katherine go into a bar and give it to the first man she sees?"

I held my breath. I didn't want it to move, but it did. To my relief, it was indecisive. Nevertheless, Rosemary liked that idea. She thought I should find a gay man who might be attuned to it and give it to him for six months. I should arrange to have him report to me if anything happened. That way, the story would continue.

"But if there's negative power in this ring or associated with it, what if something happens to him? Then I'm responsible." I was thinking of Jeff in New Orleans.

It was clear that Rosemary liked her idea best.

At that point, someone knocked at the door. It was Miss Kitty, a young woman who was part of the small group of vampires who had known Susan Walsh, the reporter whose disappearance had started my adventures. We had invited her to join us, thinking that she would add to the room's energy. Her makeup perfect, she wore black knit leggings and a bulky blue turtleneck sweater. As she removed her leather cap and ran a hand through her long brown hair, I noted how long and manicured her nails were. Everything about her seemed poised, feminine, and confident.

Kitty told me her own philosophy of ghosts. Like many I've encountered, she felt certain that ghosts couldn't and wouldn't harm anyone. They weren't negative. She had even had sex with spirits—good sex.

I asked her to describe it.

"It's nice," she said. "When you've had a busy week and haven't had time to get a release, or you don't have a lover at the moment, it works well. They give you a better experience than any man can."

"So how do you get them to come?" (No pun intended.)

"You just ask. They'll do that for you."

Another disappointing response. It never worked that way for me. Ask, beg, use the Ouija, load up on potassium—nothing worked.

She and Rosemary decided to do some energy exercises, asking me to take pictures to see if it drew the spirits. When they hugged, several orbs floated near them, and when they sat on the bed to perform a more elaborate ritual, I got one photo in which the orb was large and pure white, like a full moon.

Then Rosemary wanted to work on me. "It's yellow right now," she said of the energy between us. "We have to make it blue." It was her contention that yellow or orange-colored orbs were murky. A blue light had purity. As I relaxed, she chanted something I couldn't understand and worked her hands close to me. No orbs in those photos. She wanted to sit on the other bed, but as she made a move to do so, she said, "No, there's a cat there. I just saw a cat." Apparently she meant a ghost cat, so we stayed where we were.

Then she told me something that affirmed my own emerging ideas about ghosts and human physiology. "Your aura is the most unusual I've ever encountered. I know why you don't see ghosts. If you were to calculate your degree of electromagnetism, you'd have the least amount of static in your aura of anyone I've ever touched. I have high electricity. I blow out lightbulbs when I'm mad and I can't wear watches. But yours is very low. I think they can't see you. Or they can't get what they need from you to materialize."

"But wait," I said. "When I used a static generator in my place, they flew away from it. They didn't seem to want to be around it."

"That kind of thing breaks them up. It's different from the electrons in the body."

I was floored. "You mean that for the rest of my life, because of my aura, I'll never get to see a ghost?"

"I don't know about that. I don't know why your aura is that way. Maybe you have to raise your metabolism."

Ah! That was the kicker. My metabolism was very low. But so was my father's, and *he'd* seen something once. So maybe there were other factors that could mitigate a depressed metabolism. No static in my aura. It was probably all in my hair.

—3—

Nothing else happened while they were there, and after they left, I watched the videocamera for over an hour. I couldn't take it into the hallways to look for Sid Vicious because they were brightly lit, with highly reflective white walls. I settled for staying in the room, hoping some "travelers" might pass through.

I sat down on the couch and looked through the viewfinder. Just then a sizable orb flew up from my right as if my sitting there had displaced it. I recalled Rosemary saying that five people were sitting on this couch. Then several orbs came out from under the bed on which I had planned to lie down, and one bounced along the top of it. Hmmm. Did I really want to sleep there? It seemed weird to be filming these things. The ones in my apartment had become familiar, but these were strangers. I was spooked—especially after Rosemary's earlier reaction.

When I finally gave up, I did some EVP to see if Christian appreciated this place. I ended up not being sure. I insisted that he had to be clear. What I got was hard to understand. Nevertheless, *I* appreciated it. I was happy to be sleeping where some other author had worked his way through characters and plot. Maybe it would inspire an ending to my story with the ring.

—4—

Dave Oester told me that the orbs in my photos at the Chelsea could be dust. It was his experience that most photos like that are not paranormal. That made little sense, because I had taken three photos of the same spot just before the one that contained the multitude of orbs. All of them were negative for orbs. But then Mark Nesbitt sent me a photograph that he had taken after beating his couch one morning to raise the dust. He got orbs all right—lots of them, and they were transparent but grayish. "I think dust looks like orbs," he said, "only when it's close to the lens and out of focus. That gives it the opaque appearance and rounded edges. These photos were also taken under special light conditions, with the sunlight angling in at almost ninety degrees from the camera. That could make a difference."

I looked again. None of the orbs in his shots were bright or truly opaque, like I had gotten, and they seemed pretty consistent in size. It looked nothing like any of the photos I had of multiple orbs. Still, I wanted to get my own results. I decided to do more dust experiments, but this time more dramatic.

One night I went into my living room, got on my knees, took a slipper, and smacked it hard against the carpet. One, two, three, a dozen times. Blam, blam, blam, as hard as I could. Then I took several still shots. To my surprise, they looked just like some of my photos of multiple orbs. I had also seen numerous "sparklies" in the flash as I was taking the shots, which clearly were dust. Hmmm.

I slammed the carpet again and ran to the other side of the room to take a shot. Negative. No orbs. I did it again, and took shots from another angle. Negative. I then turned on the infrared videocam and slammed the carpet right in front of it. I watched through the viewer for twenty minutes but did not see any of the orbs I was used to seeing. I then got out a dust mop, shook it into the carpet, slammed it again with the slipper, and watched through the viewer. Nothing. Just tiny dust particles.

I then hit the rug again numerous times and took still digital photos. Nothing! How could that be? How was it that this time I did not even get a single orb, let alone a multitude? Had raising the dust disturbed the ghosts, or was it all a matter of a camera angle?

The next day I developed the two photos that I had gotten from the one angle. I compared the dust with other "orbs" that I had gotten in that room. In too many ways, there were similarities. However, there were some interesting differences and a total lack of logic that bothered me. I'd looked at the dust photos on Dave Oester's site. They looked nothing like the photos I'd gotten here in my room, but his had been outside. Mine also did not look like those that Nesbitt had gotten.

This raised a lot of questions. First, how was it possible that on one night, after nothing had moved in the room for an hour, I got a photo of multiple orbs similar to a photo I got only after beating the carpet multiple times? Then how could it be that on the same night with the same method, I got multiple orbs in several shots and then none at all? And why not from other angles? And if orbs were just dust, why wasn't everyone getting them all the time? Why wasn't I getting them in other people's homes the way I was getting them here? We certainly had dust in the air all the time and I walked around a lot in those other places. When my sister had photographed inside our room at the hotel in Gettysburg, the only photos in which there was an orb were those with me in them. Did the dust just disappear for all the other photos? And what about those photos where the orbs appeared to be dividing? Or the one where the orb was behind the leg of the TV stand. That meant that it was not right against the lens, so that also meant that it was some six inches or so in diameter. I never saw dust that large in my house. And what of the orb that had formed into a rod, or the one that looked like a worm, or the very bright one that seemed to be vibrating? And the one I had on regular film, large and white, right smack in front of me?

I went back over some of my photos and knew that many of the orbs, especially those outside, were not dust. However, I did conclude that many of my inside shots could very well be dust. It was beginning to appear that perhaps ghosts were not everywhere, as some believed. Perhaps they were in selected areas, but looked sufficiently similar to dust that many people confused dust with an orb. I mean, when you get a head-sized orb out in the dark on the grass-covered Gettysburg battlefield, that hardly seems like dust—especially when there is some kind of reading on meters or an image on night-vision scopes. If it was dust, there would be more of them. However, when you get a lot of orbs in a room where there is activity, I'm suspicious. It's ambiguous enough not to be an orb.

Even so, two of my indoor photographs of multiple orbs, though they look similar to the dust pictures, make no logical sense as dust. One was taken after there was no activity in the room for a considerable period, and the other was the one I got after three photos in a row in the Hotel Chelsea showed nothing. I wondered if it was possible that dust had been raised by some spirit activity that I couldn't see but that was sufficiently similar to slamming my slipper into the rug.

In addition, there was the issue of the vortex, when you see orbs all lined up in a perfect row. I don't think dust behaves that way. Nor did the infrared images behave like dust.

This was all so intriguing, but I was learning to be very careful with digital photography. If someone was moving around, an orb could just be dust. If it was cold, ecto could just be breath. If there was any moisture in the air, that could explain photographic anomalies. These results did not wipe out the possibility that orbs are real (or that they are spirits), but did make suspect many of the photos that purported to be of orbs. I imagined that the authentic orb, whatever it really was, was much less prevalent than many ghost hunters believed. In a way, that made stalking orbs more interesting and much more of a skill than I had realized.

Even so, I admit that I lost my motivation for a while. I stopped taking photos every night in my apartment. It wasn't that I had stopped believing that ghosts might be around. In fact, the dust experiments had convinced me that I did have something other than dust at certain times in there. However, I was tired. I had tried hard to find a way to get Christian to communicate with me and I had pretty much failed. These weird voices on my recorder were too indecipherable to get excited about. I didn't want to fall into the trap of deciding what they said based on what I wanted to hear. So I left things alone for a while.

Then something happened to make me pay attention.

I had made a date with friends, Tom and Paul, to come to their house for dinner on Saturday evening. When I got there, Tom told me that he'd had a dream the night before and felt compelled to tell me. He wanted to know what I thought it could mean.

"I was in a black Edsel with three girls," he said. "They were around age twelve or thirteen, and there was a blond man who was tall and muscular, around twenty-four. He had piercing blue eyes."

I stopped him. "Wait, wait," I said. "Did you read my vampire book?"

"No," he said with a puzzled look. Then I realized that I had not included Christian's murder of two girls around that age. I urged him to continue.

"This man wore nice clothing and had Scandinavian features, like high cheekbones. Also a tattoo or blue mark somewhere on his arm. He seemed to be able to communicate without saying anything."

Just what Wraith had said, I thought to myself.

"We went to a farmhouse, where there was also a baby. It seemed to be a trashy place with cheap furniture. There was also a radio playing seventies music. The girls warned me not to disturb the blond man because he would kill us. I had no real feeling from them; they were amorphous, but two of them appeared to be sisters, close in age."

I swallowed. This was too much like Christian.

"It was my feeling," Tom went on, "that he would kill me either way. He had several knives and a sword lying out on a green-enameled table. I sensed a lot of anger from him. Sometimes he would speak loudly in one-word type of responses, like screaming."

Like my EVP.

"I was afraid of him and thought that he was evil, but I was also attracted to him. He lay down, winked at me, and seemed to be inviting me to come and be with him. I chose that moment to leave. I ended up back in the car driving in a small town and there was an accident. Nearby was a river and I saw body parts floating down the steam, including a man's head with the glasses still on. All of this floated into a sewer."

Just like Christian's first victim, floating down a river. I didn't know what to say, but I was alert to the possibility that this dream had been meant not for Tom but for me.

"What does it mean?" Tom asked. "I can't stop thinking about it."

I shook my head. "It sounds like my ghost. You've described him perfectly, and different aspects of your dream fit him. According to what I've been told, he used knives, he killed some girls, he sent one victim down a river, he cut another one up, and he was dangerous but gorgeous."

I didn't say what it meant, but I wondered if it was Christian's way of telling me, "I could kill you but I've chosen not to."

When I went home, I got out the recorder. I was disturbed by the dream, but I wanted to affirm that Christian was communicating in this way. I asked him to tell me what he wanted. The four-syllable response was deep, emphatic, and seemingly angry. I thought I heard, "Bring the ring," but could not make out the last word.

—5—

The tarot had said that ultimately what I decided to do was up to me, and now I felt it was time. I'd been getting a lot of phone calls lately from someone who did not speak or just hung up, and I feared that Wraith had lost his patience. Since I usually get my best inspirations from literature, I turned to one that seemed appropriate: Tolkien's trilogy, *The Lord of the Rings*. Bilbo Baggins, a hobbit, acquires a ring that turns out to belong to Sauron, the powerful Dark Lord. He lost it and wants it back. Should it come into his hands, however, he can force the entire realm into his dark ways.

Gandalf, a wizard, warns the hobbits that Sauron greatly desires it, "but must not get it." The ring offers long life and absolute power, but corrupts those who wear it. Sauron would never imagine that any-one would destroy it, but that's what must be done.

Bilbo's nephew, Frodo, insists that had he known what this ring was, he'd have destroyed it. Gandalf invites him to go ahead and try. With the intention of throwing it into the hottest part of the fire, Frodo picks up the ring. He makes a move as if to toss it, but ends up putting it back into his pocket. He feels compelled to keep it.

Gandalf knows that to force him to destroy it would break his mind; it must be done by his own free will. What's worse, he must take it to the Crack of Doom on the mountain of fire and throw it in—a quest replete with hardship and danger.

Frodo agrees to do it. At first he has companions, but most of them drop away. Then after an arduous journey, during which the ring becomes increasingly more heavy as Sauron grows aware of him, he manages to get to this desolate place. He need only get to the edge of the Crack of Doom, he believes, to finally be rid of the ring. He's wrong. He's too attached to it and cannot bring himself to let it be destroyed.

I wondered the same about myself.

When I'd first acquired this ring, it had been merely a "souvenir of the night," as Wraith had called it. I had no idea that it would lead me into such adventures. I also did not realize it might put me at risk. Even if there were no ghost of the ring, even if all of the reactions to it and the dreams inspired by it were purely psychological, there was still the danger that, as Rosemary's reading indicated, I had some need for it. I could keep Christian alive, so to speak, just because I wanted to. Merlin had told me the ring was a test. It seemed better to be rid of it.

I thought of one thing that surely would bring closure to my situation. It had long been my belief that I should return the ring to the spot where Christian had died. I actually had wanted to find out where his grave was, but of course Wraith wasn't revealing identities: Once I had Christian's full name, I had ways of getting his and that meant too much risk for him. (Or it meant I might find out that his story about Christian was not altogether true.) It seemed that my only recourse, then, was to try to find my way back to the spot where Christian had killed himself. I wasn't sure I could. I'd tossed out those directions long ago. I might be able to locate the bar where I'd thought I was meeting Wraith before he'd instructed me to go to yet another place, but from there it would be tricky.

I posted some messages on various vampire bulletin boards on the Internet that I wanted Wraith to call me. I used code. "Will give you what you want. Meet me where I first saw you." I didn't know if he ever looked at these things, but I figured that it couldn't hurt. I mentioned a date, with an indication that I'd meet him at his favorite bar.

However, I had no intention of meeting him there. I just wanted to make him think I'd be there so I could get rid of the ring safely. If he was at the bar waiting for me, then he wouldn't be out in the woods.

The interesting thing was going to be Christian's role in all of this. Would he play it out? That is, if he really existed and also had contact with Wraith, would he reveal what I was up to? I suppose that would depend on what he wanted me to do with the ring. It would also depend on whether he was around to even care.

In the end, what mattered most was that the plan didn't work exactly as I'd hoped.

I went to my destination and rented a nondescript car. It didn't take long to find the bar where I'd first seen Wraith, and I had most of the afternoon to carry out my mission. I figured that he didn't go out during the day. Then came the hard part: driving around to find the spot where he'd told me his story. If I could find that, then I thought I could figure out where the rock was on which Christian's body had been found. It felt creepy to go there now after being sort of familiar with him as a ghost. It was like undressing him.

Well, maybe that wouldn't be so bad.

To make a long afternoon short, I drove and drove all over the countryside looking for that parking area near the river. I found the river on a map, but for the life of me, I couldn't figure out where along its banks I'd stood while Wraith told me about the first murder in which Christian allegedly had involved him. By late in the day, I was utterly frustrated. I wondered if I might be approaching the river from the wrong side, so I found a bridge. Although I had no recollection of crossing it before, I reminded myself that it had been dark out that night and I might not have noticed. I drove for a while longer and spotted what looked like a pull-off area. I drove over and parked.

This was nothing like I remembered. Nevertheless, it did have a light, just like the other place.

I decided to drive a little longer. If this was the spot where we had met, then Christian's rock was not more than twenty minutes away. We'd turned onto a crossroad, I remembered that, so I'd have to look for something like that.

Once again, I drove around, wasting precious time, and had no luck. I returned to the parking area. It was now early dusk and I was tempted to use the recorder to see if Christian might direct me. I reached for it and was about to press the record button, but then I chickened out. What if he said something that would really scare me? What if his voice was clear and he told me that this was it, I was going to die? I didn't need that.

After all I'd been through, I was still afraid he hadn't yet revealed his power.

I found the area, parked the car, and got out. Checking to see that the ring was still with me, I unfastened the chain from around my neck. I'd sort of expected it to be hot or something, being this close to the spot where it came from. Or heavy, the way Sauron's ring had become when Frodo got close to the place where the ring was forged. However, it was the same as always. I removed it from the chain and put it into my pocket, noticing again how ordinary it was. Just a plain silver band with a few strange things scratched into it. Nothing special.

I listened for the noise of water. I could hear it, but it didn't sound as close as it had that night. That might be due to some shift in acoustics, or perhaps there hadn't been much rain. I took a walk in the direction of the sound. It wasn't long before I reached the bank, although it seemed longer than it had before. I felt sure this was not the right place. Nevertheless, I believed it was the right river—the one into which Christian had shoved a man after cutting his throat. At least, according to Wraith. Anyway, it would do.

I found the running water easily enough. I even found a place on the bank that looked like the place we had stood as Wraith had told me the gruesome story. It occurred to me that I should have looked for the tree we had climbed that night. But it was now getting dark. I needed to attend to this thing and get it over with.

I wondered if I should do some sort of ceremony. It seemed to lack respect to just toss the ring into the river. It had led me into some pretty incredible adventures. Not only that, but there was some possibility that Christian was not the person Wraith had described, and that he'd been murdered. I felt I should give a little credence to that.

I recalled my fight with Wraith that night. I remembered asking him if he'd murdered his partner and he'd adamantly denied it. Then I had accused him of causing Christian's death with a psychological trigger, planted and then reinforced with hours of discussions about blood and death. Wraith had been amused. He'd then said, "I've been talking to you for some time now. Aren't you afraid I might have planted a trigger in you?"

In fact, I had wondered about that. From time to time, it had occurred to me that he could somehow manipulate me into doing something I wouldn't think to do on my own—such as standing out here at this time of night on a river that he knew better than I did. Yet when it became clear that he was angry about my having the ring and writing further about the story, I figured he was as powerless as he seemed. Or maybe he'd played me all along, making me think that so I'd feel safe doing this.

Yet the cards had said the opposite. *There's a pissed-off man and a woman who has the power.* That was about Wraith and me. I was sure of that. And so far, it didn't look like I was going to have to get away from him.

Okay, quit stalling, I told myself. Just drop it in the water and leave.

But I just wasn't sure. So many people had urged me to get rid of it, from an antiques dealer who'd had some bad experiences to Mariah and Karyol, who sensed psychically that I would endanger myself if I did not. But danger from what? Christian hadn't done anything to me. Wraith had never ventured to where I lived. No one had threatened me and I certainly had not been possessed. Even those who had assured me that spirits would come if I called them forth had been wrong.

Nothing had come, not apparitions or demons or anything that really bothered me. Orbs and EVP in my home did not affect me sufficiently to believe what all the spiritualists insisted would happen to me. Of course, I hadn't followed Merlin's instructions and sent my astral form out to meet my ghost, but without a chair to protect me, I wasn't about to expose myself to any skin-walkers.

After all of this, I did have a stronger belief in ghosts, but I believed less in Christian's desire or ability to do me any damage—if he was even around. I'd given him plenty of opportunities to demonstrate his existence, but hadn't been convinced. It could be that Michael or some guardian spirit prevented him from doing much. It could also be that he enjoyed being with me. It could be that he wasn't there.

Wraith told me once that Christian wanted to kill me. "He wants to bring you into his wake and drag you through what he created with me." Even that now seemed a distant memory.

I took the ring from my pocket and looked at it. "Hey, Christian," I said. "If you want this ring to be returned, then do something to move it out of my hand. Or show yourself. Give me a sign."

Just as I figured, no sign was forthcoming. I bounced it in my hand a couple of times in case he needed it in the air. My heart stopped when I nearly dropped it. I stared at it, knowing I didn't want to do this. Now that I was there, I didn't really know why.

Then I heard a car. Over the noise of evening birds and running water, I heard an engine that sounded like it was pulling up next to my car.

I gripped the ring and searched for a place to hide. I looked frantically along the bank and saw that I was more or less trapped. Then I heard a car door slam.

Geez, was it him? How could he have found me? How would he even know what kind of car I'd rented?

Quickly, I shoved the ring in my jeans pocket and plunged into the water. It was cold and rose quickly up past my knees. I struggled, going from one slippery underwater rock to another, hoping I wouldn't lose my footing. I headed toward a cluster of weeds growing out from the bank, aiming to get a foothold there. If it was Wraith, he wouldn't follow me into the water. Even if he did, he'd have to struggle, giving me time to jump out and run.

I got to the weeds, feeling like an idiot, and found some solid ground. Then I turned around. No one was there. Just the ominous woods.

But it was darker now, hard to tell.

"Who's there?" I called out.

No one answered.

I saw movement in the shadows. I didn't know what it meant. I backed into my weedy patch, ready to flee into thicker brush to my right. Wraith had been perfectly at home in the dark, so I didn't expect to see a flashlight.

"What do you want?" I shouted.

No answer. But I'd heard a car. I knew someone was there. Or maybe they'd seen my car, stopped to offer help, found no one around, and drove off.

I hadn't heard a car leave.

"Nothing's changed," I said. "I know you think I changed the story, but I haven't. I still don't know anything."

I felt watched. It was the same creepiness I'd experienced in Savannah and New Orleans. Someone was there, I was sure of it.

There was only one thing to do. I couldn't. But I had to. I thought quickly.

"Look, look!" I shouted. "I have the ring." There was just enough light that I hoped he could see it glinting off the silver. There was now no time for a ceremony. "He goes with the ring, you said. If that's true, then watch."

With that, I tossed the silver ring as far as I could out into the river. I watched it hit the water with a small pinging splash and disappear. Even if he hadn't seen it very well, he'd heard it. If Wraith wanted it, he'd have a heck of a time dredging that river for it.

But now there was no reason to follow me. Just to be sure, I said, "My book is already at my publisher's. My editor has it. There's nothing you can do about it." Anyway, it was all there except this part— and I hoped it wouldn't end like the Blair Witch or Susan Walsh story.

I listened for movement but heard nothing. It was getting too dark now, and too cold to keep standing here. I had to make my move or he'd be able to trap me. This was his territory, not mine, and I needed to go deeper into the woods so I could circle around and get to my car. I was sure he'd be watching it. That was the obvious thing for him to do, but if I could sneak up on him by hiding behind trees, I might be able to get past him and get away.

Oh, what was that third part of those cards that Rosemary had dropped? *Someone is trying to get away.* I wish she'd have dropped a fourth one that would have told me the outcome.

I shoved my way through some thorny brush, praying there was no poison ivy or oak around there, and then stopped to listen. My heart was pounding too hard for me to hear. I took some breaths to try to quiet myself. It was crucial that I be able to pay attention to the nuances of the woods.

I thought I heard something, but it was faint. I vaguely recalled that Wraith had studied Native American customs. I wondered if he knew how to move through the woods like a breeze—or if he would be able to track me.

But what would he want with me now? If he killed me, then my book would become a news item, spreading this tale about Christian even further. That couldn't be what he wanted. No, he'd wanted the ring. He wanted Christian back. He had no more use for me.

I waited there for what seemed like hours, despite bugs crawling on me and biting me. Sometimes I heard the rustle of foliage, but nothing seemed to come close. I saw no searchlights. I figured he must be gone.

Finally, I ventured back in the direction that I judged was the right one to return to my car. It wasn't easy to get back there, but I had to be careful. Every second I expected Wraith to step out or jump down from a tree and grab me. It wasn't his style to shoot me, but he could certainly have a knife. I remembered all those dreams of slashed throats.

Carefully, I emerged from the woods and made my way to where I had parked the car. When I got there, still in hiding behind some shrubs, I was surprised to see that it was the only one sitting in that little space. Whoever had come had driven away. Or else had a partner who had driven away while he waited.

But Wraith wouldn't partner with someone else. He wouldn't come here for Christian in the company of anyone.

I watched for a while, though I was shivering from wet clothes and cold night air. There was barely a moon, and just enough glow from the one light out there to see how lonely the car looked. It was so close, but not close enough that a run for it would get me to safety. He could very well ambush me. Perhaps he was on the other side, or under it, or in the backseat.

But I'd stopped feeling as if I were being watched. In fact, I felt very much alone.

"Are you here?" I called out.

There was no response. Wraith. I'd named him well when I had searched for something to call him. He was just like an elusive, ghostly wraith.

I decided to brave it and venture out. He'd seen the ring go into the river. What more could he want from me?

Just as I reached for the car door, I felt the chill of something coming up behind me. I whirled around, ready to stab him with my car keys.

No one. Just my imagination.

Or Christian.

I checked the backseat, saw nothing in there, and opened the door. I got in, locked the doors, shoved the key into the ignition, and lit out of there. It was not until I was actually on the plane back home that I felt safe again. Even in the airport, I kept expecting Wraith to jump me.

Anyway, that was the end of that.

When I got home, there was a message on my recorder. I knew before I listened that it would be from him. He'd been there, of that I was sure.

"It pays to have a friend who rents cars," he said in that polished, whispery voice. He obviously wanted me to know how he'd figured it out. Then he went on, "It doesn't really matter, you know. He gets what he wants. He always gets what he wants."

I looked at the recorder and wondered what I would hear if I turned it on.

I thought about the ring, recalling Frodo's struggle to give up the one he had. When he'd made the gesture to throw it away, it had ended up back in his pocket. Even when he reached his destination, he'd been too attached to follow through.

I knew how he felt. If he'd had to make the decision alone, I think he wouldn't have thrown the ring into the pit. In the end, he had help with that. A creature named Golem had grabbed it and gone into the pit. I'd had no such assistance. But what I did have—or had—was a silver ring on my finger that had looked remarkably like Christian's. I'm sorry to have sacrificed it, but I had to do something.

I checked my pocket. Christian's ring was still there. And it was time to make a "phone call."

Epilogue

—1—

I returned to the Gettysburg ghost conference a full year after I'd first learned these techniques. I still had questions and I hoped for further enlightenment. Surely those more advanced than I was would have things to share, for they had been out doing their own investigations. One thing I did learn was that several cameras, both digital and video, that had been trained on the same area apparently had captured similar anomalies. That was interesting, but that was about the only new development. Rick Fisher had an extraordinary video he had taken in a haunted tunnel near his home. It showed orbs in motion in a way I had never seen: They looked like comets at times, and one seemed to be a squiggly illuminated tube. My enthusiasm was renewed. I'd certainly go out ghosting with Rick again. It surprised me that of all the people there with similar equipment, he was the only one with such results.

I listened again to the admonition to look for natural explanations before accepting the possibility of a paranormal event. It seemed a noble principle, but it didn't seem to have a lot of influence. People were on the lookout for any kind of ghostly experience. If a cold breeze passed by, they wanted it to be a spirit, not the result of a shifting weather front. If they experienced sadness on some part of the battlefield, they preferred to think they had been affected by some deceased soldier's melancholy. Not that they weren't, but the emphasis was so much on having an experience that there was no room for ambiguity. I didn't blame them. Gettysburg was such a perfect place to encounter a spirit. Still, I was careful not to get caught up.

There were 150 people here, but unfortunately, that meant that numerous people were out on the field, lighting it up with their flash cameras like Christmas at Macy's. They also laughed, talked together, and exclaimed over their pictures. Not very conducive to serious work—especially when trying for some EVP. I had learned that ghosting was best done with a small group, all of whom agreed to stay quiet. Yet even when I tried to go off alone, it was like finding a good fishing spot: Someone always noticed and came over to take pictures.

Excitement filled the air as people scattered on their investigations. I tried interviewing some folks and found that no one doubted what they were doing. Orbs were spirits of the dead, plain and simple. They got them on film. Why did I question it?

By the end of the conference, it seemed that people were determined to support the notion that they were in a haunted place. They gathered in the conference room to give testimonials, and little attempt was made to extract what might truly be paranormal from what was merely based on feelings and wishful thinking. A lot of people felt "cold spots," but then again, temperatures were in the twenties, with a breeze. Nurses in one spot smelled "old blood"—apparently from the battle 140 ago! No one suggested that it might be animal blood from a much more recent trauma. Several people all heard what they took to be a "phantom train" that was clearly not running on the Gettysburg tracks. No one brought up the possibility of acoustic echoes that trick the senses, although someone finally did point out that a jackhammer had been at work on the highway. Some people heard "drums" or a whispered Confederate name, or else smelled pipe tobacco. Cameras malfunctioned and batteries drained. It was all so exciting for those who accepted that ghosts were the obvious culprits. However, I was disappointed with the apparent need to create the supernatural out of what might have been natural phenomena, and I realized why those who want real proof dismiss these ventures. They're just not that convincing.

In some ways I was back where I had started: I was listening to subjective tales the way mediums told them and I could either believe them or not. No proof would be forthcoming, aside from more pictures of orbs and ecto.

—2—

When I first started ghosting, I didn't take it that seriously. In a sense I was trying to see if it was all a trick or a treat. To me, it was a challenge to see if I could get results. It was also fun to be scared. However, the more I learned and experienced, the more I realized that if all of this is true, something quite serious is at stake. Now that I have so much behind me, what do I really think?

First, as frustrated as I am that I never quite got the full experience of an apparition, I'm pleased that ghosts seem to guard their elusive mystique. I can keep trying.

Second, I learned a lot about the potential realm beyond and I hope to continue to learn more. I believe that EVP is real, that there's more to it than the skeptics allow, and that it will be improved with better technology. Whether we'll discover its true source is not for me to guess. However, I'm convinced that the results are influenced in some way by the researcher, possibly through physiology or spiritual capacity. In that case, we should pay as much attention to improving the human instrument as to improving the machine.

Perhaps the most startling revelation to me was the apparent communication from "them"—those who had died—that the way we live here affects the way we may exist over there. If we don't like who we are, we'd better make some changes. According to one report, it's more difficult to change over there. If true, that really makes one think about what might make eternity worth the experience and what might make it miserable.

As to the various visual manifestations, I believe that there are very credible people who have seen the apparitions of those who have died. The idea that this comes from psychological projection fails to fit the evidence—especially when the witness does not know the person. If anything is a ghost, it's those appearances. I would also accept ectoplasmic forms as ghosts.

I don't know what to make of the idea that apparitions can change their appearance. I don't doubt my mother's memory that on the two separate occasions when she saw the apparition of her deceased father, each time he was wearing something different. The first time he was in a shimmery white robe, the second in his ordinary work clothes. Both times he had his hair, although when he died, he had lost most of it to the cancer treatments. Was one experience a time slippage? If it was and he saw her, why didn't he speak to her? He noticed her and waved, but said nothing, and then he just disappeared.

I also don't know what I think of orbs and vortexes. I don't believe that thirty or forty souls of dead people are hanging out in my apartment, and I think that some of my photos are certainly dust. But there are others for which that is an unlikely explanation, and the infrared videos show a phenomenon in there that appears to act with awareness.

I talked with one ghost hunter, Troy Taylor, author of *The Ghost Hunter's Guidebook.* He runs the American Ghost Society in the Midwest with nearly five hundred members and is developing a ghost museum in Illinois. He's been at this for ten years and he distrusts digital cameras. It's too easy, he says, to manipulate the image, and there's no negative to check. He believes that orbs are a natural energy phenomenon that may or may not be a ghost, yet he doesn't see how we can know for sure until we become ghosts ourselves. Until EVP improves, I tend to agree.

Another ghost hunter simply stated that since both orbs and ghosts were energy anomalies, then orbs were ghosts. The logic leaves much to be desired. That's like saying cats are animals and so are dogs, so cats are dogs. While it may be true that logic is not the best tool in the paranormal realm, logical leaps or glaring errors do mar credibility.

After seeing the dramatic photo I got in New Hope, I wondered if orbs might just be floating ectoplasm that can be drawn together by an otherwise invisible spirit with enough energy to make an apparition. Sort of like a bunch of hydrogen and oxygen molecules that have not yet become water. Looking at the size of the orbs in that photo and at the way they seemed to join to form a column that could indeed become an apparition, I began to rethink the idea that I have a whole crowd of spirits around me. What I think I have, if it's a spirit at all, is one that isn't wholly there. Perhaps he's attempting to form but doesn't have the power (which might be due to my limited electromagnetism). He can make the ectoplasmic parts react but has a harder time using them to fully materialize. He may have a voice, but it might not be coming from an orb. I recall once setting up the videocam for the night. Just before I pushed the record button, I saw what looked like a wave of some kind of substance moving away from me. I also once saw what appeared to be a tiny fist. I wondered if either of these might have been something attempting to put itself together. I read one theory that the "phone calls from the dead" weren't real voices but electrical impulses from a vibration. Couldn't orbs be something similar? Might they be evidence of a paranormal presence, but not necessarily be the ghost itself?

I know that theory will not sit well with many ghost hunters. Yet the fact that the orbs seem to hover around my electrical systems tells me they're drawn to energy. (My utility bill did go up, but it was also winter.) Even if they're all individual souls of some kind—people, animals, bugs—I'm still not satisfied. If they're around me, if they're registering on my recorder and EMF meter, if they want me to pay attention to them, then why can't they *move* something or show themselves to me in some definitive way? (Enigmatic marks on the television screen are not definitive.) They do that with others, whether or not those people even want to see a ghost. They shove things off tables, make alarms ring, choke, grab, push, laugh, pinch, call out a name. Why is it that the orbs in my place (or even in other places) are so weak that they can't manage to do any of those things—even after I invite them to? They can even choke me if they want. I'll accept that.

I suppose it's because I live alone, or have too little static. It's been said that the more people there are the more ectoplasm and electrical energy there is available for an apparition. However, I've never seen an obvious ghost when I was with a group, either, and these orbs do seem to show up in a lot of places—and not just as dust.

About the only thing I can say for their responsiveness is that they will often move in front of the camera if I ask them to. But not always. And they do seem to dissipate quickly when I use a flash camera. Someone mentioned to me that possibly each time I took a photo I was dispersing the fragile energy. I hope that's not true. I don't want to believe that each time I take a shot, I kill orbs like a sneeze kills brain cells.

And so much for the idea that if you go looking for ghosts, they'll come looking for you. If I didn't have this equipment, I wouldn't even know they were there. If they want me to know them or their story, they need to do something dramatic. I'm not settling for explanations that I'm too left brain, or I'm trying too hard, or I'm not the right kind of person to see a ghost. I have counter examples to all of those theories. If they are spirits with intelligence and intention, and if they can hear me, then they know what I want and I know that they can show themselves. They don't.

———

—3—

In the meantime, I have to deal with people who claim to know what this is all about and insist that everyone else go along with their theories. While I do not intend to psychologize the realm of spirits, I want to point out what seems evident in the many approaches that I've encountered. To my mind, a dogmatic stance damages the collective attempts to take ghosts seriously, particularly when so many people who are *certain* end up contradicting others who are just as certain.

For example, one person said that ghosts never lie.

Another insisted they can, and sometimes do.

One person said she could conjure up Christian and put me in touch with him.

Another told me that no one can conjure up ghosts; they come and go as they please, while yet another insisted that whoever said they can conjure up a ghost is violating the rules.

Rules? Oh, yes, there are people who know the rules and insist that everyone else abide by them. As I mentioned in the beginning, I broke all the rules because each person I met had a set of procedures that differed from someone else's. And since I had not yet made up my mind about ghosts, I was willing to do whatever it took to find out more. Had I had some definitive proof that any given theory or approach was the key, or that exorcism was better for ghosts than resolution, I'd have accepted it. However, it seemed to me that all of these belief systems rely on an initial leap of faith: You buy into an ideology and you acquire a set of doctrines from which you can then speak with authority on how to define any given phenomenon.

However, to go out seeking to know a phenomenon that is inherently elusive requires an open, flexible mind that is tolerant of mystery. We need to embrace the actual experience, not blur it with abstract ideas. I believe one must defer the need for definitive answers and most especially the need to be an authority. Having listened to many people who claim it, I don't know that anyone has genuine clarity on these issues, let alone the ground from which to make pronouncements about what others should or should not be doing. That they believe they have such ground has a lot to do, I think, with the way we process information.

—4—

This brings me to the Suggestibility Effect. I define that as the tendency to be so easily persuaded of an unproven reality that one attributes all events to it, thereby "forgetting" the essential ambiguity.

People whose first thought when a machine malfunctions is that ghosts are behind it are prone to the Suggestibility Effect. They don't even think of other possibilities. They have guided their perception to be attuned to one thing and closed off other possibilities.

I wonder if the reason that "ghosts see only what they want to see," according to the kid in *The Sixth Sense,* is that they did that as people, too. Rick Fisher's approach to first eliminate other reasonable explanations may be too cautious for some, but it provides a credible bridge between believers and those unconvinced seekers who want to know more. Clearly, the ghost world is as prone to developing myopic worldviews as any other human endeavor. This happens in part because we're more comfortable with a belief system than without, and because we tend to create mental shortcuts to make information manageable. Let me present a few that seem to apply.

1. *People interpret information through what's familiar. One influencing factor is our associations, such as connecting the report of an apparition with a violent death. Repeated experience with these associations strengthens them in our minds, making them seem true. We then "script" situations from expectations, which guides us to selectively attend to only those aspects of a situation that conform.*

2. *Another shortcut occurs when people form a strong initial impression that then blocks later information that contradicts it—with the result that the subsequent information fails to alter the impression, even if it's more accurate. I have seen this at work in the claims of skeptics, ghost hunters, and mediums. They stick to what they "know" and refuse new information, believing that the first impression is the truth.*

Mental shortcuts can result in judgment errors that we may not even realize. They can actually undercut our better reasoning processes.

Add to that the research that indicates that we unconsciously turn information into narratives that have a storylike construction. We hear some information and anticipate a plot that will bring closure in accordance with our beliefs. Based on childhood tales, for example, we think the presence of a paranormal effect means some dead person has unfinished business. We may then look for evidence to confirm that and to interpret it in a storylike way.

Those experiences related as stories are more vivid and distinct. They influence how we listen. When someone describes an event, we make sense of it in terms of what we anticipate. Seeking plausibility, we then stretch evidence to form a story: We leave out details, exagger-ate others, and perhaps add things that did not happen just to make it work. That becomes our truth.

Thus, to do our best work with the ambiguous paranormal world, I believe we need to pay attention to how we process information. We must take care not to impose easy frameworks on the facts. While it's true that theories must be devised and tested before they can be discarded, it's too easy for us to stick to those that resonate to our mental shortcuts or story arcs. To work with such elusive phenomena, we have to be educated about ourselves, and vigilant.

—5—

I admire those who research this realm with tenacity and in-genuity. I sincerely hope that increasingly more breakthroughs are made—and I hope I make a few. To my mind, research should take the direction of increased attention to the physiology of the recipient of paranormal events and to the development of better attunement capac-ities within ourselves. Perhaps biofeedback could be used in this regard. I know that some people use hypnosis, but having used that tool in therapy, I think it leaves too much open to the Suggestibility Effect. For myself, I plan to pursue the EVP angle. It seems the most intriguing and potentially informative.

Some will ask me if, after all I've seen, heard, and done, I can honestly say that I experienced paranormal events. I suppose I would admit that the stacked-up coins, the television drawings, the EVP, and a few of my photographs make for a package convincing enough to inspire me to continue to explore. Just recently, I heard a whisper on my recorder that chilled me to the bone. I want to know who that was and why he's trying to communicate.

The fact is, if our souls and personalities do continue, I'd love to be on the forefront of those who find out more about what this is like. I'd also like to receive a communication from someone who has died who once made this study his or her life's work. If anyone could tell us some interesting things, it would be those people. Much as I've always wanted to see an apparition, I'd trade that experience for some good solid EVP.

So what is—or was—Christian? Is he just a thoughtform—a psy-chic entity created by a mind and endowed with psychokinetic powers? Is he some stranded dissociated memory? Is he a demon? A ghost in a sorry state? I wish I knew. I'll just have to keep calling him and see what he reveals.

resources

The following is a brief list of contact information. Many more can be found on the Internet, such as at The Dark Side of the Net, and many of the sites listed below have more links.

International Ghost Hunters Society—
Dave Oester and Sharon Gill
PMB 8377
P.O. Box 2428
Pensacola, FL 32513
Ghostweb@ghostweb.com

Pennsylvania Ghost Hunters Society—
Rick Fisher
users.desupernet.com/rfisher/pghs/html

Ghosts of Gettysburg
271 Baltimore Street
Gettysburg, PA 17325
717-337-0445
www.ghostsofgettysburg.com

Dorothy Fiedel
717 Kinderhook Road
Columbia, PA 17512
Ghostlady@dejazzd.com

Ed Okonowitz
1386 Fair Hill Lane
Elkton, MD 21921
Edo@udel.edu

American Ghost Society
Troy Taylor
515 East Third Street
Alton, IL 62002
Ghosts of the Prairie
www.prairieghosts.com

North Florida Paranormal Research—
Jeff Reynolds and Kris Mattson
www.ghosttracker.com

Haunted History Tours, New Orleans—
Kat Smith
www.hauntedhistorytours.com

Sarah Estep
AAEVP@prodigy.net

Tom and Lisa Butler, AA-EVP Directors
(taking over from Sarah Estep)
3415 Socrates Drive
Reno, Nevada 89512
Aaevp@aol.com
dreamwater.com/aaevp

Princeton Paranormal Research Society
P.O. Box 3314
Princeton, NJ 08543-3314
princetonprs.tripod.com

Ghost Stalker's Guide
www.ghoststalkers.com

Elizabeth Baron (medium)
New Life Center
Charleston, SC 29422
843-762-2123
www.ElizabethBaron.com

Whitley Strieber
Unknowncountry.com
Dreamland
5150 Broadway
San Antonio, TX 78209

Chanda Wright, Ordained Spiritual
Counselor
National Ghost Hunters Society
www.nationalghosthunters.com
chandachanda@yahoo.com

Sister Mimi Lansou
Esoterica Occult Goods
541 Rue Dumaine
New Orleans, LA 70116
504-581-7711
800-353-7001
www.onewitch.com
Esoterica@onewitch.com

HAUNTED PLACES TO STAY

Lizzie Borden B&B
92 Second Street
Fall River, MA
508-675-7333

The Logan Inn
10 West Ferry Street
New Hope, PA 18938
215-862-2300
www.loganinn.com

The Farnsworth House
401 Baltimore Street
Gettysburg, PA 17325
717-334-8838
farnhaus@cvn.net

Jerome Grand Hotel
800-817-6788
www.jeromegrandhotel.net

Inn at Jerome
309 Main Street
Jerome, AZ 86331
800-634-5094

Herr Tavern and Publick House
900 Chambersburg Road
Gettysburg, PA 17325
800-362-9849
www.herrtavern.com

17 Hundred 90 Inn
307 E. President St.
Savannah, GA 31401
800-497-1790

bibliography

Adams, Charles III. *Bucks County Ghost Stories*. Reading, PA: Exeter House, 1999.

————. *New York City Ghost Stories*. Reading, PA: Exeter House, 1996.

Andrews, Ted. *How to Develop and Use Psychic Touch*. St. Paul, MN: Llewellyn, 1999.

Bander, Peter. *Voices from the Tapes: Recordings from the Other World*. New York: Drake Publishers, 1973.

Barflinecht, Gary. *Unexplained Michigan Mysteries*. Davison, MI: Freide Publications, 1993.

Becker, Robert, and Gary Selden. *The Body Electric: Electromagnetism and the Foundation of Life*. New York: William Morrow, 1985.

Berendt, John. *Midnight in the Garden of Good and Evil*. New York: Random House, 1994.

Blackman, W. Haden. *The Field Guide to North American Hauntings*. New York: Three Rivers Press, 1998.

Brewer, James. *Jerome: Story of Mines, Men, and Money*. Tucson, AZ: Southwest Parks and Monuments Association, 1993.

Broughton, Richard. *Parapsychology: The Controversial Science*. New York: Ballantine, 1991.

Cahill, Robert E. *New England's Ghostly Haunts*. Peabody, MA: Chandler-Smith Publishing, 1983.

Cohen, Daniel. *The Encyclopedia of Ghosts*. New York: Dodd, Mead & Co., 1984.

DeBolt, Margaret W. *Savannah Spectres*. Atglen, PA: Donning Company, 1984.

De Felitta, Frank. *The Entity*. New York: Warner, 1978.

Eason, Cassandra. *Ghost Encounters: Finding Phantoms and Understanding Them*. London: Blandford, 1997.

Estep, Sarah. AA-EVP newsletters, Annapolis, MD, 1999.

———. *How to Tape-Forward Voices*, Annapolis, MD 21401.

———. *Voices of Eternity*. New York: Fawcett, 1988.

Fiedel, Dorothy Burtz. *Living with Ghosts*. Euphrata, PA: Science Press, 1999.

———. *Haunted Lancaster County, Pennsylvania*. Euphrata, PA: Science Press, 1994.

———. *True Ghost Stories of Lancaster County*. Euphrata, PA: Science Press, 1995.

Finucane, R. C. *Ghosts: Appearances of the Dead and Cultural Transformation*. Amherst, NY: Prometheus Books, 1996.

Fiore, Edith. *The Unquiet Dead*. New York: Ballantine, 1987.

Foreman, Laura, Ed. *Haunted Holidays*. London: Discovery Communications, 1999.

Fuller, John G. *The Ghost of Flight 401*. New York: Berkley, 1976.

———. *The Ghost of 29 Megacycles*. New York: Signet, 1981.

Garcez, Antonio. *Arizona Ghost Stories*. Truth or Consequences, NM: Red Rabbit Press, 1998.

The Ghost Orchid CD. The Parapsychic Acoustic Research Cooperative, 1999.

Gill, Sharon, and Dave Oester. *The Haunted Reality*. St. Helens, OR: StarWest, 1996.

Gilmore, Mikal. *Shot in the Heart*. New York: Doubleday, 1994.

Guiley, Rosemary E. *The Encyclopedia of Ghosts and Spirits*. New York: Facts on File, 1992.

Holzer, Hans. *Are You Psychic?* Garden City Park, NY: Avery, 1997.

———. *Ghosts: True Encounters with the World Beyond*. New York: Black Dog & Leventhal, 1997.

Hufford, David J. *The Terror That Comes in the Night: An-Experience-Centered Study of Supernatural Assault Traditions*. Philadelphia, PA: University of Pennsylvania Press, 1982.

Hunt, Stoker. *Ouija: The Most Dangerous Game*. New York: HarperCollins, 1992.

Jeffrey, Adi-Kent Thomas. *Ghosts in the Valley*. Southampton, PA: Hamptom Publishing, 1971.

Keyes, Edward. *The Michigan Murders*. New York: Pocket, 1976.

Kuntsler, William. *The Hall-Mills Murder Case*. New Brunswick, NJ: Rutgers University Press, 1996.

Lapham, Dave. *Ghosts of St. Augustine*. Sarasota, FL: Pineapple Press, 1997.

Mack, Carol, and Dinah Mack. *A Field Guide to Demons, Fairies, Fallen Angels, and Other Subversive Spirits*. New York: Arcade, 1998.

Mead, Robin. *Haunted Hotels*. Nashville, TN: Routledge Hill Press, 1995.

Meek, George. *After We Die, Then What?* Columbus, OH: Ariel Press, 1987.

Moody, Raymond. *Reunions: Visionary Encounters with Departed Loved Ones*. New York: Villard, 1993.

Moore, Joyce E. *Haunt Hunter's Guide to Florida*. Sarasota, FL: Pineapple Press, 1998.

Nesbitt, Mark. *Ghosts of Gettysburg*. Gettysburg, PA: Thomas Publications, 1991.

———. *More Ghosts of Gettysburg*. Gettysburg, PA: Thomas Publications, 1992.

———. *Ghosts of Gettysburg III*. Gettysburg, PA: Thomas Publications, 1995.

———. *Ghosts of Gettysburg IV*. Gettysburg, PA: Thomas Publications, 1998.

Oester, Dave, and Sharon Gill. *Home Study Course Manual for Certified Ghost Hunter*. Crooked River Ranch, OR: self-published, 1998.

———. *Photo Analysis CD*. International Ghost Hunters Society, 1999.

Okonowitz, Ed. *Crying in the Kitchen*. Elkton, MD: Myst and Lace, 1998.

———. *Horror in the Hallway*, Elkton, MD: Myst and Lace, 1999.

———. *Opening the Door*. Elkton, MD: Myst and Lace, 1995.

———. *Possessed Possessions*. Elkton, MD: Myst and Lace, 1996.

———. *Possessed Possessions II*. Elkton, MD: Myst and Lace, 1998.

———. *Presence in the Parlor*. Elkton, MD: Myst and Lace, 1997.

———. *Pulling Back the Curtain*. Elkton, MD: Myst and Lace, 1994.

———. *Up the Back Stairway*. Elkton, MD: Myst and Lace, 1999.

———. *Welcome Inn*, Elkton, MD: Myst and Lace, 1995.

Pert, Candace. *Molecules of Emotion*. New York: Scribner, 1987.

Price, Charles Edwin. *Haunted Tennessee*. Johnson City, TN: Overmountain Press, 1995.

Ramsland, Katherine. *Dean Koontz: A Writer's Biography*. New York: HarperPrism, 1997.

———. *Piercing the Darkness: Undercover with Vampires in America Today*. New York: HarperPrism, 1998.

Rauber, A. J. *Ghosts, Poltergeists, and the Electronic Voice*. North Brunswick, NJ: Expanding Perceptions, 1996.

Raudive, Konstantin. *Breakthrough: An Amazing Experiment in Electronic Communication with the Dead*, trans. Nadia Fowler. New York: Taplinger, 1971.

Rawlings, Maurice S. *The Hell and Back: Life After Death—Startling New Evidence*. Nashville, TN: Thomas Nelson, 1993.

Rebello, Leonard. *Lizzie Borden, Past and Present*, self-published, 1999.

Robson, Ellen, and Dianne Halicki. *Haunted Highways: The Spirits of Route 66*. Phoenix, AZ: Golden West Publishers, 1999.

Rogo, D. Scott, and Ray Bayless. *Phone Calls from the Dead*. Englewood Cliffs, NJ: Prentice-Hall, 1979.

Roth, Andrew. *Infamous Manhattan*. New York: Citadel, 1996.

Sinisi, Ralph. "There Is a Place, a Very Evil Place," *Weird New Jersey*, no. 11, 1998.

Smith, Katherine. *Journey Into Darkness: Ghosts and Vampires of New Orleans*. New Orleans, LA: De Simonin Publications, 1998.

Spencer, John, and Anne Spencer. *The Encyclopedia of Ghosts and Spirits*. London: Headline, 1992.

Spencer, John, and Tony Wells. *Ghost Watching: The Ghost Hunter's Handbook*. London: Virgin Books, 1994.

Taylor, Troy. *The Ghost Hunter's Guidebook*. Alton, IL: Whitechapel Productions, 1999.

Underwood, Peter. *The Ghost Hunter's Guide*. London: Javelin, 1986.

USA Weekend editors. *I Never Believed in Ghosts Until . . .* New York: Contemporary Books, 1992.

Warren, Joshua P. "Ghost Bait," *Fate*, July 1999.

Waters, Colin. *Sexual Hauntings Through the Ages*. New York: Dorset, 1993.

Welch, William Addams. *Talks with the Dead*. New York: Pinnacle, 1975.

Whedbee, Charles H. *Legends of the Outer Banks and Tarheel Tidewater*. Winston-Salem, NC: John F. Blair, 1966.

Wilson, Colin. *Strange but True Ghost Sightings*. London: Robinson, 1997.

Winer, Richard, and Nancy Osborn. *Haunted Houses*. New York: Bantam, 1979.

———. *More Haunted Houses*. New York: Bantam, 1981.

index